Learning Angular
Third Edition

A no-nonsense beginner's guide to building web applications with Angular 10 and TypeScript

Aristeidis Bampakos

Pablo Deeleman

BIRMINGHAM—MUMBAI

Learning Angular
Third Edition

Commissioning Editor: Pavan Ramchandani
Acquisition Editor: Ashitosh Gupta
Senior Editor: Mohammed Yusuf Imaratwale
Content Development Editor: Keagan Carneiro
Technical Editor: Shubham Sharma
Copy Editor: Safis Editing
Project Coordinator: Kinjal Bari
Proofreader: Safis Editing
Indexer: Manju Arasan
Production Designer: Nilesh Mohite

First published: May 2016
Second edition: December 2017
Third edition: September 2020

Production reference: 1040920
Published by Packt Publishing Ltd.
Livery Place
35 Livery Street
Birmingham
B3 2PB, UK.

ISBN 978-1-83921-066-2

`www.packt.com`

To my wonderful wife Ria for being supportive and compassionate and for helping me keep focused on the good things in our life.

– Aristeidis Bampakos

Angular bicycle - Photo by Giannis Smirnios (@GiannisSmirnios)

Contributors

About the authors

Aristeidis Bampakos is an experienced frontend web developer and a contributor to the Angular documentation. For the last 8 years, he has mainly focused on developing web applications with the AngularJS and Angular frameworks, Typescript, and Angular Material. He has also been involved in the development of hybrid mobile applications using the Ionic framework. Currently, at Plexscape, he is working on integrating GIS technologies with Angular and Electron.

I want to thank my parents and the Angular Athens Meetup core team for their full support and encouragement throughout my writing journey.

Pablo Deeleman is a former UI/UX designer who fell in love with JavaScript and CSS back in 1998, during the old days of Netscape Navigator and Microsoft Internet Explorer 3. The discovery of Node.js back in 2011 became a turning point in his career. From that moment on he started focusing on JavaScript application development, with a special focus on creating single-page applications and interaction development.

With sound expertise in front-end libraries and frameworks, such as Backbone.js, Knockout.js, Polymer, React, Svelte, AngularJs, and Angular, Pablo has developed his career as a JavaScript practitioner across a broad range of successful start-ups as well as large enterprise corporations such as Gameloft, Red Hat or Dynatrace, just to name a few. He currently works as a Senior Software Engineer and Angular specialist for Dynatrace, a Gartner quadrant leader in the Application Performance Monitoring field.

Pablo Deeleman has contributed to the dev community with several books on Angular since 2016, all published by Packt Publishing.

About the reviewer

Pawel Czekaj has Bachelor's degree in Computer Science. He has 10 years of experience as a frontend developer. Currently, he works as Lead Frontend Developer at Ziflow Ltd. He specializes in AngularJS, Angular, Amazon Web Services, Auth0, NestJS, and many others. Currently, he is building enterprise-level proofing solutions based fully on Angular.

Sridhar Rao Chivukula is a technical lead at Mindtree Ltd and is based out of New York City. He brings with him more than a decade of rich hands-on experience in all aspects of frontend engineering. He has worked with leading companies such as Oracle, Tech Mahindra, and Cognizant Technology Solutions. He has a Bachelor's degree in Information Technology. He is the author of the books *Expert Angular* and *PHP and script.aculo.us Web 2.0 Application Interfaces*, published by Packt.

Packt is searching for authors like you

If you're interested in becoming an author for Packt, please visit `authors.packtpub.com` and apply today. We have worked with thousands of developers and tech professionals, just like you, to help them share their insight with the global tech community. You can make a general application, apply for a specific hot topic that we are recruiting an author for, or submit your own idea.

Table of Contents

Section 2: Components – the Basic Building Blocks of an Angular App

3

Component Interaction and Inter-Communication

4
Enhance Components with Pipes and Directives

5
Structure an Angular App

6

Enrich Components with Asynchronous Data Services

Section 3: User Experience and Testability

7

Navigate through Components with Routing

8

Orchestrating Validation Experiences in Forms

9

Introduction to Angular Material

10
Giving Motion to Components with Animations

11
Unit test an Angular App

Section 4: Deployment and Practice

12
Bringing an Angular App to Production

13

Develop a Real-World Angular App

Other Books You May Enjoy

Index

Preface

Angular, loved by millions of web developers, is one of the top JavaScript frameworks thanks to its regular updates and new features that enable fast, cross-platform, and secure frontend web development.

Updated to Angular 10, this third edition of the *Learning Angular* book covers new features and modern web development practices to address the current frontend web development landscape. If you are new to Angular, this book will give you a comprehensive introduction to help you get you up and running in no time. You'll learn how to develop apps by harnessing the power of the Angular command-line interface (CLI), write unit tests, style your apps by following the Material Design guidelines, and finally deploy them to a hosting provider. The book is especially useful for beginners to get to grips with the bare bones of the framework needed to start developing Angular apps.

Who this book is for

The book is intended for any JavaScript or full stack developer who wants to enter the world of frontend development with Angular or migrate to the Angular framework to build professional web applications. Familiarity with web and programming concepts will assist with understanding the content covered in the book.

What this book covers

Chapter 1, Building Your First Angular App, covers the setup of the development environment by installing Angular CLI 10 and explains how to use schematics (commands) to automate tasks such as code generation and application building. We create a new simple application using the Angular CLI 10 and build it. We also learn about how Angular tooling has been improved in some of the most widely known IDEs and emphasize the importance of Visual Studio Code.

Chapter 2, Introduction to TypeScript, explains what TypeScript is, the language that is used when creating Angular applications, and what the most basic building blocks are, such as types, template strings, lambdas, and classes. We learn to use the decorators that are widely used in Angular classes and ES6 modules and take a look at some of the advanced types available and the latest features of the language.

Chapter 3, Component Interaction and Inter-Communication, covers how a component is connected to its template and how we can use an Angular decorator to configure it. We take a look at how components communicate each other by passing data from one component to another using input and output bindings and learn about the different strategies to detect changes in a component. We will then see, what are some of the available ways to apply styles to a component. Finally, we investigate the hook events that are available in the life cycle of a component.

Chapter 4, Enhance Components with Pipes and Directives, covers the available built-in directives and pipes, and we build our own custom pipes and leverage them to a sample component that demonstrates their use. We learn the difference between attribute and structural directives.

Chapter 5, Structure an Angular App, explains how an Angular 10 application is organized into a tree of components, and how to group components into modules and use the dependency injection mechanism to create and use services in components. We find out about the different types of modules and their purpose as well as the different scopes for services.

Chapter 6, Enrich Components with Asynchronous Data Services, examines the RxJS library and observables that are fundamental to the HTTP client of Angular. We learn how to access a remote backend API, get some data and display it to the component, and how to overcome the problem of not having the actual backend API ready yet (how to design our application without a real API). We also investigate how to set additional headers to an HTTP request and intercept such a request to act before sending the request or upon completion.

Chapter 7, Navigate through Components with Routing, explains how to use the Angular router in order to activate different parts of an Angular 10 application from a URL. We find out how to pass parameters through the URL and what are the available events of the router that we can hook. We learn to break an application into routing modules that can be lazy loaded. We then learn how to guard against our components and how to prepare data prior to initialization of the component.

Chapter 8, Orchestrating Validation Experiences in Forms, explains how to use Angular reactive forms in order to integrate HTML forms and how to set them up using FormGroup and FormControl. We track the interaction of the user in the form and validate input fields, and then create a simple login form to illustrate the use of forms.

Chapter 9, Introduction to Angular Material, covers how to integrate Google Material Design guidelines in an Angular 10 application using a library called Angular Material that has been developed by the Angular team. We take a look at some of the core components of the library and their usage and discuss the available themes that are bundled with the library and how to install them.

Chapter 10, Give Motion to Components with Animations, explains how animation works with pure vanilla CSS and how to animate components of an Angular 10 application using the built-in AnimationBuilder or a custom directive.

Chapter 11, Unit Test an Angular App, covers how to test Angular 10 artifacts and override them in a test, what the different parts of a test are, and which parts of a component should be tested.

Chapter 12, Bringing an Angular App to Production, sets out the available hosting providers that are supported by the Angular CLI. We perform optimizations prior to deployment, and we use Angular CLI 10 to deploy to GitHub pages.

Chapter 13, Develop a Real-World Angular App, puts into practice many aspects of what we have learned in the previous chapters to create a full-blown, real-world Angular 10 application.

To get the most out of this book

You will need a version of Angular 10 installed on your computer, preferably the latest minor one. All code examples have been tested using Angular 10.0.0 on a Windows OS, but they should work with any future release of Angular as well. The book uses the TypeScript 3.9 version as it is supported by Angular 10.

You will find the latest code files for the book, updated with the latest versions of the technology on GitHub: `https://github.com/PacktPublishing/Learning-Angular--Third-Edition`

If you are using the digital version of this book, we advise you to type the code yourself or access the code via the GitHub repository (link available in the next section). Doing so will help you avoid any potential errors related to the copying and pasting of code.

Download the example code files

You can download the example code files for this book from your account at `www.packt.com`. If you purchased this book elsewhere, you can visit `www.packtpub.com/support` and register to have the files emailed directly to you.

You can download the code files by following these steps:

1. Log in or register at `www.packt.com`.
2. Select the **Support** tab.
3. Click on **Code Downloads**.
4. Enter the name of the book in the **Search** box and follow the onscreen instructions.

Once the file is downloaded, please make sure that you unzip or extract the folder using the latest version of:

- WinRAR/7-Zip for Windows
- Zipeg/iZip/UnRarX for Mac
- 7-Zip/PeaZip for Linux

The code bundle for the book is also hosted on GitHub at `https://github.com/PacktPublishing/Learning-Angular--Third-Edition`. In case there's an update to the code, it will be updated on the existing GitHub repository.

We also have other code bundles from our rich catalog of books and videos available at `https://github.com/PacktPublishing/`. Check them out!

Conventions used

There are a number of text conventions used throughout this book.

`Code in text`: Indicates code words in text, database table names, folder names, filenames, file extensions, pathnames, dummy URLs, user input, and Twitter handles. Here is an example: "Open the `hero.component.html` file and add a `button` element named `Add hero` before the button that adds powers."

A block of code is set as follows:

```
addBio() {
  this.heroDetails.patchValue({
    biometricData: {
      age: 35,
      hair: <#ff0000>
    },
  })
}
```

When we wish to draw your attention to a particular part of a code block, the relevant lines or items are set in bold:

```
export class LoginComponent {
  username: string;
  password: string;
}
```

Any command-line input or output is written as follows:

```
npm install -g @angular/cli@10.0.0
```

Bold: Indicates a new term, an important word, or words that you see on screen. For example, words in menus or dialog boxes appear in the text like this. Here is an example: " Click on the **Username** field and then on the **Password**."

> **Tips or important notes**
> Appear like this.

Get in touch

Feedback from our readers is always welcome.

General feedback: If you have questions about any aspect of this book, mention the book title in the subject of your message and email us at `customercare@packtpub.com`.

Errata: Although we have taken every care to ensure the accuracy of our content, mistakes do happen. If you have found a mistake in this book, we would be grateful if you would report this to us. Please visit `www.packtpub.com/support/errata`, selecting your book, clicking on the Errata Submission Form link, and entering the details.

Piracy: If you come across any illegal copies of our works in any form on the internet, we would be grateful if you would provide us with the location address or website name. Please contact us at `copyright@packt.com` with a link to the material.

If you are interested in becoming an author: If there is a topic that you have expertise in, and you are interested in either writing or contributing to a book, please visit `authors.packtpub.com`.

Reviews

Please leave a review. Once you have read and used this book, why not leave a review on the site that you purchased it from? Potential readers can then see and use your unbiased opinion to make purchase decisions, we at Packt can understand what you think about our products, and our authors can see your feedback on their book. Thank you!

For more information about Packt, please visit `packt.com`.

Section 1: Getting Started with Angular

This section explains how to use the Angular CLI 10 to scaffold a simple Hello World application and covers the basics of TypeScript the language used when writing Angular applications.

This part comprises the following chapters:

- *Chapter 1, Building Your First Angular App*
- *Chapter 2, Introduction to TypeScript*

1
Building Your First Angular App

To better understand how to develop an Angular application, we need to learn some basic but essential things so that we can have a great experience on our journey with the Angular framework. One of the basic things that we should know is **semantic versioning**, which is the way that the Angular team has chosen to deal with changes between different versions of the framework. It will hopefully make it easier to find the right solutions to future app development challenges when you visit the official Angular documentation website (`https://angular.io`) or other sites (such as Stack Overflow) to search for solutions.

Another important but sometimes painful topic is that of project setup. It is a necessary evil that needs to be done at the beginning of a project, but getting this right early on can reduce a lot of friction as your application grows. Therefore, a large part of this chapter is dedicated to **Angular CLI**, a tool developed by the Angular team that provides scaffolding and automation tasks in an Angular app, demystifying the process and enabling you as a developer to save yourself from facing future frustrations and migraines. We will use the Angular CLI to create our first application from scratch, get a feel for the anatomy of an Angular application, and take a sneak peek at how Angular works under the hood.

Working with an Angular project without an **Integrated Development Environment (IDE)** can be painful. Our favorite code editor can provide us with an agile development workflow that includes TypeScript compilation at runtime, static type checking, and introspection, code completion, and visual assistance for debugging and building our app. We will highlight some popular code editors and take a bird's eye view of how each one of them can assist us when developing Angular applications.

To sum up, here are the main topics that we will explore in this chapter:

- Semantic versioning, why it matters, and Angular's take on it
- How to set up an Angular project using Angular CLI 10
- How to use Angular CLI commands to accomplish certain tasks, such as building and serving an Angular app
- How to create our first application and begin to understand the core concepts in Angular
- The available tooling for Angular in popular IDEs

Technical requirements

- **GitHub link**: `https://github.com/PacktPublishing/Learning-Angular--Third-Edition/tree/master/ch01`
- **Node.js**: `http://nodejs.org/`
- **Node Package Manager (npm)**: Included with Node.js
- **Git**: `https://git-scm.com/downloads`
- **Visual Studio Code (VS Code)**: `https://code.visualstudio.com/download`

It's just Angular – introducing semantic versioning

Using semantic versioning is about managing expectations. It's about managing how the user of your application, or library, reacts when a change happens to it. Changes happen for various reasons, either to fix something broken in the code or to add/alter/remove a feature. Authors of frameworks or libraries use a way to convey what impact a particular change has by incrementing the version number of the software in different ways.

A piece of production-ready software traditionally has version 1.0, or 1.0.0 if you want to be more specific.

There are three different levels of change that can happen when updating your software. Either you patch it and effectively correct something, make a minor change that essentially means you add functionality, or make a major change that might completely change how your software works. Let's look at these changes in more detail in the following sections.

Patch change

A patch change means that we increment the rightmost digit by one. Changing software from 1.0.0 to 1.0.1 is a small change, and usually implies a bug fix. As a user of that software, you don't really have to worry; if anything, you should be happy that something is suddenly working better. The point is that you can safely start using 1.0.1.

Minor change

A minor change means that the software version increases from 1.0.0 to 1.1.0. We deal with more severe changes as we increase the middle digit by one. This number should increase when new functionality is added to the software, and it should still be backward compatible with the 1.0.0 version. In this case, it should be safe to start using the 1.1.0 version of the software.

Major change

With a major change, the version number increases from 1.0.0 to 2.0.0. Things might have changed so much that constructs have been renamed or removed. It might not be compatible with earlier versions. Please note that many software authors still ensure that there is decent backward compatibility, but the main point here is that there is no warranty, no contract guaranteeing that it will still work.

What about Angular?

Most people knew the first version of Angular as Angular 1; it later became known as AngularJS, but many still refer to it as Angular 1. It did not use semantic versioning.

Then Angular 2 came along, and in 2016 it reached production readiness. Angular decided to adopt semantic versioning, and this caused a bit of confusion in the developer community, especially when it announced that there would be an Angular 4 and 5 and so on. The Angular team, as well as the network of their Google Developer Experts, started to explain that we should call the latest version of the framework Angular—just Angular. You can argue the wisdom of that decision. Still, the fact remains that the new Angular uses semantic versioning, which means that Angular is the same platform as Angular 2, as well as Angular 10, and so on. Adopting semantic versioning means that you, as a user of the framework, can rely on things working the same way until Angular decides to increase the major version. Even then, it's up to you whether you want to remain on the latest major version or upgrade your existing apps.

Introducing Angular

Angular represents a full rewrite of the AngularJS framework, introducing a brand-new application architecture built entirely from scratch in **TypeScript**, a strict superset of **JavaScript** that adds optional static typing and support for interfaces and decorators.

In a nutshell, Angular applications are based on an architecture design that comprises trees of web components interconnected by their particular I/O interface. Under the hood, each component takes advantage of a completely revamped dependency injection mechanism.

To be fair, this is a simplistic description of what Angular really is; however, the simplest project ever made in Angular is formed by these definition traits. We will focus on learning how to build interoperable components and manage dependency injection in the following chapters before moving on to more advanced topics, such as routing, web forms, and HTTP communication. We will not make explicit references to AngularJS throughout the book; it makes no sense to waste time and pages referring to something that does not provide any useful insights on the topic. Besides, we assume that you might not know about Angular 1.x, so such knowledge does not have any value here.

Setting up our workspace with Angular CLI

Setting up a frontend project today is more cumbersome than ever. We used to manually include the necessary JavaScript and **CSS** files in our **HTML**. Life used to be simple. Then frontend development became more ambitious: we started splitting up our code into modules and using special tools called **preprocessors** for both our code and CSS.

All in all, our projects became more complicated, and we started to rely on build systems to bundle our applications. As developers, we are not huge fans of configuration—we want to focus on building awesome apps. Modern browsers, however, do more to support the latest web standards, and some of them have even started to support modules. That said, this is far from being widely supported. In the meantime, we still have to rely on tools for bundling and module support.

Setting up a project with Angular can be tricky. You need to know what libraries to import and ensure that files are processed in the correct order, which leads us to the topic of scaffolding. Scaffolder tools almost become a necessity as complexity grows, but also where every hour counts towards producing business value rather than fighting configuration problems.

The primary motivation behind creating the Angular CLI was to help developers focus on app building, eliminating the boilerplate of configuration. Essentially, with a simple command, you should be able to initialize an application, add new artifacts to it, run tests, and create a production-grade bundle. The Angular CLI supports all of this with the use of special commands.

Prerequisites

Before we begin, we need to make sure that our development environment includes a set of software tools that are essential to the Angular development workflow.

Node.js

Node.js is a JavaScript runtime built on top of Chrome's v8 JavaScript engine. Angular requires a current or LTS version. If you have already installed it, you can run `node -v` in the command line to check which version you are running. If not, you can get it from `https://nodejs.org`.

Angular CLI uses Node.js to accomplish specific tasks, such as serving, building, and bundling your application.

Npm

Npm is a software package manager that is included by default in Node.js. You can check this out by running `npm -v` in the command line. The Angular framework is an ecosystem of various libraries, called **packages**, that are available in a central place called **npm registry**. The npm client downloads and installs the libraries that are needed to run your application from the registry.

Git

Git is a client that allows us to connect to distributed version-control systems, such as *GitHub*, *Bitbucket*, and *GitLab*. It is optional from the perspective of the Angular CLI. You should install it in case you want to upload your Angular project in a Git repository, which is something that you might want to do.

Installing Angular CLI

The Angular CLI is part of the Angular ecosystem and is available to download from the npm package registry. Since it is used for creating Angular apps and projects, we need to install it globally in our system. Open a terminal and run the following command:

```
npm install -g @angular/cli@10.0.0
```

> **Important Note**
> On some Windows systems, you may need to have elevated permissions to do this, in which case you should run your command-line window as an administrator. In Linux/macOS systems, run the command using the `sudo` keyword: `sudo npm install -g @angular/cli@10.0.0`.

The command that we used to install Angular CLI uses the npm client followed by a set of runtime arguments:

- `install` or `i`: Denotes the installation of a package
- `-g`: Denotes that the package will be installed to the system globally
- `@angular/cli`: Denotes the name of the package to install
- `@10.0.0`: Denotes the version of the package to install

CLI commands

Angular CLI is a command-line interface tool that automates specific tasks during development, such as serving, building, bundling, and testing an Angular project. As the name implies, it uses the command line to invoke the `ng` executable and run commands using the following syntax:

```
ng command [options]
```

Here, `command` is the name of the command to be executed and `[options]` denotes additional parameters that can be passed to each command. To view all available commands, you can run the following:

```
ng help
```

Some commands can also be invoked using an alias instead of the actual command name. In this book, we revise the most common ones (the alias of each command is shown inside parentheses):

- `new (n)`: Creates a new Angular application from scratch.
- `build (b)`: Compiles an Angular application and outputs generated files in a predefined folder.
- `generate (g)`: Creates new files that comprise an Angular application.
- `serve (s)`: Builds an Angular application and serves it from a preconfigured web server.
- `test (t)`: Runs unit tests of an Angular application.
- `deploy`: Deploys an Angular application to a web-hosting provider. You can choose from a collection of providers that are included in the Angular CLI.
- `add`: Installs a third-party library to an Angular application.
- `update`: Updates an Angular application along with its dependencies. Dependencies are libraries, npm packages, that are needed for the Angular application to run.

> **Important Note**
> A library must be compatible with the Angular CLI that is to be used with add and update commands. The way that a library adds compatibility is out of the scope of this book.

Angular CLI follows the same major version of Angular, as all other packages of the framework do. The version that we use in this book and the accompanying source code is 10. You can check which version you have installed by running `ng version` or `ng v` in the command line.

Angular CLI uses modern web techniques to orchestrate an Angular application and provide us with a fantastic development experience. It uses **Webpack** under the hood, a popular module bundler for modern JavaScript applications. We do not interact directly with Webpack, but through the Angular CLI interface.

Creating a new project

Now that we have prepared our development environment, we can start creating magic by scaffolding our very first Angular application. We use the `new` command of the Angular CLI and pass the name of the application that we want to create as an option. To do so, go to a folder of your choice and type the following:

```
ng new my-app
```

Creating a new Angular application is an easy and straightforward process. The Angular CLI will ask you for some details about the application that you want to create so that it can scaffold the Angular project as best as it can. Initially, it will ask you if you want to include routing in your app.

Would you like to add Angular routing? (y/N)

Routing is related to navigating from one view of your application to another, and it is something that we will learn about later in *Chapter 7, Navigate through Components with Routing*. For now, answer *No* to the question and press *Enter*.

The next question is related to the styling of your application.

Which stylesheet format would you like to use? (Use arrow keys)

It is common to use CSS for styling Angular applications. You can, however, use preprocessors, such as **SCSS** or **Less**, that can provide added value to your development workflow. In this book, we work with CSS directly, so you can accept the default choice, `CSS`, and press *Enter*.

The process may take some time depending on your internet connection. During this time, Angular CLI will download and install all of the necessary dependencies, as well as create default files for your Angular application. When finished, it will have created a folder called `my-app`. Navigate to the newly created folder and start your application with the following command:

```
ng serve
```

Angular CLI compiles the Angular project and starts a web server that watches for changes in project files. This way, whenever you make a change, the web server rebuilds the project to reflect the new changes.

To preview the application, open your browser and go to `http://localhost:4200`

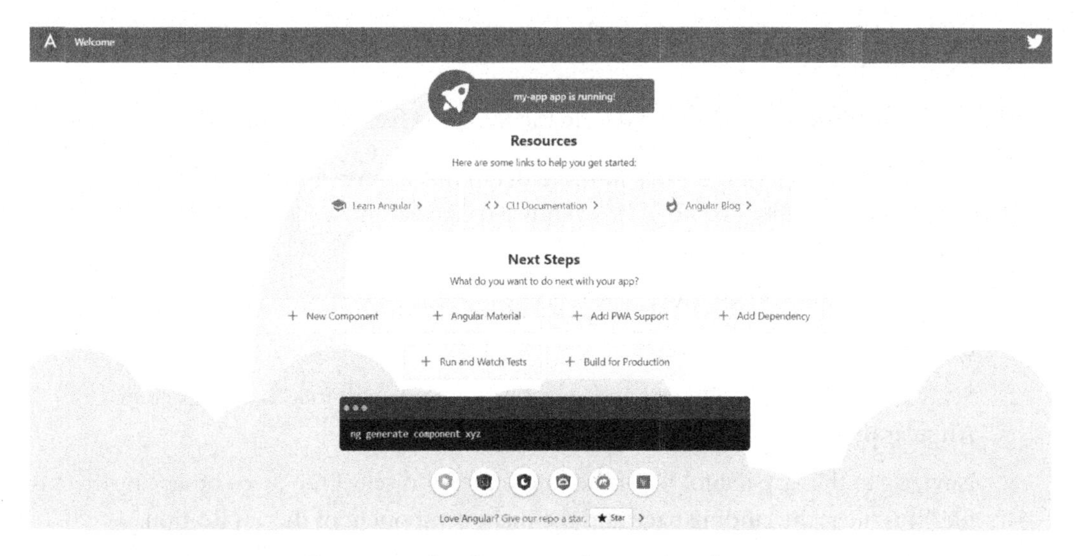

Figure 1.1 – Landing page of a new Angular app

When we create a new Angular application from scratch, the Angular CLI displays, by default, a landing page that contains useful links, such as where to look for additional resources and documentation about the Angular framework or the next steps to start building our application. In the next section, we will explore how Angular makes the whole process work and learn how to make a change to this landing page.

Hello Angular

We are about to take the first trembling steps into extending our first Angular application. The Angular CLI has already scaffolded our project, and has thereby carried out a lot of heavy lifting. All we need to do is fire up our favorite IDE and start working with the Angular project. We are going to use **Visual Studio Code (VS Code)** in this book, but feel free to choose any editor you are comfortable with. VS Code is a very popular IDE in the Angular community because of the powerful tooling that it provides to developers. You will learn more details about IDEs later in the *IDEs and plugins* section.

The landing page of our application is an Angular **component** that consists of the following parts:

- **Component class**: Contains the presentation logic of the component and handles interaction with its template
- **HTML template**: The actual UI of the component that interacts with the component class
- **CSS styles**: Specific styles that define the look and feel of the component

We will learn about each of the parts in more detail in *Chapter 3, Component Interaction and Inter-Communication*. For now, let's venture into customizing some of the aforementioned parts of our landing page:

1. Open VS Code and select **File | Open Folder** or just **Open** for Mac users from the main menu.
2. Search for the `my-app` folder and select it. VS Code will load the associated Angular project.
3. Navigate to the `app` subfolder of the `src` folder and select the `app.component.ts` file. This file is the landing page and the main component of the application.

> **Important Note**
> An Angular application has at least one main component called `AppComponent`, as a convention.

4. Locate the property `title` and change its value to `Hello Angular 10`:

app.component.ts

```
import { Component } from <@angular/core>;

@Component({
  selector: 'app-root',
  templateUrl: './app.component.html',
  styleUrls: ['./app.component.css']
})
export class AppComponent {
  title = 'Hello Angular 10';
}
```

5. Save the file and wait for Angular to do its thing. It recompiles the project and refreshes the browser. The landing page should reflect the change that you have just made:

Figure 1.2 – Title of landing page

Congratulations! You have successfully used the Angular CLI to create an Angular application and interact with a component. What you have just experienced is only the tip of the iceberg. There are so many things that happen under the hood, so let's get started by explaining how Angular worked its way to display the actual page on the browser.

Components

Each web application has a main HTML file. For an Angular application, this is the `index.html` file that exists inside the `src` folder:

index.html

```
<!doctype html>
<html lang="en">
<head>
  <meta charset="utf-8">
  <title>MyApp</title>
  <base href="/">
  <meta name="viewport" content="width=device-width,
  initial-scale=1">
  <link rel="icon" type="image/x-icon" href="favicon.ico">
</head>
<body>
  <app-root></app-root>
</body>
</html>
```

When the Angular CLI builds an Angular app, it first parses `index.html` and starts identifying HTML tag elements inside the `body` tag. An Angular application is always rendered inside the `body` tag and comprises a tree of components. When the Angular CLI finds a tag that is not a known HTML element, such as `app-root`, it starts searching through the components of the application tree. But how does it know which components belong to the app?

Modules

Angular organizes components into self-contained blocks of functionality called **modules**. An Angular application has at least one main module called `AppModule`, as a convention:

app.module.ts

```
import { BrowserModule } from '@angular/platform-browser';
import { NgModule } from '@angular/core';

import { AppComponent } from './app.component';

@NgModule({
  declarations: [
    AppComponent
  ],
  imports: [
    BrowserModule
  ],
  providers: [],
  bootstrap: [AppComponent]
})
export class AppModule { }
```

Angular components should be registered with a module so that they are discoverable by the framework. The `declarations` property is the place where we define all components that exist inside a module. Failure to add a component in this property will mean that it will not be recognized by the framework, and it will throw errors when we try to use it. We will learn more about modules and their properties later in *Chapter 5, Structure an Angular App*.

As soon as the application knows about all of the available components that it can search, it needs to identify which element tag belongs to which component. That is, it needs to find a way to match the tag with a component.

Selector

Angular matches HTML tags with components via a **selector**. It is the name that you give to a component so that it is correctly identified in HTML:

```
selector: 'app-root'
```

When Angular finds an unknown element tag in an HTML file, it searches through the selectors of all registered components to check whether there is a match. As soon as it finds a matching selector, it renders the template of the component in place of the element tag. You can think of a selector as an anchor that tells Angular where to render a component.

Template

The HTML content of a component is called the **template** and is defined in the `templateUrl` property. It denotes the path of the HTML file of the component relative to the component class file:

```
templateUrl: './app.component.html'
```

Angular parses the template of the component and replaces the selector it found with the HTML content of this file.

The template of the component is written in valid HTML syntax and contains standard HTML tag elements, some of them enriched with Angular template syntax. It is the Angular template language that extends HTML and JavaScript and customizes the appearance or adds behavior to existing HTML tag elements. To get a glimpse of the Angular template syntax, in VS Code, select the `app.component.html` file and go to line 330:

```
<span>{{ title }} app is running!</span>
```

The `{{ }}` syntax is one example of the Angular template language, called **interpolation**. It reads the `title` property of the component class, converts its value to text, and renders it on the screen as the following:

Hello Angular 10 app is running

Bootstrapping

You have learned how Angular works under the hood to display a component such as the landing page. But how does it know where to start? What is responsible for booting up the process of rendering a page on the screen? This method is called **bootstrapping**, and it is defined in the `main.ts` file inside the `src` folder:

main.ts

```
import { enableProdMode } from '@angular/core';
import { platformBrowserDynamic } from '@angular/platform-browser-dynamic';

import { AppModule } from './app/app.module';
import { environment } from './environments/environment';

if (environment.production) {
  enableProdMode();
}

platformBrowserDynamic().bootstrapModule(AppModule)
  .catch(err => console.log(err));
```

The starting point of an Angular application is always a module. The main task of the bootstrapping file is to define this module. It calls the `bootstrapModule` method of browser platform and passes `AppModule` as the entry point of the application.

> **Important Note**
>
> Angular is a cross-platform framework. It can support different types of platforms, such as browser, server, web worker, and native mobile. In our case, we are using the `platformBrowserDynamic` to target the browser platform.

By now, you should have a basic understanding of how Angular works and what the basic building blocks of the framework are. As a reader, you had to swallow a lot of information at this point and take our word for it. Don't worry: you will get a chance to get more acquainted with the components and Angular modules in the upcoming chapters. For now, the focus is to get you up and running by giving you a powerful tool in the form of the Angular CLI and show you how just a few steps are needed to render an app to the screen.

IDEs and plugins

An IDE is a term that we use for something more powerful than Notepad or a simple editor. Writing code means that we have different requirements than if we were to write an essay. The editor needs to be able to indicate when we type something wrong, provide us with insights about our code, and preferably give us autocompletion that gives us a list of possible methods once we start typing the first letter. A coding editor can and should be your best friend.

For frontend development, there are a lot of great choices out there, and no environment is better than any other; it all depends on what works best for you. This book uses VS Code because of its popularity among the Angular community and the rich collection of plugins that are available from its marketplace. Let's embark on a journey of discovery so that you can be the judge of what environment will best suit you.

Atom

Developed by GitHub, the highly customizable environment and ease of installation of new packages has turned Atom into the IDE of choice for many people.

To optimize your experience with TypeScript when coding Angular apps, you need to install the Atom TypeScript package either via the Atom Package Manager CLI or by using the built-in package installer. It contains a variety of functionalities, such as automatic code hints, static type checking, code introspection, and automatic build-upon saving, to name a few. On top of these, this package also includes a convenient built-in generator to help you easily configure TypeScript for your project.

Sublime Text

Sublime Text is probably one of the most widespread code editors nowadays, although it has lost some momentum lately with users favoring other rising competitors, such as VS Code. To provide support for TypeScript code editing, you need to install Microsoft's TypeScript plugin, available at `https://github.com/Microsoft/TypeScript-Sublime-Plugin`. Please refer to this page to learn how to install the plugin and all the shortcuts and key mappings.

Once successfully installed, it only takes you pressing *Ctrl* + *Space bar* to display code hints based on type introspection. On top of this, you can trigger the build process and compile source files to JavaScript by hitting the *F7* key. Real-time code-error reporting is another fancy functionality that you can enable from the command menu.

WebStorm

WebStorm is an excellent code editor supplied by IntelliJ that is great for coding Angular apps. It comes with built-in support for TypeScript out of the box so that you can start developing Angular components from day one. WebStorm also implements a built-in transpiler with support for file watching, so you can compile your TypeScript code into pure vanilla JavaScript without relying on any third-party plugins.

Visual Studio Code

Visual Studio Code, or VS Code as it is more widely known, is an open source code editor backed by Microsoft that is gaining momentum as a serious contender in the Angular community, mostly because of its robust support for TypeScript out of the box. TypeScript has been, to a great extent, a project driven by Microsoft, so it makes sense that one of its popular editors was conceived with built-in support for this language. It means that all the nice features that we might want are already baked in, including syntax, error highlighting, and automatic builds. Another reason for its broad popularity is the various extensions available in the marketplace that enrich the Angular development workflow. What makes VS Code so great is not only its design and ease of use, but also the access to a ton of plugins, and there are some great ones for Angular development. The most popular are included in the Angular Essentials extension pack. To get it, go through the following steps:

1. Navigate to the Extensions menu of VS Code.
2. Search for the **Angular Essentials** keyword.
3. Click the **Install** button of the first entry item:

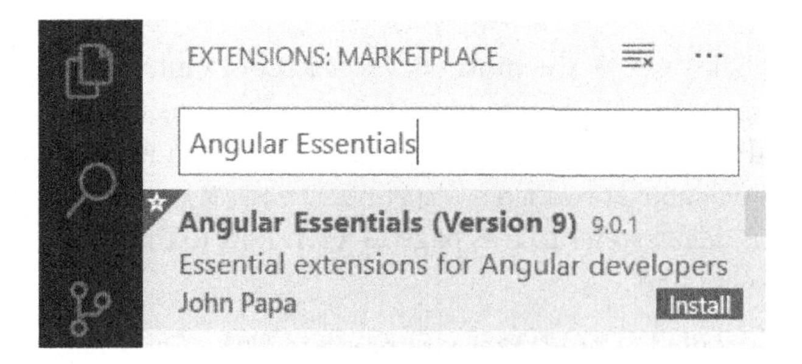

Figure 1.3 – Angular Essentials

Alternatively, you can install it automatically, since it is already included in the repository of this book's source code. When you download the project from GitHub and open it in VS Code, it will prompt you to view and install the recommended extensions:

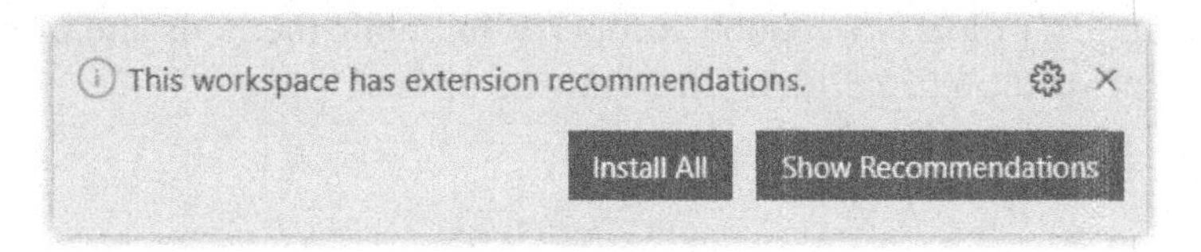

Figure 1.4 – Recommended extensions prompt

Let's now look at some of the extensions that are included in the Angular Essentials extension pack in the following sections.

Angular Language Service

The Angular Language Service extension is developed and maintained by the Angular team and provides code completion, navigation, and error detection inside Angular templates. It is included in the Angular Essentials extension pack, but it is also available for WebStorm and Sublime Text editors as a standalone plugin. It enriches IDEs with the following features:

- Code completion
- Go-to definition
- Quick info
- AOT diagnostic messages

To get a glimpse of the powerful capabilities of the extension, let's have a look at the code completion feature. Suppose that we want to display a new property called `description` in the template of `AppComponent`. We can set this up by going through the following steps:

1. Define the new property in the component class:

```
export class AppComponent {
  title = 'Hello Angular 10';
  description = 'Hello World';
}
```

2. Start typing the name of the property in the template. The Angular Language Service will find it and suggest it for you automatically:

Figure 1.5 – IntelliSense in the template

The `description` property is a public property. In public methods and properties, we can omit the keyword `public`. Take the following phrase:

```
description = 'Hello World';
```

This phrase is equivalent to the following:

```
public description = 'Hello World';
```

Code completion works only for public properties and methods. If the property had been declared as `private description = 'Hello World';`, then the Angular Language Service would not have been able to find it.

You may have noticed that as you were typing, a red line appeared instantly underneath the HTML element. This is an effect of the AOT diagnostic messages feature. The Angular Language Service did not recognize the property until you typed it correctly and gave you a proper indication of this lack of recognition. If you hover over the red indication, it displays a complete information message about what went wrong:

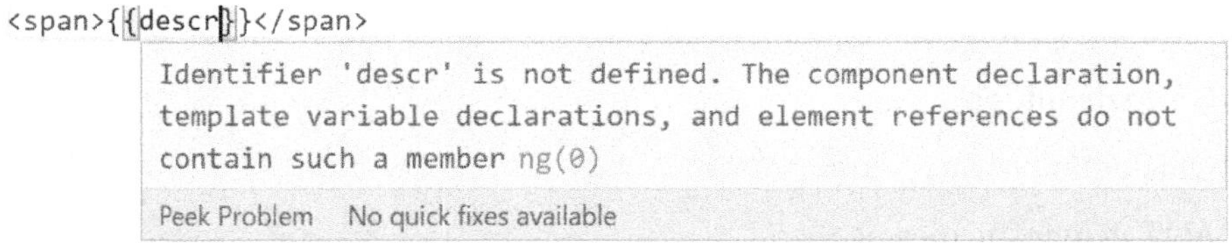

```
<span>{{descr}}</span>
Identifier 'descr' is not defined. The component declaration,
template variable declarations, and element references do not
contain such a member ng(0)
Peek Problem    No quick fixes available
```

Figure 1.6 – Error handling in the template

Angular Snippets

The Angular Snippets extension contains a collection of TypeScript and HTML code snippets for various Angular artifacts, such as components. To create the TypeScript class of an Angular component using the extension, go through the following steps:

1. Open VS Code and select **File | New File**.
2. Select **File | Save As** and give it a proper name with the `.ts` extension, which is the extension for TypeScript files.
3. Type `a-component` inside the file and press *Enter*.

The extension builds the TypeScript code for you automatically. Change the class name and the selector to something more appropriate, and you are ready to start using it in your project:

```
import { Component, OnInit } from '@angular/core';

@Component({
```

```
    selector: 'selector-name',
    templateUrl: 'name.component.html'
})

export class NameComponent implements OnInit {
    constructor() { }

    ngOnInit() { }
}
```

All available Angular snippets start with the `a-` prefix.

Nx Console

Nx Console is an interactive UI for the Angular CLI that aims to assist developers that are not very comfortable with the command-line interface or do not want to use it at all. It works as a wrapper over Angular CLI commands, and it helps developers concentrate on delivering outstanding Angular applications instead of trying to remember the syntax of every CLI command they want to use.

The extension is automatically enabled when you open an Angular CLI project. If you click on the Nx Console menu of VS Code, it displays a list of Angular CLI commands that you can execute:

Figure 1.7 – Nx Console

TSLint

TSLint is a tool that performs static analysis of TypeScript code and enforces readability, maintainability, and error checking by applying a set of rules. These rules are defined in the `tslint.json` configuration file, which can be found in the root folder of an Angular CLI project. It is maintained by Microsoft and must be installed separately:

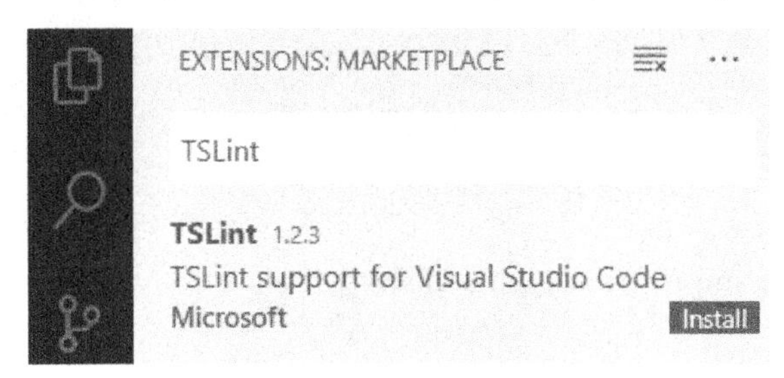

Figure 1.8 – TSLint

Development teams can significantly benefit from its use, as it can govern the coding style that a team uses internally. Developers of a team can agree on a specific set of rules beforehand. When the coding style of a developer does not respect one of these rules, TSLint displays a warning related to the violation. This method ensures that the application code is written consistently by all members of the team and that onboarding new developers on an Angular project becomes an easy process.

Material icon theme

VS Code has a built-in set of icons that it uses to display different types of files in a project. This extension provides additional icons that conform to the Material Design guidelines by Google; a subset of this collection targets Angular-based artifacts.

Using this extension, you can easily spot the type of Angular files in a project, such as components and modules, and increase developer productivity, especially in large projects with lots of files:

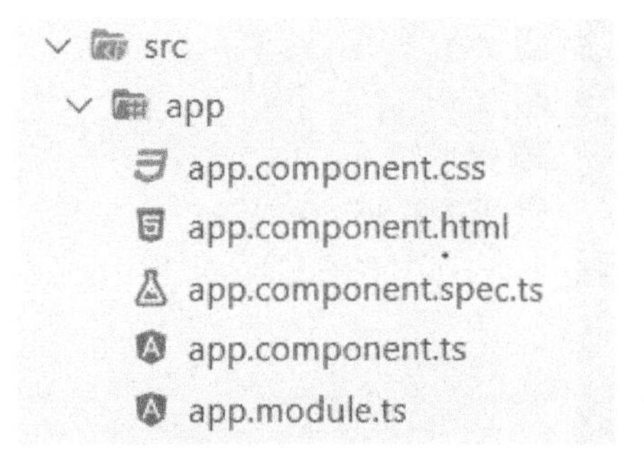

Figure 1.9 – Material icon theme

> **Important Note**
>
> You need to reload VS Code after this extension is installed for the icon changes to take effect.

EditorConfig

VS Code editor settings, such as indentation or spacing, can be set at a user or project level. **EditorConfig** can override these settings using a configuration file called `.editorconfig`, which can be found in the root folder of an Angular CLI project. You can define unique settings in this file to ensure the consistency of the coding style across your team.

Summary

That's it! Your journey to the world of Angular has just begun. Let's recap the features that you have learned so far. We looked at semantic versioning and how modern JavaScript frameworks such as Angular use it. We looked over the brief history of the Angular framework and learned how semantic versioning helps the Angular team to deliver up-to-date high-quality features.

We saw how to set up our working space and where to go to find the tools that we need to bring TypeScript into the game and use the Angular framework in our projects, going through the role of each tool in our application. We introduced the Angular CLI tool, the Swiss Army knife for Angular, that automates specific development tasks, and we used some of the most common commands to scaffold our very first Angular application. We had a glimpse of the structure of an Angular component and learned how to interact with it.

Our first application gave us a basic understanding of how Angular works internally to render our app on a web page. We embarked on our journey, starting with the main HTML file of an Angular application. We saw how Angular parses that file and starts searching the component tree to match HTML elements with component selectors and templates. We learned that components that share similar functionality are grouped into modules and looked at how Angular bootstraps the very first module of the application.

Finally, we met some of the most popular IDEs and learned how they can empower you as a software developer. There are many choices for editors, some of which we have chosen to cover in more detail, such as VS Code. There are also many plugins and snippets that save quite a few keystrokes. At the end of the day, your focus and energy should be spent on solving the problem and structuring your solution, not making your fingers tired. We encourage you to learn more about your editor and its possibilities because this will make you faster and more efficient.

In the next chapter, you will learn all about TypeScript, everything from the basics to the professional level. The chapter will cover what problems can be solved by introducing types, but also the language construct itself. TypeScript, as a superset of JavaScript, contains a lot of powerful concepts and marries well with the Angular framework, as you are about to discover.

2
Introduction to TypeScript

As we learned in the previous chapter, where we built our very first Angular application, the code of an Angular project is written in TypeScript. Writing in TypeScript and leveraging its static typing gives us a remarkable advantage over other scripting languages. This chapter is not a thorough overview of the TypeScript language. Instead, we'll just focus on the core elements and study them in detail on our journey through Angular. The good news is that TypeScript is not all that complex, and we will manage to cover most of its relevant parts.

In this chapter, we will cover the following topics:

- Look at the background and rationale behind TypeScript
- Discover online resources to practice with while we learn
- Recap on the concept of typed values and their representation
- Build our custom types, based on classes and interfaces
- Emphasize the use of advanced types in an Angular project
- Learn to organize our application architecture with modules

Let's get started!

The history of TypeScript

Transforming small web applications into thick monolithic clients was not possible due to the limitations of earlier JavaScript versions, such as the ECMAScript 5 specification. In a nutshell, large-scale JavaScript applications suffered from serious maintainability and scalability problems as soon as they grew in size and complexity. This issue became more relevant as new libraries and modules required seamless integration into our applications. The lack of proper mechanisms for interoperability led to cumbersome solutions that never seemed to fit the bill.

As a response to these concerns, ECMAScript 6 (also known as **ES6** or ES2015) promised to solve these issues by introducing better module loading functionalities, an improved language architecture for better scope handling, and a wide variety of syntactic sugar to better manage types and objects. The introduction of class-based programming turned into an opportunity to embrace a more OOP approach when building large-scale applications.

Microsoft took on this challenge and spent nearly 2 years building a superset of the language, combining the conventions of ES6 and borrowing some proposals from the next version of the specification, ES7. The idea was to launch something that would help build enterprise applications with a lower error footprint using static type checking, better tooling, and code analysis. After 2 years of development led by Anders Hejlsberg, lead architect of C# and creator of Delphi and Turbo Pascal, TypeScript 0.8 was finally introduced in 2012 and reached version 1.0 2 years later. It was not only running ahead of ES6 – it also implemented the same features and provided a stable environment for building large-scale applications. It introduced, among other features, optional static typing through type annotations, thereby ensuring type checking at compile-time and catching errors early in the development process. Its support for declaration files also allows developers to describe the interface of their modules so that other developers can better integrate them into their code workflow and tooling.

The benefits of TypeScript

As a superset of JavaScript, one of the main advantages of embracing TypeScript in your next project is the low entry barrier. If you know JavaScript, you are pretty much all set, since all the additional features in TypeScript are optional. You can pick and introduce any of them to achieve your goal. Overall, there is a long list of strong arguments for advocating for TypeScript in your next project, and all of them apply to Angular as well.

Here is a short rundown, to name a few:

- Annotating your code with types ensures a consistent integration of your different code units and improves code readability and comprehension.

- The built-in type-checker analyzes your code at runtime and helps you prevent errors even before executing your code.
- The use of types ensures consistency across your application. In combination with the previous two, the overall code error footprint gets minimized in the long run.
- TypeScript extends classes with long-time demanded features such as class fields, private members, and enumerations.
- The use of decorators allows you to extend your classes and implementations in unique ways.
- Creating interfaces ensures a smooth and seamless integration of your libraries in other systems and code bases.
- TypeScript support across different IDEs is terrific, and you can benefit from features such as highlighting code, real-time type checking, and automatic compilation at no cost.
- The syntax is familiar to developers coming from other OOP-based backgrounds such as Java, C#, and C++.

Introducing TypeScript resources

Let's have a look at where we can get further support to learn and test drive our new knowledge of TypeScript.

> **Important Note**
> In this book we will be using TypeScript 3.9 as it is supported by Angular 10

The TypeScript official site

Our first stop is the official website of the language: `https://www.typescriptlang.org`.

There, we can find more extensive documentation of the language, along with a playground that gives us access to a quick tutorial to get up to speed with the language in no time. It includes some ready-made code examples that cover some of the most common traits of the language. We encourage you to leverage this tool to test the code examples we'll cover throughout this chapter.

The TypeScript official wiki

The code for TypeScript is fully open sourced at GitHub, and the Microsoft team has put reasonable effort into documenting the different facets of the code in the wiki available on the repository site. We encourage you to take a look at it any time you have a question, or if you want to dive deeper into any of the language features or form aspects of its syntax. The wiki is located at `https://github.com/Microsoft/TypeScript/wiki`.

Types in TypeScript

Working with TypeScript or any other coding language means working with data, and such data can represent different sorts of content that are called **types**. Types are used to represent the fact that such data can be a text string, an integer value, or an array of these value types, among others. You may have already met types in JavaScript since we have always been working implicitly with them but in a flexible manner. This also means that any given variable could assume (or return, in the case of functions) any value. Sometimes, this leads to errors and exceptions in our code because of type collisions between what our code returned and what we expected it to return type-wise. We can enforce this flexibility using **any** type, as we will see later in this chapter. However, statically typing our variables gives our IDE and us a good picture of what kind of data we are supposed to find in each instance of code. It becomes an invaluable way to help debug our applications at compile time before it is too late.

String

One of the most widely used primitive types is `string`, which populates a variable with a piece of text:

```
var brand: string = 'Chevrolet';
```

Check out the type definition next to the variable name, which is separated by a colon. This is how we annotate types in TypeScript. We can use either single or double quotes for the value of a `string`. Feel free to choose either and stick with it within your team. We can define multiline text strings with support for text interpolation with placeholder variables by using backticks:

```
var brand: string = 'Chevrolet';
var message: string = `Today it's a happy day! I just bought a
new ${brand} car`;
```

In this case, any variables that we may use inside the multiline text must be surrounded by the curly braces of the placeholder `${}`.

Declaring variables

TypeScript, as a superset of JavaScript, supports expressive declaration nouns such as `let`, which denotes that the scope of the variable is the nearest enclosing block (either a `function`, `for` loop, or any enclosing statement). On the other hand, `const` indicates that the value of the declared variable has the same type or value once set.

The let keyword

Traditionally, developers have been using `var` to declare objects, variables, and other artifacts, but this is discouraged when you start using ES6 or TypeScript. The reason for this is that ES5 only has a `function` scope; that is, a variable is unique within the context of a `function`, like so:

```
function test() {
    var a;
}
```

There can be no other a variable in this function. If you do declare one, then you effectively redefine it. However, there are cases in which scoping is not applied, such as in for loops. In Java, you would write the following and ensure that a variable will never leak outside of the `for` loop:

```
var i = 3;
for (var i = 0; i < 10; i++) {
}
```

That is, the `i` variable outside of the `for` loop will not affect the `i` variable inside it; they would have a separate scope. But this is not the case with ES5. Thus, ES6 introduced a new feature to fix this flaw, called the `let` keyword. Consider the following piece of code:

```
let i = 3;
for (let i = 0; i < 10; i++) {
}
```

TypeScript compiles it and generates the following JavaScript code:

```
var i = 3;
for (var i_1 = 0; i_1 < 10; i_1++) {
}
```

It essentially renames the variable within the `for` loop so that a name collision doesn't happen. So, remember, no more `var`; use the `let` keyword wherever possible.

The const keyword

The `const` keyword is a way to indicate that a variable should never change. As a code base grows, changes may happen by mistake, and such a mistake might be costly. The `const` keyword can prevent these types of mistakes through compile-time support. Consider the following code snippet:

```
const PI = 3.14;
PI = 3;
```

When the compiler tries to run it, it displays the following error message:

Cannot assign to 'PI' because it is a constant

Notice that this works only at the top level. You need to be aware of this if you declare objects as constants, like so:

```
const obj = {
    a: 3
};

obj.a = 4;
```

Declaring `obj` as a constant does not freeze the entire object from being edited, but rather what it points to. So, the preceding code is valid.

In the following example, we're actively changing the reference of `obj`, not one of its properties. Therefore, it is not allowed, and we get the same compiler error that we got previously:

```
obj = {};
```

> **Important Note**
>
> `const` versus `let`: Prefer to use the `const` keyword over `let` when you are sure that the properties of an object will not change during its lifetime. This prevents the object from accidentally changing at runtime and enforces data immutability, a hot topic in Angular applications.

Number

`number` is probably the other most widespread primitive data type, along with `string` and `boolean`:

```
const age: number = 7;
const height: number = 5.6;
```

It defines a floating-point number, as well as hexadecimal, decimal, binary, and octal literals.

Boolean

The `boolean` type defines a variable that can have a value of either `true` or `false`:

```
const isZeroGreaterThanOne: boolean = false;
```

The result of the variable represents the fulfillment of a boolean condition.

Array

Handling exceptions that arise from errors such as assigning wrong member types in a list can now be easily avoided with the **array** type, where it defines a list of items that contain certain types only. The syntax requires the postfix `[]` in the type annotation, as follows:

```
const brand: string[] = ['Chevrolet', 'Ford', 'General
Motors'];
const ages: number[] = [8, 5, 12, 3, 1];
```

If we try to add a new item to the `ages` array with a type other than `number`, the runtime type checker will complain, making sure our typed members remain consistent and that our code is error-free.

Dynamic typing with any type

Sometimes, it is hard to infer the data type out of the information we have at any given point, especially when we are porting legacy code to TypeScript or integrating loosely typed third-party libraries and modules. TypeScript supplies us with a convenient type for these cases. The `any` type is compatible with all the other existing types, so we can type any data value with it and assign any value to it later:

```
let distance: any;
distance = '1000km';
```

```
distance = 1000;

const distances: any[] = ['1000km', 1000];
```

However, this great power comes with great responsibility. If we bypass the convenience of static type checking, we are opening the door to type errors when piping data through our modules. It is up to us to ensure type safety throughout our application.

> **Important Note**
> The `null` and `undefined` literals require special treatment. In a nutshell, they are typed under the `any` type, which makes it possible to assign these literals to any other variable, regardless of its original type.

Custom types

In TypeScript, you can come up with your own type if you need to by using the `type` keyword in the following way:

```
type Animal = 'Cheetah' | 'Lion';
```

It is essentially a type with a finite number of allowed values. Let's create a variable from this type:

```
const animal: Animal = 'Cheetah';
```

This is perfectly valid as `Cheetah` is one of the allowed values and works as intended.

The interesting part happens when we give our variable a value it does not expect:

```
const animal: Animal = 'Turtle';
```

This results in the following compiler error:

```
Type '"Turtle"' is not assignable to type 'Animal'.
```

Enum

The enum type is a set of unique numeric values that we can represent by assigning user-friendly names to each of them. Its use goes beyond assigning an alias to a number. We can use it as a way to list the different variations that a specific type can assume, in a convenient and recognizable way. It is defined using the enum keyword and begins numbering members, starting at 0, unless explicit numeric values are assigned to them:

```
enum Brands { Chevrolet, Cadillac, Ford, Buick, Chrysler, Dodge
};
const myCar: Brands = Brands.Cadillac;
```

Inspecting the value of myCar returns 1 (which is the index held by Cadillac). As we mentioned already, we can assign custom numeric values in enum:

```
enum BrandsReduced { Tesla = 1, GMC, Jeep };
const myTruck: BrandsReduced = BrandsReduced.GMC;
```

Inspecting myTruck yields 2, since the first enumerated value, Tesla, was set to 1 already. We can extend value assignation to all the enum members as long as such values are integers:

```
enum StackingIndex {
    None = 0,
    Dropdown = 1000,
    Overlay = 2000,
    Modal = 3000
};
const mySelectBoxStacking: StackingIndex = StackingIndex.
Dropdown;
```

One last point worth mentioning is the possibility to look up the enum member mapped to a given numeric value:

```
enum Brands { Chevrolet, Cadillac, Ford, Buick, Chrysler, Dodge
};
const myCarBrandName: string = Brands[1];
```

It should also be mentioned that from TypeScript 2.4 and onward, it is possible to assign string values to enums. This is something that is preferred in Angular projects because of its extended support in template files.

Void

The `void` type represents the absence of a type, and its use is constrained to annotating functions that do not return an actual value:

```
function test(): void {
    const a = 0;
}
```

Therefore, there is no return type in `function` either.

Type inference

Typing is optional since TypeScript is smart enough to infer the data types of variables and function return values out of context with a certain level of accuracy. When this is not possible, it will assign the dynamic `any` type to the loosely-typed data at the cost of reducing type checking to a bare minimum. The following is an example of this:

```
const brand = 'Chevrolet';
```

This holds the same effect; that is, it leads to a compilation error if you try to assign a non-compatible data type to it.

Functions, lambdas, and execution flow

Functions are the processing machines we used to analyze input, digest information, and apply the necessary transformations to data that's provided either to transform the state of our application or to return an output that will be used to shape our application's business logic or user interactivity.

Functions in TypeScript are not that different from regular JavaScript, except for the fact that, just like everything else in TypeScript, they can be annotated with static types. Thus, they improve the compiler by providing it with the information it expects in their signature and the data type it aims to return, if any.

Annotating types in our functions

The following example showcases how a regular `function` is annotated in TypeScript:

```
function sayHello(name: string): string {
    return 'Hello, ' + name;
}
```

We can see two main differences from the usual `function` syntax in regular JavaScript. First, we annotate the parameters declared in the `function` signature, which makes sense since the compiler will want to check whether the data provided holds the correct type. In addition to this, we also annotate the returning value by adding the `string` type to the `function` declaration.

As mentioned in the previous section, the TypeScript compiler is smart enough to infer types when no annotation is provided. In this case, the compiler looks into the arguments provided and return statements to infer a returning type from it.

Functions in TypeScript can also be represented as expressions of anonymous functions, where we bind the `function` declaration to a variable:

```
const sayHello = function(name: string): string {
    return 'Hello, ' + name;
}
```

However, there is a downside to this syntax. Although typing `function` expressions this way is allowed, thanks to type inference, the compiler is missing the type definition of the declared variable. We might assume that the inferred type of a variable that points to a `function` typed as a `string` is a string. Well, it's not. A variable that points to an anonymous `function` ought to be annotated with a `function` type:

```
const sayHello: (name: string) => string = function(name: 
string): string {
    return 'Hello, ' + name;
}
```

The `function` type informs us of the types expected in the `function` payload and the type returned by the execution of `function`, if any. This whole block, which is of the form *(arguments: type) => returned type*, becomes the type annotation our compiler expects.

Function parameters in TypeScript

Due to the type checking performed by the compiler, `function` parameters require special attention in TypeScript.

Optional parameters

Parameters are a core part of the type checking that's applied by the TypeScript compiler. TypeScript defines that a parameter is optional by adding the `?` symbol as a postfix to the parameter name we want to make optional:

```
function greetMe(name: string, greeting?: string): string {
    if(!greeting) {
        greeting = 'Hello';
    }
    return greeting + ', ' + name;
}
```

Thus, we can omit the second parameter in the `function` call:

```
greetMe('John');
```

So, an optional parameter is set unless you explicitly do so. It is more of a construct so that you can get help with deciding what parameters are mandatory and which ones are optional. Let's exemplify this:

```
function add(mandatory: string, optional?: number) {}
```

You can invoke this `function` in the following ways:

```
add('some string');
add('some string', 3.14);
```

Both versions are valid. Be aware that optional parameters should be placed last in a `function` signature. Consider the following `function`:

```
function add(optional?: number, mandatory: string) {}
```

This creates a situation where both parameters would be considered mandatory. Let's say you call your `function` like so:

```
add(1);
```

Here, the compiler would complain that you have not provided a value for the `mandatory` argument. Remember, optional arguments are great, but place them last.

Default parameters

TypeScript gives us another feature to cope with default parameters, where we can set a default value that the parameter assumes when it's not explicitly passed upon executing the function. The syntax is pretty straightforward, as we can see when we refactor the previous example:

```
function greetMe(name: string, greeting: string = 'Hello'):
string {
    return `${greeting}, ${name}`;
}
```

Just as with optional parameters, default parameters must be put right after the required parameters in the `function` signature.

Rest parameters

One of the big advantages of the flexibility of JavaScript when defining functions is its ability to accept an unlimited non-declared array of parameters in the form of the arguments object. In a statically typed context such as TypeScript, this might not be possible, but it is actually using the **rest** parameter's object. We can define, at the end of the arguments list, an additional parameter prefixed by ellipsis `...` and typed as an array:

```
function greetPeople(greeting: string, ...
names: string[]): string {
    return greeting + ', ' + names.join(' and ') + '!';
}
```

So, rest parameters are your friend when you don't know how many arguments you have.

Function overloading

Method and `function` overloading is a common pattern in other languages, such as C#. However, implementing this functionality in TypeScript clashes with the fact that JavaScript, which TypeScript is meant to compile to, does not implement any elegant way to integrate it out of the box. So, the only workaround possible requires writing `function` declarations for each of the overloads and then writing a general-purpose `function` that wraps the actual implementation, whose list of typed arguments and return types are compatible with all the others:

```
function hello(names: string): string {}
function hello(names: string[]): string {}
function hello(names: any, greeting?: string): string {
```

```
    let namesArray: string[];
    if (Array.isArray(names)) {
        namesArray = names;
    } else {
        namesArray = [names];
    }

    if (!greeting) {
        greeting = 'Hello';
    }
    return greeting + ', ' + namesArray.join(' and ') + '!';
}
```

In the preceding example, we are creating three different `function` signatures, and each of them features different type annotations. We could even define different return types if there was a case for that. To do so, we should have annotated the wrapping `function` with any type.

Arrow functions

ES6 introduced the concept of fat arrow functions (also called lambda functions in other languages such as Python, C#, Java, or C++) as a way to simplify the general `function` syntax and to provide a bulletproof way to handle the scope of the functions. This is something that is traditionally handled by the infamous scope issues of tackling with the `this` keyword. The first thing we notice is its minimalistic syntax, where, most of the time, we see arrow functions as single-line, anonymous expressions:

```
const double = x => x * 2;
```

The function computes the double of a given number `x` and returns the result, although we do not see any `function` or `return` statements in the expression. If the `function` signature contains more than one argument, we need to wrap them all between braces:

```
const add = (x, y) => x + y;
```

Arrow functions can also contain statements. In this case, we want to wrap the whole implementation in curly braces:

```
const addAndDouble = (x, y) => {
    const sum = x + y;
    return sum * 2;
}
```

Still, what does this have to do with scope handling? The value of `this` can point to a different context, depending on where we execute the function. This is a big deal for a language that prides itself on excellent flexibility for functional programming, where patterns such as callbacks are paramount. When referring to `this` inside a callback, we lose track of the upper context, which usually leads us to using conventions such as assigning its value to a variable named `self` or `that`. It is this variable that is used later on within the callback. Statements containing interval or timeout functions make for a perfect example of this:

```
function delayedGreeting(name): void {
    this.name = name;
    this.greet = function(){
        setTimeout(function() {
            console.log('Hello ' + this.name);
        }, 0);
    }
}

const greeting = new delayedGreeting('John');
greeting.greet();
```

Executing the preceding script won't give us the expected result of **Hello John**, but an incomplete string highlighting a pesky greeting to *Mr. Undefined*! This construction screws the lexical scoping of `this` when evaluating the function inside the timeout call. Porting this script to arrow functions will do the trick, though:

```
function delayedGreeting(name): void {
    this.name = name;
    this.greet = function() {
        setTimeout(() =>
            console.log('Hello ' + this.name)
        , 0);
    }
}
```

Even if we break down the statement contained in the arrow function into several lines of code wrapped by curly braces, the lexical scoping of `this` keeps pointing to the proper context outside the `setTimeout` call, allowing for more elegant and clean syntax.

Common TypeScript features

There are some general features in TypeScript that don't apply specifically to classes, functions, or parameters, but instead make coding more efficient and fun. The idea is that the fewer lines of code you have to write, the better it is. It's not only about fewer lines but also about making things more straightforward. There are a ton of such features in ES6 that TypeScript has also implemented. In the following sections, we'll name a few that you are likely going to use in an Angular project.

Spread parameter

A spread parameter uses the same ellipsis syntax as the rest parameters but in a different way. It's not used as a parameter inside of a `function`, but rather inside its body. Let's illustrate this with an example:

```
const newItem = 3;
const oldArray = [1, 2];
const newArray = [...oldArray, newItem];
```

What we do here is add an item to an existing array without changing the old one. `oldArray` still contains 1, 2, but `newArray` contains 1, 2, 3. This general principle is called **immutability**, which essentially means don't change, but rather create a new state from the old state. It's a principle used in functional programming as a paradigm, but also for performance reasons. You can also use a rest parameter on objects, like this:

```
const oldPerson = { name : 'John' };
const newPerson = { ...oldPerson, age : 20 };
```

This is a merge between the two objects. Just like with the example of the list, we don't change the previous variable, `oldPerson`. The `newPerson` variable takes the information from `oldPerson` and adds its new values to it.

Template strings

Template strings are all about making your code clearer. Consider the following:

```
const url = 'http://path_to_domain' +
    'path_to_resource' +
    '?param=' + parameter +
    '=' + 'param2=' +
    parameter2;
```

So, what's wrong with this? The answer is readability. It's hard to imagine what the resulting string will look like, but it is also easy for you to edit the previous code by mistake, and suddenly, the result will not be what you want. Most languages use a format `function` for this, and that is exactly what template strings are. This can be used in the following way:

```
const url =
`${baseUrl}/${path_to_
resource}?param=${parameter}&param2={parameter2}`;
```

This is a much more condensed expression and much easier to read.

Generics

Generics is an expression for indicating a general code behavior that we can employ, regardless of the type of data. They are often used in collections because they have similar behavior, regardless of the type. They can, however, be used on constructs such as methods. The idea is that generics should indicate if you are about to mix types in a way that isn't allowed:

```
function method<T>(arg: T): T {
    return arg;
}

method<number>(1);
```

In the preceding example, the type of `T` is not evaluated until you use the method. As you can see, its type varies, depending on how you call it. It also ensures that you are passing the correct type of data. Suppose that the preceding method is called in this way:

```
method<string>(1));
```

We specify that `T` should be a string, but we insist on passing it a value of the `number` type. The compiler clearly states that this is not correct. You can, however, be more specific on what `T` should be. You can make sure that it is an array type so that any value you pass must adhere to this:

```
function method<T>(arg: T[]): T[] {
    console.log(arg.length);
    return arg;
}

```

```
class CustomPerson extends Array {}
class Person {}

const people: Person[] = [];
const newPerson = new CustomPerson();
method<Person>(people);
method<CustomPerson>(newPerson);
```

In this case, we decide that `T` should be the `Person` or `CustomPerson` type, and that the parameter needs to be of the array type. If we try to pass an object, the compiler will complain:

```
const person = new Person();
method<Person>(person);
```

So, why do we do this? We want to ensure that various array methods are available, such as `length`, and that we, in a given moment, don't care if we operate on something of the `CustomPerson` or `Person` type. You can also decide that `T` should adhere to an `interface`, like this:

```
interface Shape {
    area(): number;
}

class Square implements Shape {
    area() { return 1; }
}
class Circle implements Shape {
    area() { return 2; }
}

function allAreas<T extends Shape>(...args: T[]): number {
    let total = 0;
    args.forEach (x => {
        total += x.area();
    });
    return total;
```

```
}

allAreas(new Square(), new Circle());
```

Generics are quite powerful to use if you have a typical behavior that many different data types can relate to. You most likely won't be writing your custom generics, at least not initially, but it's good to know what is going on.

Classes, interfaces, and inheritance

Now that we have overviewed the most relevant bits and pieces of TypeScript, it's time to see how everything falls into place when building TypeScript classes. These classes are the building blocks of Angular applications.

Although `class` was a reserved word in JavaScript, the language itself never had an actual implementation for traditional POO-oriented classes as other languages such as Java or C# did. JavaScript developers used to mimic this kind of functionality by leveraging the `function` object as a `constructor` type and instantiating it with the `new` operator. Other standard practices, such as extending `function` objects, were implemented by applying prototypal inheritance or by using composition.

Now, we have an actual `class` functionality, which is flexible and powerful enough to implement the functionality our applications require. We already had the chance to tap into classes in the previous chapter. We'll look at them in more detail now.

Anatomy of a class

Property members in a `class` come first, and then a `constructor` and several methods and property accessors follow. None of them contain the reserved `function` word, and all the members and methods are annotated with a type, except `constructor`. The following code snippet illustrates what a `class` could look like:

```
class Car {
    private distanceRun: number = 0;
    private color: string;

    constructor(private isHybrid: boolean, color: string =
    'red') {
        this.color = color;
    }

```

```
    getGasConsumption(): string {
        return this.isHybrid ? 'Very low' : 'Too high!';
    }

    drive(distance: number): void {
        this.distanceRun += distance;
    }

    static honk(): string {
        return 'HOOONK!';
    }

    get distance(): number {
        return this.distanceRun;
    }
}
```

The `class` statement wraps several elements that we can break down:

- **Members**: Any instance of the `Car` class will contain three properties: `color` typed as a `string`, `distanceRun` typed as a `number`, and `isHybrid` as a `boolean`. Class members will only be accessible from within the class itself. If we instantiate this `class`, `distanceRun`, or any other member or method marked as `private`, it won't be publicly exposed as part of the object API.
- **Constructor**: The `constructor` executes right away when we create an instance of the class. Usually, we want to initialize the `class` members here, with the data provided in the `constructor` signature. We can also leverage the `constructor` signature itself to declare `class` members, as we did with the `isHybrid` property. To do so, we need to prefix the `constructor` parameter with an access modifier such as `private` or `public`. As we saw when analyzing functions in the previous sections, we can define rest, optional, or default parameters, as depicted in the previous example with the `color` argument, which falls back to red when it is not explicitly defined.
- **Methods**: A method is a special kind of member that represents a `function` and, therefore, may return a typed value. It is a `function` that becomes part of the object API but can be `private` as well. In this case, they are used as helper functions within the internal scope of the class to achieve the functionalities required by other `class` members.

- **Static members**: Members marked as `static` are associated with the `class` and not with the object instances of that `class`. We can consume `static` members directly, without having to instantiate an object first. Static members are not accessible from the object instances, which means they cannot access other `class` members using the `this` keyword. These members are usually included in the `class` definition as helper or factory methods to provide a generic functionality not related to any specific object instance.
- **Property accessors**: To create property accessors (usually pointing to internal `private` fields, as in the example provided), we need to prefix a typed method with the name of the property we want to expose using the `set` (to make it writable) and `get` (to make it readable) keywords.

Constructor parameters with accessors

Typically, when creating a `class`, you need to give it a name, define a `constructor`, and create one or more backing fields, like so:

```
class Car {
    make: string;
    model: string;

    constructor(make: string, model: string) {
        this.make = make;
        this.model = model;
    }
}
```

For every field you want to add to the class, you usually need to do the following:

- Add an entry to the `constructor`
- Add an assignment in the `constructor`
- Declare the field

This is boring and not very productive. TypeScript eliminates this boilerplate by using accessors on the `constructor` parameters. You can now type the following:

```
class Car {
    constructor(public make: string, public model: string) {}
}
```

TypeScript will create the respective `public` fields and make the assignment automatically. As you can see, more than half of the code disappears; this is a selling point for TypeScript as it saves you from typing quite a lot of tedious code.

Interfaces

As applications scale and more classes and constructs are created, we need to find ways to ensure consistency and rules compliance in our code. One of the best ways to address the consistency and validation of types is to create interfaces. In a nutshell, an `interface` is a blueprint of the code that defines a particular field's schema. Any artifacts (classes, `function` signatures, and so on) that implement these interfaces should comply with this schema. This becomes useful when we want to enforce strict typing on classes generated by factories, or when we define `function` signatures to ensure that a particular typed property is found in the payload.

Let's get down to business! In the following code, we're defining the `Vehicle` interface. It is not a `class`, but a contractual schema that any `class` that implements it must comply with:

```
interface Vehicle {
    make: string;
}
```

Any `class` implementing this `interface` must contain a member named `make`, which must be typed as a `string`:

```
class Car implements Vehicle {
    make: string;
}
```

Interfaces are, therefore, beneficial to defining the minimum set of members any artifact must fulfill, becoming an invaluable method for ensuring consistency throughout our code base.

It is important to note that interfaces are not used just to define minimum `class` schemas, but any type out there. This way, we can harness the power of interfaces by enforcing the existence of specific fields, as well as methods in classes and properties in objects, that are used later on as `function` parameters, `function` types, types contained in specific arrays, and even variables.

An `interface` may contain optional members as well. The following is an example of defining an `Exception` interface that contains a required `message` and optional `id` property members:

```
interface Exception {
    message: string;
    id?: number;
}
```

In the following code, we're defining the blueprint for our future `class`, with a typed array and a method with its returning type defined as well:

```
interface ErrorHandler {
    exceptions: Exception[];
    logException(message: string, id?: number): void
}
```

We can also define interfaces for standalone object types. This is quite useful when we need to define templated `constructor` or method signatures:

```
interface ExceptionHandlerSettings {
    logAllExceptions: boolean;
}
```

Let's bring them all together:

```
class CustomErrorHandler implements ErrorHandler {
    exceptions: Exception[] = [];
    logAllExceptions: boolean;

    constructor(settings: ExceptionHandlerSettings) {
        this.logAllExceptions = settings.logAllExceptions;
    }

    logException(message: string, id?: number): void {
        this.exceptions.push({message, id });
    }
}
```

We define a custom error handler `class` that manages an internal array of `exceptions` and exposes a `logException` method to log new exceptions by saving them into the array. These two elements are defined in the `ErrorHandler` interface and are mandatory.

So far, we have seen interfaces as they are used in other high-level languages, but interfaces in TypeScript are on steroids; let's exemplify that. In the following code, we're declaring an `interface`, but we're also creating an instance from an `interface`:

```
interface A {
    a
}

const instance = <A> { a: 3 };
instance.a = 5;
```

This is interesting because there are no classes involved. This means you can create a mocking library very easily. Let's explain a what we mean when talking about a mock library. When you are developing code, you might think in terms of interfaces before you even start thinking in terms of concrete classes. This is because you know what methods need to exist, but you might not have decided exactly how the methods should carry out a task.

Imagine that you are building an order module. You have logic in your order module and you know that, at some point, you will need to talk to a database service. You come up with a contract for the database service, an `interface`, and you defer the implementation of this `interface` until later. At this point, a mocking library can help you create a mock instance from the interface. Your code, at this point, might look something like this:

```
interface DatabaseService {
    save(order: Order): void
}

class Order {}

class OrderProcessor {

    constructor(private databaseService: DatabaseService) {}

```

```
    process(order) {
        this.databaseService.save(order);
    }
}

let orderProcessor = new OrderProcessor(mockLibrary.
mock<DatabaseService>());
orderProcessor.process(new Order());
```

So, mocking at this point gives us the ability to defer implementation of `DatabaseService` until we are done writing `OrderProcessor`. It also makes the testing experience a lot better. Where in other languages we need to bring in a mock library as a dependency, in TypeScript, we can utilize a built-in construct by typing the following:

```
const databaseServiceInstance = <DatabaseService>{};
```

This creates an instance of `DatabaseService`. However, be aware that you are responsible for adding a `process` method to your instance because it starts as an empty object. This will not raise any problems with the compiler; it is a powerful feature, but it is up to us to verify that what we create is correct. Let's emphasize how significant this TypeScript feature is by looking at some more cases, where it pays off to be able to mock away things.

Let's reiterate that the reason for mocking anything in your code is to make it easier to test. Let's assume your code looks something like this:

```
class Stuff {
    srv:AuthService = new AuthService();

    execute() {
        if (srv.isAuthenticated()) {}
        else {}
    }
}
```

A better way to test this is to make sure that the `Stuff` class relies on abstractions, which means that `AuthService` should be created elsewhere and that we use an `interface` of `AuthService` rather than the concrete implementation. So, we would modify our code so that it looks like this:

```
interface AuthService {
    isAuthenticated(): boolean;
}

class Stuff {

    constructor(private srv:AuthService) {}

    execute() {
        if (this.srv.isAuthenticated()) {}
        else {}
    }
}
```

To test this `class`, we would typically need to create a concrete implementation of `AuthService` and use that as a parameter in the `Stuff` instance, like this:

```
class MockAuthService implements AuthService {
    isAuthenticated() { return true; }
}

const srv = new MockAuthService();
const stuff = new Stuff(srv);
```

It would, however, become quite tedious to write a mock version of every dependency that you wanted to mock away. Therefore, mocking frameworks exist in most languages. The idea is to give the mocking framework an `interface` from which it would create a concrete object. You would never have to create a mock `class`, as we did previously, but that would be something that would be up to the mocking framework to do internally.

Class inheritance

Just like a class can be defined by an interface, it can also extend the members and functionality of other classes as if they were its own. We can make a class inherit from another by appending the extends keyword to the class name, including the name of the class we want to inherit its members from:

```
class Sedan extends Car {
    model: string;

    constructor(make: string, model: string) {
        super(make);
        this.model = model;
    }
}
```

Here, we're extending from a parent Car class, which already exposes a make member. We can populate the members already defined by the parent class and even execute their constructor by executing the super method, which points to the parent constructor. We can also override methods from the parent class by appending a method with the same name. Nevertheless, we are still able to execute the original parent's class methods as it is still accessible from the super object.

Decorators in TypeScript

Decorators are a very cool functionality, initially proposed by Google in AtScript (a superset of TypeScript that finally got merged into TypeScript back in early 2015). They are a part of the current standard proposition for ECMAScript 7. In a nutshell, decorators are a way to add metadata to class declarations for use by dependency injection or compilation directives. By creating decorators, we are defining special annotations that may have an impact on the way our classes, methods, or functions behave or just simply altering the data we define in fields or parameters. In that sense, they are a powerful way to augment our type's native functionalities without creating subclasses or inheriting from other types. It is, by far, one of the most interesting features of TypeScript. It is extensively used in Angular when designing directives and components or managing dependency injection, as we will learn later in *Chapter 4, Enhance Components with Pipes and Directives*.

The @ prefix can easily recognize decorators in a name, and they are usually located as standalone statements above the element they decorate.

We can define up to four different types of decorators, depending on what element each type is meant to decorate:

- Class decorators
- Property decorators
- Method decorators
- Parameter decorators

We'll look as these types of decorators in the following subsections.

> **Important Note**
> The Angular framework defines its own decorators, which we are going to use during the development of an application.

Class decorators

Class decorators allow us to augment a `class` or perform operations over its members. The decorator statement is executed before the `class` gets instantiated. Creating a `class` decorator requires defining a plain `function`, whose signature is a pointer to the `constructor` belonging to the `class` we want to decorate, typed as a `function` (or any other type that inherits from the `function`). The formal declaration defines a `ClassDecorator`, as follows:

```
declare type ClassDecorator = <TFunction extends
Function>(Target:TFunction) => TFunction | void;
```

It's complicated to grasp what this gibberish means, isn't it? Let's put everything in context through a simple example, like this:

```
function Banana(target: Function): void {
    target.prototype.banana = function(): void {
        console.log('We have bananas!');
    }
}

@Banana
class FruitBasket {
    constructor() {}
```

```
}

const basket = new FruitBasket();
basket.banana();
```

As we can see, we have gained a `banana` method, which was not originally defined in the `FruitBasket` class, by properly decorating it with the `@Banana` decorator. It is worth mentioning, though, that this won't compile. The compiler will complain that `FruitBasket` does not have a `banana` method, and rightfully so because TypeScript is typed. So, at this point, we need to tell the compiler that this is valid. So, how do we do that? One way is that, when we create our `basket` instance, we give it the `any` type, like so:

```
const basket: any = new FruitBasket();
```

Another way of essentially accomplishing the same effect is to type this instead:

```
const basket = new FruitBasket();
(basket as any).banana();
```

Here, we are doing a conversion on the fly with the `as` keyword, and we tell the compiler that this is valid.

Extending a class decorator

Sometimes, we might need to customize the way our decorator operates upon instantiating it. We can design our decorators with custom signatures and then have them returning a `function` with the same signature we defined when designing `class` decorators with no parameters. The following piece of code illustrates the same functionality as the previous example, but it allows us to customize the message:

```
function Banana(message: string) {
    return function(target: Function) {
        target.prototype.banana = function(): void {
            console.log(message);
        }
    }
}

@Banana('Bananas are yellow!')
class FruitBasket {
    constructor() {}
}
```

As a rule of thumb, decorators that accept parameters require a `function` whose signature matches the parameters we want to configure and returns another `function` whose signature matches that of the decorator we want to define.

Property decorators

Property decorators are applied to `class` fields and are defined by creating a `PropertyDecorator` `function`, whose signature takes two parameters:

- `target`: The prototype of the `class` we want to decorate
- `key`: The name of the property we want to decorate

Possible use cases for this specific type of decorator consist of logging the values assigned to `class` fields when instantiating objects of such a `class`, or when reacting to data changes in such fields. Let's see an actual example that showcases both behaviors:

```
function Jedi(target: Object, key: string) {
    let propertyValue: string = this[key];
    if (delete this[key]) {
        Object.defineProperty(target, key, {
            get: function() {
                return propertyValue;
            },
            set: function(newValue){
                propertyValue = newValue;
                console.log(`${propertyValue} is a Jedi`);
            }
        });
    }
}

class Character {
    @Jedi
    name: string;
}
const character = new Character();
character.name = 'Luke';
```

The same logic for parameterized `class` decorators applies here, although the signature of the returned `function` is slightly different so that it matches that of the parameterless decorator declaration we saw earlier. The following example depicts how we can log changes on a given `class` property:

```
function NameChanger(callbackObject: any): Function {
    return function(target: Object, key: string): void {
        let propertyValue: string = this[key];
        if (delete this[key]) {
            Object.defineProperty(target, key, {
                get: function() {
                    return propertyValue;
                },
                set: function(newValue) {
                    propertyValue = newValue;
                    callbackObject.changeName.call(this,
                    propertyValue);
                }
            });
        }
    }
}

class Character {
    @NameChanger ({
        changeName: function(newValue: string): void {
            console.log(`You are now known as ${newValue}`);
        }
    })
    name: string;
}

var character = new Character();
character.name = 'Anakin';
```

A custom `function` is triggered upon changing that `class` property.

Method decorators

This decorator can detect, log, and intervene in terms of how methods are executed. To do so, we need to define a `MethodDecorator function` whose payload takes the following parameters:

- `target`: Represents the decorated method (object).
- `key`: The actual name of the decorated method (`string`).
- `value`: This is a property descriptor of the given method. It's a hash object containing, among other things, a property named value with a reference to the method itself.

In the following example, we're creating a decorator that displays how a method is called:

```
function Log(){
    return function(target, propertyKey: string, descriptor: 
PropertyDescriptor) {
        const oldMethod = descriptor.value;
        descriptor.value = function newFunc( ...args:any[]){
            let result = oldMethod.apply(this, args);
            console.log(`${propertyKey} is called with ${args.
            join(',')} and result ${result}`);
            return result;
        }
    }
}

class Hero {
    @Log()
    attack(...args:[]) { return args.join(); }
}

const hero = new Hero();
hero.attack();
```

This also illustrates what the arguments were upon calling the method, and what the result of the method's invocation was.

Parameter decorator

Our last decorator covers the `ParameterDecorator` `function`, which taps into parameters located in `function` signatures. This sort of decorator is not intended to alter the parameter information or the `function` behavior, but to look into the parameter value and perform operations elsewhere, such as logging or replicating data. It accepts the following parameters:

- `target`: This is the object prototype where the `function`, whose parameters are decorated, usually belongs to a `class`.
- `key`: This is the name of the `function` whose signature contains the decorated parameter.
- `parameterIndex`: This is the index in the parameters array where this decorator has been applied.

The following example shows a working example of a parameter decorator:

```
function Log(target: Function, key: string, parameterIndex:
number) {
    const functionLogged = key || target.prototype.constructor.
    name;
    console.log(`The parameter in position ${parameterIndex} at
    ${functionLogged} has been decorated`);
}

class Greeter {
    greeting: string;

    constructor (@Log phrase: string) {
        this.greeting = phrase;
    }
}
```

You have probably noticed the weird declaration of the `functionLogged` variable. This is because the value of the target parameter varies, depending on the `function` whose parameters are decorated. Therefore, it is different if we decorate a `constructor` parameter or a `method` parameter. The former returns a reference to the `class` prototype, while the latter returns a reference to the `constructor` `function`. The same applies to the `key` parameter, which is undefined when decorating the `constructor` parameters.

Parameter decorators do not modify the value of the parameters decorated or alter the behavior of the methods or constructors where these parameters live. Their purpose is usually to log or prepare the container object for implementing additional layers of abstraction or functionality through higher-level decorators, such as a method or `class` decorator. Usual case scenarios for this encompass logging component behavior or managing dependency injection.

Advanced types

In the *Types in Typescript 3.9* section, we learned about some of the basic types in the TypeScript language, which we usually meet in other high-level languages as well. In this section, we'll take a look at some of the advanced types that will help us in the development of an Angular application.

Partial

We use this type when we want to create an object from an `interface` but include some of its properties, not all of them:

```
interface Hero {
    name: string;
    power: number;
}

const hero: Partial<Hero> = {
    name: 'Iron man'
}
```

In the preceding snippet, we can see that the `hero` object does not include `power` in its properties.

Record

Some languages, such as C#, have a reserved type when defining a key-value pair object or dictionary, as it is known. In TypeScript, there is no such thing. If we want to define such a type, we declare it as follows:

```
interface Hero {
    powers: {
        [key: string]: number
```

```
    }
}
```

However, this syntax is not clear. In a real-world scenario, interfaces have many more properties. Alternatively, we can use the `Record` type to define the interface:

```
interface Hero {
    powers: Record<string, number>
}
```

It defines `key` as a `string`, which is the name of the power in this case, and the value, which is the actual power factor, as a `number`.

Union

We've alrady learned about generics and how they help us when we want to mix types. A nice alternative, when we know what the possible types are, is the `Union` type:

```
interface Hero {
    name: string;
    powers: number[] | Record<string, number>;
}
```

In the preceding snippet, we defined the `powers` property as an array of numbers or a key-value pair collection, nothing more.

Nullable

We mentioned earlier, in the *Types in TypeScript 3.9* section, that TypeScript contains two particular basic types, `null` and `undefined`, for assigning a variable to anything. We can leverage these types, along with the `Union` type, to indicate that a property is nullable:

```
interface Hero {
    powers: number[] | null | undefined;
}
```

If we want to use the `powers` property in an object that's of the `Hero` type, we need to check for nullable values:

```
const hero: Hero = {
    powers: [10, 20]
```

```
}

if (hero.powers !== null && hero.powers !== undefined) {
    for (let i = 0; i < hero.powers.length; i++) {
    }
}
```

Imagine what happens if we have many nullable properties. We need to type `if-else` statements for each one separately, which is a cumbersome process. A new feature recently that was added to TypeScript 3.9 comes to the rescue here, known as optional chaining. Essentially, it allows us to write our code so that TypeScript knows to stop execution automatically when it runs into a nullable value. To use it, we need to place the `?` postfix in the nullable property, as follows:

```
for (let i = 0; i < hero.powers?.length; i++) {
}
```

Now, the `if-else` statement to check for nullable values is not needed anymore.

Modules

As our applications scale and grow in size, there will be a time when we need to organize our code better and make it sustainable and more reusable. Modules are responsible for this need, so let's take a look at how they work and how we can implement them in our application.

A module works at a file level, where each file is the module itself, and the module name matches the filename without the `.ts` extension. Each member marked with the `export` keyword becomes part of the module's public API:

my-service.ts

```
export class MyService {
    getData() {}
}
```

To use this module and its exported `class`, we need to import it:

```
import { MyService } from './my-service';
```

Notice that the ./my-service path is relative to the location of the file that imports the module. If the module exports more than one artifact, we place them inside the curly braces one by one, separated with a comma:

```
export class MyService {
    getData() {}
}
export const PI = 3.14;

import { MyService, PI } from './my-service';
```

In the preceding example, MyService exports the getData method and the PI variable in one go.

Summary

This was a long read, but this introduction to TypeScript was necessary to understand the logic behind many of the most brilliant parts of Angular. It gave us the chance to not only introduce the language syntax, but also explain the rationale behind its success as the syntax of choice for building the Angular framework.

We reviewed its type architecture and how we can create advanced business logic when designing functions with a wide range of alternatives for parameterized signatures, and we even discovered how to bypass issues related to scope by using the powerful new arrow functions. Probably the most relevant part of this chapter encompassed our overview of classes, methods, properties, and accessors and how we can handle inheritance and better application design through interfaces. Modules and decorators were some other significant features we explored in this chapter. As we will see very soon, having sound knowledge of these mechanisms is paramount to understanding how dependency injection works in Angular.

With all this knowledge at our disposal, we can now resume our investigation of Angular and confront the relevant parts of component creation, such as style encapsulation, output formatting, and so on, with confidence.

The next chapter will expose us to the basics of a component, how to pass data between components, and how to communicate with them. These features will allow us to put our newly gained knowledge of TypeScript into practice.

Section 2: Components – the Basic Building Blocks of an Angular App

This section explains how to organize an Angular 10 application into components and modules, and how to use the HTTP client to get data from a backend API and leverage built-in directives and pipes to enhance components.

This part comprises the following chapters:

- *Chapter 3, Component Interaction and Inter-Communication*
- *Chapter 4, Enhance Components with Pipes and Directives*
- *Chapter 5, Structure an Angular App*
- *Chapter 6, Enrich Components with Asynchronous Data Services*

3

Component Interaction and Inter-Communication

So far, we have had the opportunity to take a bird's eye overview of the Angular framework. We learned how to create a new Angular application using Angular CLI 10, and how the Angular framework works under the hood. TypeScript turns out to be the perfect companion for this endeavor.

We seem to have everything that we need to explore further possibilities that Angular brings to the game with regard to creating interactive components and how they can communicate with each other.

In this chapter, we will do the following:

- Learn how to create components for an Angular application
- Discover all the syntactic possibilities at our disposal to bind content in our templates
- Create public APIs for our components so that we can benefit from their properties and event handlers
- See how to implement data binding in Angular

- Reduce the complexity of CSS management with view encapsulation
- Learn how to adjust change detection inside components
- Take an overview of the component lifecycle

Technical requirements

GitHub link: `https://github.com/PacktPublishing/Learning-Angular--Third-Edition/tree/master/ch03`.

Creating our first component

Components are the basic building blocks of an Angular application. They control different parts of a web page called **views**, such as a list of products or a registration form. An Angular application consists of a tree of components that can interact with each other:

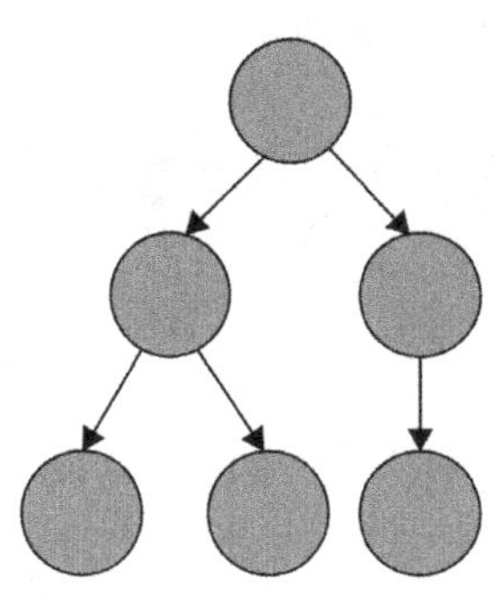

Figure 3.1 – Component architecture

The architecture of an Angular application is based on components. Each Angular component can communicate and interact with one or more components in the component tree. As we can see in the previous diagram, a component can simultaneously be a parent of some child components and a child of another parent component.

One of the most commonly used commands of the Angular CLI is the `generate` command, which we use to create certain Angular artifacts. We define the `<type>` of the artifact and its `<name>` in the following syntax:

```
ng generate <type> <name>
```

You can find a list of available types at `https://angular.io/cli/generate#ng-generate`.

In this chapter, we are interested in the component type. We will learn how to create other types of artifacts in the following chapters. To create a component, navigate to the root folder of an Angular CLI project and run the following in the command line:

```
ng generate component hero
```

If you are using VS Code, consider using the integrated terminal for running Angular CLI commands. Select **Terminal | New Terminal** from the main menu to open it.

> **Important Note**
> In Windows, the integrated terminal of VS Code uses **PowerShell** by default, which may prevent you from running Angular CLI commands due to security reasons. To change it, click on the dropdown that reads **1: powershell**, choose the **Select Default Shell** option, and select **Command Prompt**.

Creating an Angular component is a two-step process. It includes the creation of the necessary files of the component and its registration with an Angular module. We'll learn more details about this process in the following sections.

Component file creation

When we run the command in the previous section to generate an Angular component, the Angular CLI creates a `hero` folder inside the `app` folder and generates the following files:

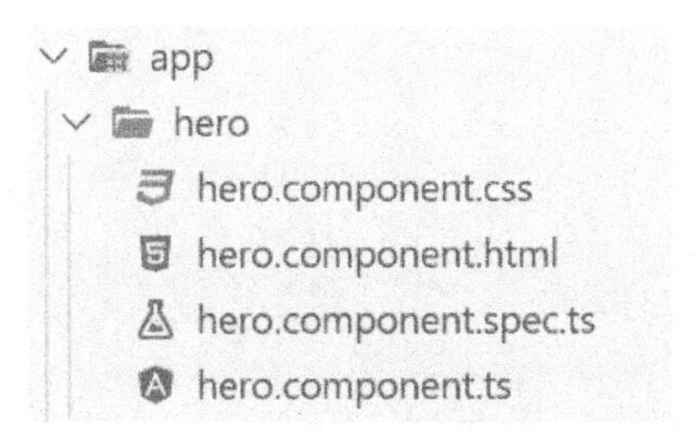

Figure 3.2 – Component folder structure

The Angular CLI appends the word `component` in each filename as a convention. It follows the same principle for all Angular artifacts, such as directives, pipes, and services so that it is easier to find them using the search feature of your IDE, among other files. A typical Angular component consists of the following files:

- **Component class**: A TypeScript file that contains the data and presentation logic of the component (`hero.component.ts`).

- **Component template**: An HTML file that is associated with the `class` and defines the view of the component (`hero.component.html`).
- **Component styles**: A set of CSS styles that are scoped, particularly to the component (`hero.component.css`). The extension of the file is dependent on the type of styling that you choose when creating a new Angular app.
- **Component unit test**: A set of unit tests that accompany the component (`hero.component.spec.ts`).

Module registration

In *Chapter 1, Building Your First Angular App*, we discussed how Angular works internally to display a component by searching through all the registered components of an Angular application. The Angular CLI registers a component automatically upon its creation by adding it to the `declarations` property of the main application module, `AppModule`:

app.module.ts

```
import { BrowserModule } from '@angular/platform-browser';
import { NgModule } from '@angular/core';

import { AppComponent } from './app.component';
import { HeroComponent } from './hero/hero.component';

@NgModule({
  declarations: [
    AppComponent,
    HeroComponent
  ],
  imports: [
    BrowserModule
  ],
  providers: [],
  bootstrap: [AppComponent]
})
export class AppModule { }
```

The `declarations` property of the `@NgModule` decorator is the place where we put Angular artifacts that we want to register with a module. These can be components, directives, and pipes. To declare them correctly, we must `import` them as ES6 modules. Luckily, the Angular CLI adds the `import` statement for us automatically. We will learn later, in *Chapter 5, Structure an Angular App*, that an Angular application can have many modules and how to configure them using the `@NgModule` decorator. Now that we have created a component, let's see how we can configure it appropriately.

Configuring a component

A component is typically a TypeScript `class` marked with the `@Component` decorator. Similar to the filename convention, the Angular CLI appends the word `Component` in the `class` name. All Angular artifacts are TypeScript classes that follow the same naming principle and have an appropriate decorator. Angular does not recognize them in the context of the framework unless we define the decorator *above* the `class` definition. The decorator is used to pass metadata to Angular so that it knows how to create a specific artifact. The metadata of the `@Component` decorator is a plain object with specific properties:

```
@Component({
  selector: 'app-hero',
  templateUrl: './hero.component.html',
  styleUrls: ['./hero.component.css']
})
```

In particular, it defines the following options:

- `selector`: The name of the component to be identified in an HTML template. It tells Angular where to create the component when it finds the corresponding tag in HTML. The Angular CLI adds the `app` prefix by default, but you can customize it when creating the Angular project using the `--prefix` option.
- `templateUrl`: The path of the component template file, relative to the component `class`. Alternatively, you can provide the template inline using the `template` property.
- `styleUrls`: The path of the component style files, relative to the component `class`. Notice that this option is an array and accepts multiple files for component styling. Alternatively, you can provide the styles inline using the `styles` property.

The component template file is an essential property of an Angular component. In the following section, we'll learn in detail how to interact with it.

Interacting with the template

In *Chapter 1, Building Your First Angular App*, we saw how Angular displays HTML content from components, but we didn't even scratch the surface of template development for Angular. As we will see later in this book, template implementation is tightly coupled with the principles of Shadow DOM design, and it brings out a lot of syntactic sugar to ease the task of binding properties and events in our views in a declarative fashion. Let's first take a look at how an Angular component can interact with its template either by displaying and getting data from it or by applying styles to it.

Displaying data from the component

We have already stumbled upon interpolation to display a property value from the `class` component to the template:

```
<span>{{ title }}</span>
```

Angular converts the `title` component property into text and displays it on the screen. An alternate way to perform interpolation is to bind `title` to the `innerText` property of the `span` HTML element, a method called **property binding**:

```
<span [innerText]="title"></span>
```

Notice that we bind to the **Document Object Model (DOM)** property of an element, not an HTML attribute, as it looks at first sight. The property inside square brackets is called the **target property** and is the property of the DOM element into which we want to bind. The variable on the right is called the **template expression** and corresponds to the `public title` property of the component. If the property is not `public`, the template will not be able to use it.

> **Important Note**
>
> When we open a web page in the browser, it parses the HTML content of the page and converts it into a tree structure, the DOM. Each HTML element of the page is converted to an object called a node, which represents part of the DOM. A node defines a set of properties and methods that represent the API of this object. `innerText` is such a property, which is used to set the text inside of an HTML element.

To better understand how the Angular templating mechanism works, we need to first understand how Angular interacts with attributes and properties. It defines attributes in HTML to initialize a DOM property, and then it uses data binding to interact with the property directly.

To set the attribute of an HTML element, we use the `attr-` syntax through property binding. For example, to set the `aria-label` attribute of an HTML element, we would write the following:

```
<p [attr.aria-label]="myText"></p>
```

Here, `myText` is a property in the corresponding Angular component. Remember that property binding interacts with properties of Angular components. Therefore, if we would like to set the value of the `innerText` property directly to the HTML, we would write the text value surrounded by single quotes:

```
<span [innerText]="'My title'"></span>
```

In this case, the value passed to the `innerText` property is a static `string`, not a component property.

Property binding is a convenient technique not only for display but also for style purposes.

Applying styles to the template

Styles in a web application can be applied either using the `class` or the `styles` attribute of an HTML element:

```
<p class="star"></p>
<p style="color: greenyellow"></p>
```

The Angular framework provides two types of property binding to set both of them dynamically, **class binding** and **style binding**. We can apply a single class to an HTML element using the following syntax:

```
<p [class.star]="isLiked"></p>
```

The `star` class will be added to the paragraph element when the `isLiked` expression is `true`. Otherwise, it will be removed from the element. If we want to apply multiple classes simultaneously, we can use the following syntax:

```
<p [class]="currentClasses"></p>
```

The `currentClasses` variable is a property of the component `class` and can be one of the following:

- A space-delimited string of class names such as `'star, active'`.
- An object with keys as the class names and values as `boolean` conditions for each key. A class is added to the element when the value of the key, with its name, evaluates to `true`. Otherwise, the class is removed from the element:

```
currentClasses = {
  star: true,
  active: false
};
```

Instead of styling our elements using CSS classes, we can set styles directly to them. Similar to the class binding, we can apply single or multiple styles simultaneously using a style binding. A single style can be set to an HTML element using the following syntax:

```
<p [style.color]="'greenyellow'"></p>
```

The paragraph element will have a `greenyellow` color. Some styles can be expanded further in the binding, such as the `width` of the paragraph element, which we can define with the measurement unit:

```
<p [style.width.px]="100"></p>
```

The paragraph element will be `100` pixels long. If we need to toggle multiple styles at once, we can use the object syntax:

```
<p [style]="currentStyle"></p>
```

`currentStyle` can be a string with styles separated by a semicolon:

```
currentStyle = 'color: greenyellow; width: 100px';
```

Alternatively, it can be an object where keys are the names of styles and values the actual style values:

```
currentStyle = {
  color: 'greenyellow',
  width: '100px'
};
```

Class and style bindings are powerful features that Angular provides out of the box when it comes to styling our components. An equally compelling feature is the ability to read data from a template into the component class.

Getting data from the template

In the previous section, we learned how to use property binding to display data from the component `class`. Real-world scenarios usually involve bidirectional data flow through components. To get data from the template back to the component, we use a method called **event binding**. Consider the following HTML snippet:

```
<button (click)="onClick()">Click me</button>
```

An event binding listens for DOM events that occur on the target HTML element and responds to those events by calling corresponding methods in the component. In this case, when the user clicks the `button`, the component calls the `onClick` method. The event inside parentheses is called the **target event** and is the event that we are listening to.

It supports native DOM events that can be found at `https://developer.mozilla.org/en-US/docs/Web/Events`.

The variable on the right is called the **template statement** and corresponds to the `onClick` `public` method of the component. Component methods must be `public` for the template to be able to call them:

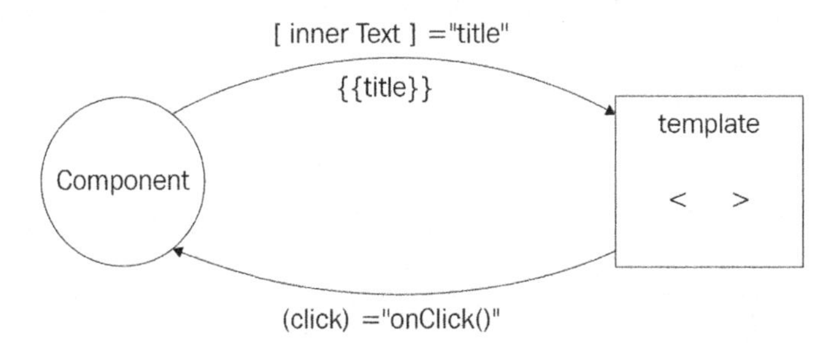

Figure 3.3 – Component-template interaction

In the previous diagram, you can see an overview of how the component interacts with its template bidirectionally. The same principle is followed when we want to communicate between components.

Communicating with other components

In a nutshell, Angular components expose a public API that allows them to communicate with other components. This API encompasses input properties, which we use to feed the component with data. It also exposes output properties we can bind event listeners to, thereby getting timely information about changes in the state of the component.

Let's take a look at how Angular solves the problem of injecting data into and removing data from components through quick and easy examples in the following sections.

Passing data using input binding

In the *Creating our first component* section, we learned how to create a new component in an Angular project. The Angular CLI created a template with static HTML content for our new component by default:

```
<p>hero works!</p>
```

To see the new component in action, do the following:

1. Navigate to the app folder that exists inside the `src` folder.
2. Open the template of the main component of the application, `app.component.html`.
3. Replace the contents of the template with the `selector` of the hero component, `<app-hero></app-hero>`.

   If we run the application, we'll see the template of our new component displayed on the screen:

Figure 3.4 – Simple Angular component

Templates that display only static information are rare in an Angular application. Let's make our hero component more interactive by displaying the name of the actual hero that works. The name will be dynamically passed from `AppComponent`. Initially, we define a property in the hero component `class` using the `@Input` decorator followed by the name of the property:

```
@Input() name: string;
```

The `@Input` decorator is a specialized TypeScript decorator created by the Angular team that is used when we want to pass data from a component *down* to another component. We first need to import it from the `@angular/core` package to use it:

```
import { Input } from '@angular/core';
```

The type of the input property, `string`, defines what type of data is going to be passed into the component.

After we have defined the input property, we use interpolation to bind the `name` property to the template of the hero component:

```
<p>{{name}} hero works!</p>
```

We have already completed most of the work; we now need to pass the value of the input property from `AppComponent`. We use property binding, as we learned earlier, in the *Interacting with the template* section, to bind the value of the `hero` property from `AppComponent` into the `name` input property of the hero component. This approach is called **input binding**:

```
<app-hero [name]="hero"></app-hero>
```

There are cases where we want to pass a static `string` or a value that we are sure will never change. In these cases, we can omit the square brackets surrounding the input property, as follows:

```
<app-hero name="Boothstomper"></app-hero>
```

The `hero` variable that we use in the input binding corresponds to a property in `AppComponent`:

```
export class AppComponent {
  title = 'my-app';
  hero = 'Drogfisher';
}
```

If we now run the application, it should display the following:

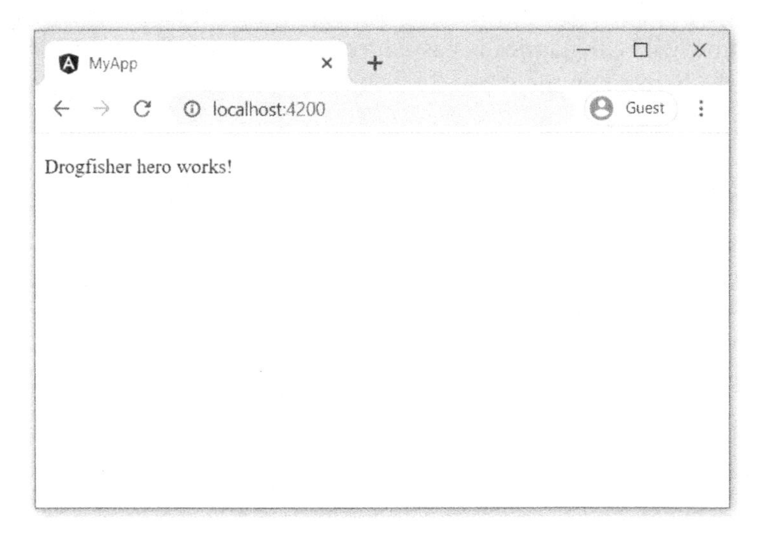

Figure 3.5 – Component with input binding

That's it! We have successfully passed data from one component to another. In the following section, we'll learn how to listen for events in a component and respond to them.

Listening for events using output binding

We learned that input binding is used when we want to pass data between components. This method is applicable in scenarios where we have two components, one that acts as the parent component and the other as the child. What if we want to communicate the other way round, from the child component to the parent? How do we notify the parent component about specific actions that occur in the child component?

Consider the scenario where the template of the hero component contains a **Like** `button` element that, when clicked, should notify `AppComponent` about the user's action. Initially, we define an output property in the hero component `class`:

```
@Output() liked = new EventEmitter();
```

The `liked` property is an `EventEmitter` marked with the `@Output` decorator, followed by the name of the property. The `@Output` decorator is a specialized TypeScript decorator created by the Angular team that is used when we want to trigger events from a component *up* to another component. We first need to import both of them from the `@angular/core` package to use them:

```
import { Output, EventEmitter } from '@angular/core';
```

> **Important Note**
>
> Many packages, Angular and non-Angular, contain an `EventEmitter` class. Make sure that you import the correct one from the `@angular/core` package.

Our button should call the `emit` method of the `liked` property to trigger the `EventEmitter`:

```
<button (click)="liked.emit()">Like</button>
```

We are almost there! We need to wire up the binding in `AppComponent` so that the two components can communicate with each other. We use event binding, as we learned earlier, in the *Interacting with the template* section, to bind the `onLike` method from `AppComponent` into the `liked` output property of the hero component. This approach is called **output binding**:

```
<app-hero [name]="hero" (liked)="onLike()"></app-hero>
```

When the user clicks the **Like** `button` in the hero component, `AppComponent` calls the `onLike` method:

```
onLike() {
    window.alert(`I like ${this.hero}`);
}
```

The application then displays the following alert message:

Figure 3.6 – Output binding that displays an alert window

Here, you can see an overview of the component communication mechanism that we have already discussed:

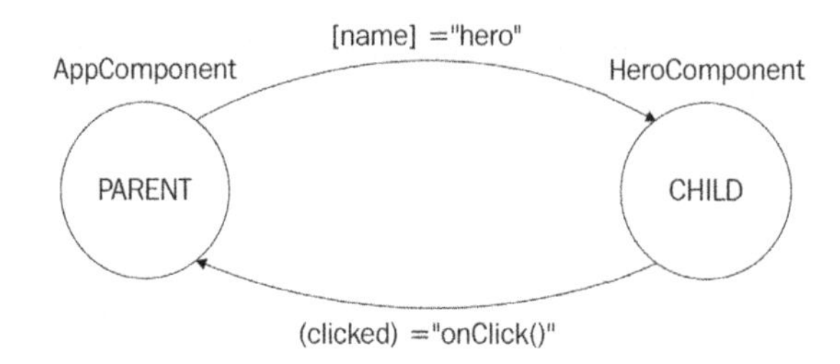

Figure 3.7 – Component inter-communication

The `liked` `EventEmitter` of the hero component does nothing more and nothing less but emits an event to the parent component, `AppComponent`. The `EventEmitter` `class` can also be used to pass arbitrary data through the `emit` method, as we will learn in the following section.

Emitting data through custom events

The `emit` method of an `EventEmitter` property can accept any data to pass up to the parent component. The proper way is initially to define the type of data that can be passed to the `EventEmitter` property.

Let's assume that the application should keep the state of the **Like** button each time it was clicked so that the user can like or dislike a hero. We would use generics of the `EventEmitter` class to declare the type of data that will be passed into `AppComponent`:

```
@Output() liked = new EventEmitter<boolean>();
```

The `click` event binding of the hero component template would call the `emit` method passing a `boolean` value as follows:

```
<button (click)="liked.emit(true)">Like</button>
```

The data would then be available in `AppComponent` through the `$event` object:

```
<app-hero [name]="hero" (liked)="onLike($event)"></app-hero>
```

The `$event` object is a reserved keyword in Angular that contains the payload data of an event emitter.

Input and output bindings are a great way to communicate between components using the public API. There are cases, though, where we want to access a property or a method of a component directly using local template reference variables.

Local references in templates

We have seen how we can bind data to our templates using interpolation with the double curly braces syntax. Besides this, we will quite often spot named identifiers prefixed by a hash symbol (#) in the elements belonging to our components or even regular HTML elements. These reference identifiers, namely **template reference variables**, are used to refer to the components flagged with them in our template views and then access them programmatically. They can also be used by components to refer to other elements in the DOM and access their properties.

In the previous section, we saw how we could listen to the `liked` event of the hero component or pass data through the `hero` property of `AppComponent`. But what if we could inspect the component in depth, or at least its `public` properties and methods, and access them without going through the input and output bindings? Well, setting a local reference on the component itself opens the door to its public facade. Let's declare the instance of our `hero` component in the template of `AppComponent` with a local reference named `#heroCmp`:

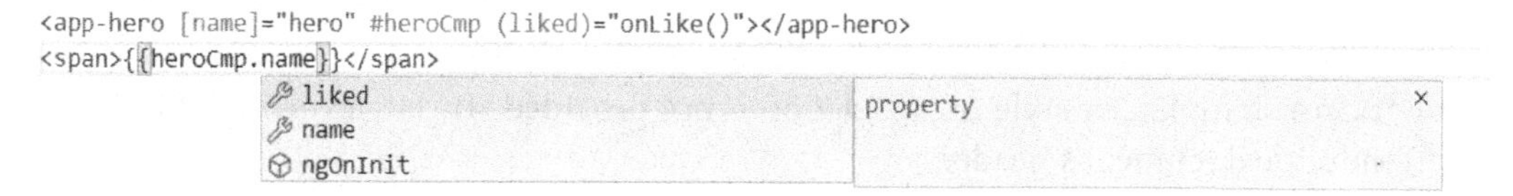

Figure 3.8 – Template reference variable in action

From that very moment, we can access the hero component's `public` properties directly and even bind it in other locations of the template. This way, we do not even need to rely on the input and output properties, and we can even manipulate the value of such properties.

We have mostly explained how the component class interacts with its template or other components, but we have barely been concerned about their styling.

Encapsulating CSS styling

To better encapsulate our code and make it more reusable, we can define CSS styling within our components. In the *Configuring a component* section, we learned how to define CSS styles to a component either using an external CSS file through the `styleUrls` property or by defining CSS styles inside the TypeScript component file with the `styles` property.

The usual rules of CSS specificity govern both ways:

`https://developer.mozilla.org/en/docs/Web/CSS/Specificity`

CSS management and specificity become a breeze on browsers that support Shadow DOM, thanks to scoped styling. CSS styles apply to the elements contained in the component, but they do not spread beyond their boundaries.

On top of that, Angular embeds style sheets at the head of the document so that they might affect other elements of our application. To prevent this from happening, we can set up different levels of view encapsulation. In a nutshell, encapsulation is the way that Angular needs to manage CSS scoping within the component for both Shadow DOM-compliant browsers and those that do not support it. It can be changed by setting the `encapsulation` property of the `@Component` decorator in one of the following `ViewEncapsulation` enumeration values:

- `Emulated`: This is the default option, and it entails an emulation of native scoping in Shadow DOM, through sandboxing the CSS rules under a specific selector that points to our component. This option is preferred to ensure that our component styles are affected by other existing libraries on our application.
- `Native`: Use the native Shadow DOM encapsulation mechanism of the renderer that works only on browsers that support Shadow DOM.
- `None`: Template or style encapsulation is not provided. The styles are injected as is into the document's header.

Let's take a look at an example of view encapsulation:

```
import { Component, ViewEncapsulation } from '@angular/core';

@Component({
  selector: 'app-hero',
  templateUrl: './hero.component.html',
  styles: ['p { color: #900; }'],
  encapsulation: ViewEncapsulation.Emulated
})
```

If we use the browser's developer tools inspector and check the generated HTML, we will discover how Angular injected the CSS inside the page `<head>` block:

```
<!doctype html>
<html lang="en">
▼<head>
    <meta charset="utf-8">
    <title>MyApp</title>
    <base href="/">
    <meta name="viewport" content="width=device-width, initial-scale=1">
    <link rel="icon" type="image/x-icon" href="favicon.ico">
  ▶<style>…</style>
  ▶<style>…</style>
...   <style>p[_ngcontent-voo-c11] { color: #900; }</style> == $0
  </head>
▶<body data-gr-c-s-loaded="true">…</body>
</html>
```

Figure 3.9 – Injected CSS styles from Angular

The injected style sheet has been sandboxed using a custom CSS selector, `_ngcontent-voo-c11`, to ensure that the global CSS rule we defined at the component only applies to matching elements scoped by the `hero` component exclusively.

> **Important Note**
>
> The custom CSS selector that starts with `_ngcontent` is created dynamically from the Angular framework and may not be the same when you run the preceding example.

Another essential property of the `@Component` decorator that we can configure is the change detection strategy of the component.

Change detection strategies

Change detection is the mechanism that Angular uses internally to detect changes that occur in component properties and reflect this change to the view. It is a non-deterministic process that is triggered on specific events such as when the user clicks on a button, an asynchronous request is completed, or a `setTimeout` and `setInterval` method is executed. Angular monkey patches these types of events by overwriting their default behavior using a library called **Zone.js**.

Every component has a change detector that detects whether a change has occurred in its properties by comparing the current value of a property with the previous one. If there are differences, it applies the change to the template of the component. In the following snippet, when the `name` input property changes, as a result of an event that we mentioned earlier, the change detection mechanism runs for this component and updates the template accordingly:

```
@Input() name: string;
```

There are use cases for which this behavior is not the desired one, such as in components that render hundreds or thousands of items in a list. In this scenario, the default change detection mechanism could introduce performance bottlenecks in the application. In this case, we could set the `changeDetection` property of the `@Component` decorator to select a different strategy from the available `ChangeDetectionStrategy` enumeration values:

```
import { Component, ChangeDetectionStrategy } from '@angular/
core';

@Component({
  selector: 'app-hero',
  templateUrl: './hero.component.html',
  changeDetection: ChangeDetectionStrategy.OnPush
})
```

The `OnPush` strategy triggers the change detection mechanism *only* when the reference of `@Input` properties change, significantly improving performance in large-scale apps.

The change detection strategy concludes our journey on how we can configure a component, but the Angular framework does not stop there. It also allows us to hook into specific times in the lifecycle of a component, as we'll learn in the following section.

Introducing the component lifecycle

Life cycle events are hooks that allow us to spy on specific stages in the lifecycle of a component and apply custom logic. They are entirely optional to use but might be of valuable help if you understand how to use them. Some hooks are considered best practice to use, while others help with debugging and understanding what happens in an Angular app. A hook comes with an `interface` that defines a method that we need to implement. The Angular framework makes sure the hook is called, provided we have implemented this method in the component. It is not obligatory to define the `interface` in the component, but it is considered a good practice. The Angular framework cares whether we have implemented the actual method or not. The available component lifecycle hooks are as follows:

- `OnInit`
- `OnDestroy`
- `OnChanges`
- `DoCheck`
- `AfterContentInit`
- `AfterContentChecked`
- `AfterViewInit`
- `AfterViewChecked`

All of the previous lifecycle hooks are available from the `@angular/core` package of the Angular framework. In this section, we cover the top three that are most frequently used in an Angular app. Some of the remaining ones will be revisited in later chapters of the book.

The first and most basic lifecycle event of a component is the `OnInit` hook.

Performing component initialization

The Angular CLI implements it by default when creating a new component:

```
import { Component, OnInit, Input, Output, EventEmitter } from
'@angular/core';

@Component({
  selector: 'app-hero',
  templateUrl: './hero.component.html',
```

```
  styleUrls: ['./hero.component.css']
})
export class HeroComponent implements OnInit {

  @Input() name: string;
  @Output() liked = new EventEmitter();

  constructor() { }

  ngOnInit(): void {
  }

}
```

The `OnInit` lifecycle hook implements the `ngOnInit` method, which is called upon the initialization of a component. At this stage, all input bindings and data-bound properties have been set appropriately, and we can safely use them. It may be tempting to use the `constructor` of the component to access them. In the following snippet, the `name` input property is undefined inside the `constructor`:

```
constructor() {
  console.log(this.name);
}
```

Constructors should be relatively empty and devoid of logic other than setting initial variables. Adding business logic inside a `constructor` also makes it challenging to mock it in testing scenarios.

Another good use of the `OnInit` hook is when we need to initialize a component with data that comes from an external source, such as an Angular service. As we will learn in *Chapter 5, Structure an Angular App*, when we want to use a method of an Angular service before component initialization, we call it inside the `ngOnInit` method.

The Angular framework provides hooks for all stages of the lifecycle of a component, from initialization to destruction.

Cleaning up resources

The `interface` that we implement to hook on the destruction event is the `OnDestroy` lifecycle hook:

```
export class HeroComponent implements OnDestroy, OnInit {

  @Input() name: string;
  @Output() liked = new EventEmitter();

  constructor() { }

  ngOnInit(): void {
  }

  ngOnDestroy() {

  }

}
```

We can use more than one lifecycle hook by separating them with a *comma*. The `OnDestroy` lifecycle hook implements the `ngOnDestroy` method that is called when a component is removed from the DOM tree of the web page. Destroying a component could be the result of one of the following:

- Using the `ngIf` directive, as we will learn in *Chapter 4, Enhance Components with Pipes and Directives*.
- Navigating away from a component using a URL, as we will learn in *Chapter 7, Navigate through Components with Routing*.

We usually perform a clean up of component resources inside the `ngOnDestroy` method, such as the following:

- Resetting timers and intervals
- Unsubscribing from observable streams, as we will learn in *Chapter 6, Enrich Components with Asynchronous Data Services*

We have already learned how to pass data down to a component using an input binding. The Angular framework provides the `OnChanges` lifecycle hook, which we can use to inspect when the value of such a binding has changed.

Detecting input changes

To better understand how it works, let's see it in action:

1. Open the `app.component.ts` file and modify the `onLike` method so that it changes the `hero` property to `Boothstomper`:

```
onLike() {
  window.alert(`I like ${this.hero}`);
  this.hero = 'Boothstomper';
}
```

2. Open the `hero.component.ts` file and add the `OnChanges` lifecycle hook in the list of implemented interfaces of the component.
3. Add the `ngOnChanges` method, which implements the `interface` that you just added.

The `ngOnChanges` method accepts an object of type `SimpleChanges` as a parameter that contains one key for each input property that changes. Each key points to another object with the properties `currentValue` and `previousValue`, which denote the new and the old value of the input property, respectively:

```
ngOnChanges(changes: SimpleChanges) {
  const hero = changes['name'];
  const oldValue = hero.previousValue;
  const newValue = hero.currentValue;
  console.log(`Hero changed from ${oldValue} to ${newValue}`);
}
```

The previous snippet tracks the `name` input property for changes, and logs both old and new values in the console window. To inspect the result, do the following:

1. Run the application using `ng serve`.
2. Open the console window from the developer tools of the browser.
3. Click on the **Like** button.

4. Dismiss the pop-up dialog and notice the output in the console window.

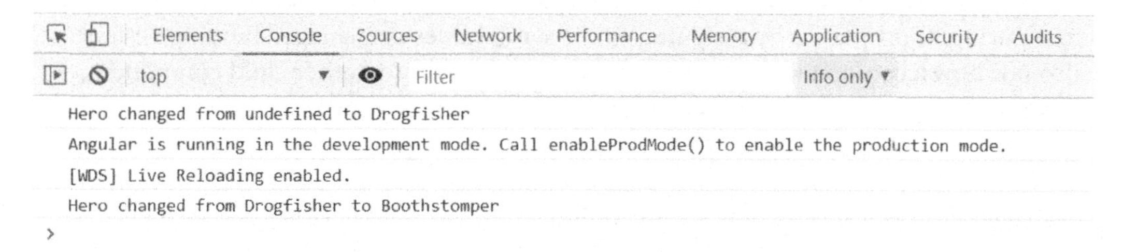

Figure 3.10 – Browser console window

In the last line, you can see the log from the `ngOnChanges` method. If you look closely, you will notice that there is an additional log in the first line stating that the name changed from **undefined** to **Drogfisher**. Why is that? We have already learned that the `ngOnChanges` method is called when an input property of the component changes. The initial value of the property is also considered a change. The old value is `undefined` since the property does not have a value yet. The new value is the first value that we set in the property – in our case, `Drogfisher`. To eliminate the unnecessary log, we can check whether this is the first change, using the `isFirstChange` method:

```
if (!hero.isFirstChange()) {
  console.log(`Hero changed from ${oldValue} to ${newValue}`);
}
```

If we rerun the application, we can see the correct log in the console window.

Summary

In this chapter, we learned how to create an Angular component using the Angular CLI and configure it using the `@Component` decorator. We discussed how we could isolate the component's HTML template in an external file to ease its future maintainability. Also, we saw how to do the same with any style sheet we wanted to bind to the component, in case we do not want to bundle the component styles inline. We also went through communication between the component and its template in a bidirectional way using property and event bindings.

We were guided through the options available in Angular for creating powerful APIs for our components, so we can provide high levels of interoperability between components, configuring its properties by assigning either static values or managed bindings. We also saw how a component can act as a host component for another child component, instantiating the former's custom element in its template, setting the ground up for larger component trees in our applications. Output parameters give the layer of interactivity we need by turning our components into event emitters so they can adequately communicate in an agnostic fashion with any parent component that might eventually host them.

Template references paved the way to create references in our custom elements that we can use as accessors to their properties and methods from within the template in a declarative fashion. An overview of the built-in features for handling CSS view encapsulation in Angular gave us some additional insights into how we can benefit from Shadow DOM's CSS scoping on a per-component basis. Finally, we learned how important change detection is in an Angular application and how we can customize it to improve its performance further.

We still have much more to learn regarding template management in Angular, mostly with regard to two concepts that you will use extensively in your journey with Angular: directives and pipes, which we cover in the next chapter.

4
Enhance Components with Pipes and Directives

In the previous chapter, we built several components that rendered data on the screen with the help of input and output properties. We'll leverage that knowledge in this chapter to take our components to the next level with the use of directives and pipes. Pipes allow us to digest and transform the information we bind in our templates. Directives allow us to conduct more ambitious functionalities such as manipulating the DOM or altering the appearance and behavior of HTML elements.

In this chapter, we will do the following:

- Have a comprehensive overview of the built-in directives of Angular.
- Discover how we can refine our data output with pipes.
- See how we can design and build custom pipes and directives.

Technical requirements

GitHub link: `https://github.com/PacktPublishing/Learning-Angular--Third-Edition/tree/master/ch04`.

Introducing directives

Angular directives are HTML attributes that extend the behavior or the appearance of a standard HTML element. When we apply a directive to an HTML element or even an Angular component, we can add custom behavior to it or alter its appearance. There are three types of directives:

- **Components** are directives with an associated template.
- **Structural directives** add or remove elements from the DOM.
- **Attribute directives** modify the appearance or define a custom behavior of a DOM element.

Angular provides us with a set of built-in directives that we can use in our components and cover most use cases.

Transforming elements using directives

The Angular framework includes a set of ready-made structural directives that we can start using straight away in our apps:

- `ngIf` adds or removes a portion of the DOM tree based on an expression.
- `ngFor` iterates through a list of items and binds each item to a template.
- `ngSwitch` switches between templates within a specific set and displays each one depending on a condition.

We describe each one of them in the following sections.

Displaying data conditionally

The `ngIf` directive adds or removes an HTML element in the DOM, based on the evaluation of an expression. If the expression evaluates to `true`, the element is inserted into the DOM. Otherwise, the element is removed from the DOM. We could enhance our `hero` component from the previous chapter by leveraging this directive:

```
<p *ngIf="name === 'Boothstomper'">{{name}} hero works!</p>
```

When the `name` property of the component `class` has the value of `Boothstomper`, the paragraph element is rendered on the screen. Otherwise, it is completely removed.

Someone could reasonably point out that we could use the hidden property of the paragraph element instead of ngIf as follows:

```
<p [hidden]="name !== 'Boothstomper'">{{name}} hero works!</p>
```

The difference is that ngIf adds or removes elements from the DOM tree where hidden hides or displays elements that exist already in the DOM tree. It is recommended to use ngIf when dealing with a large amount of data, such as lists with hundreds of items or elements that contain advanced presentation logic in their child elements. In such cases, it performs better because Angular does not need to keep data or elements in memory, runtime, as it does with the hidden property. If we inspect our application using the browser's developer tools, we can see the following:

```
▼<app-hero _ngcontent-oxw-c17 _nghost-oxw-c11 ng-reflect-name="Boothstomper">
   <p _ngcontent-oxw-c11>Boothstomper hero works!</p>
   <!--bindings={
     "ng-reflect-ng-if": "true"
   }-->
 </app-hero>
```

Figure 4.1 – Inspect the HTML element with the ngIf directive

The template in the comments represents the ngIf portion. Angular adds comments in place of structural directives that act as placeholders to help the framework recognize where it should place the appropriate templates.

> **Important Note**
>
> When using expressions that evaluate to a boolean value, it is best to use triple equality, ===, over the usual == because === checks not only whether values are equal but also whether types match. For example, 0 == '0' is truthy, whereas 0 === '0' is falsy.

You have probably noticed the asterisk, *, that prepends ngIf. Structural directives have such an asterisk. It is syntactic sugar that acts as a shortcut for a more complicated syntax. Angular embeds the HTML element marked with the ngIf directive in an ng-template element, which is used later on to render the actual content on the screen. The ng-template element is neither added in the DOM tree nor rendered on the screen but rather acts as a wrapper for other elements. These elements are not rendered automatically on the screen, but structural directives trigger them. Consider the scenario where we want to display a default message when the name of the hero is not Boothstomper. We need to create another paragraph element:

```
<p *ngIf="name === 'Boothstomper'">{{name}} hero works!</p>
<p *ngIf="name !== 'Boothstomper'">Hero was not found</p>
```

The approach of using multiple `ngIf` statements has drawbacks:

- It is error-prone because it is easy to make a mistake when composing them.
- The syntax is not readable.
- It goes against the **Do not Repeat Yourself (DRY)** syntax.

Alternatively, we can use `ng-template` to compose an if-else statement in the template of our component:

hero.component.html

```
<p *ngIf="name === 'Boothstomper'; else noHero">{{name}} hero
works!</p>
<ng-template #noHero>
  <p>Hero was not found</p>
</ng-template>
```

We have added another statement in the template expression of the `ngIf` directive, the `else` statement of the if-else syntax. It is separated from the first one using a semicolon.

> **Important Note**
> You can chain multiple statements in a template expression by separating them using semicolons.

The `else` statement refers to a `noHero` variable that is activated if the condition of the `ngIf` directive is not satisfied. The `noHero` variable is a template reference variable, as we learned in *Chapter 3, Component Interaction and Inter-Communication* pointing to an `ng-template` element that contains a paragraph element. The paragraph element is displayed on the screen only when the `else` statement becomes active.

The `ngIf` directive is a useful asset to our toolchain when it comes to displaying particular pieces of the user interface. It is common to combine it with the `ngFor` directive when we want to display multiple pieces of data.

Iterating through data

The `ngFor` directive allows us to loop over a collection of items and render a template for each one, where we can define convenient placeholders to interpolate item data. Each rendered template is scoped to the outer context, where the loop directive is placed so that we can access other bindings. We can think of `ngFor` as the `for` loop for HTML templates.

Suppose that we have an array of `Hero` objects that we want to display. We can enlist them using `ngFor` in the following syntax:

```
<ul>
  <li *ngFor="let hero of heroes">
    {{hero.name}}
  </li>
</ul>
```

We turn each object fetched from the `heroes` array into a `hero` local reference so that we can easily bind the `name` property in our template using interpolation. The properties of the `hero` object are defined in the `Hero interface`:

hero.model.ts

```
export interface Hero {
  id: number;
  name: string;
  team: string;
}
```

We can create an `interface` in Angular using the following `generate` command of the Angular CLI:

```
ng generate interface <name>
```

The `name` argument parameter indicates the name of the `interface`, which, in our case, is `hero`.

> **Important Note**
>
> You might be surprised that we define an `interface` for our model entity rather than a `class`. It is perfectly fine when the model does not feature any business logic requiring the implementation of methods or data transformation in a `constructor` or setter/getter function. When the latter is not required, an `interface` suffices since it provides the static typing we require in a simple and more lightweight fashion.

The `ngFor` directive observes changes in the underlying collection and adds, removes, or sorts the rendered templates as items are added, removed, or reordered in the collection.

Besides just looping all the items in a collection, it is possible to keep track of other useful properties as well. Such a property can be used by adding another statement after the main template statement:

```
<li *ngFor="let hero of heroes; property as variable"></li>
```

The `variable` is a local reference that we can use later in our template, and the `property` can have the following values:

- `index` indicates the index of the item in the array, starting at 0 (`number`).
- `first/last` indicates whether the current item is the first or last item of the array (`boolean`).
- `even/odd` indicates whether the index of the item in the array is even or odd (`boolean`).

In the following snippet, Angular assigns the value of the `index` property in the `myIndex` local variable. The `myIndex` variable is later used to display the `heroes` array as a numbered list:

```
<ul>
  <li *ngFor="let hero of heroes; index as myIndex">
    {{myIndex+1}}. {{hero.name}}
  </li>
</ul>
```

During the execution of `ngFor`, data may change, elements may be added or removed, and even the whole list may be replaced. Angular must take care of these changes by creating/removing elements to sync changes to the DOM tree. It is a process that can become very slow and expensive at the time and will eventually result in the poor performance of your application.

Angular deals with variations to a collection by keeping DOM elements in memory. Internally, it uses something called object identity to keep track of every item in the collection. We can, however, use a specific property of the iterable items instead of the internal Angular object identity using the `trackBy` property:

```
<li *ngFor="let hero of heroes; trackBy: trackByHeroes"></li>
```

The trackBy property defines the trackByHeroes method that is declared in the component class and accepts two parameters, the index of the current item and the actual item. It returns the property of the item that we want to use as the object identity:

```
trackByHeroes(index: number, hero: Hero): number {
  return hero.id;
}
```

We use ngIf and ngFor most of the time during development. Another structural directive that is not so commonly used is the ngSwitch directive.

Switching through templates

We learned that structural directives such as ngIf and ngFor are prefixed with an asterisk. The ngSwitch directive is an exception to this rule. It is used to switch between templates and display each one depending on a defined value. You can think of ngSwitch as an ordinary switch statement. It consists of a set of other directives:

- ngSwitchCase adds/removes a template from the DOM tree depending on the value of the ngSwitch directive.
- ngSwitchDefault adds a template in the DOM tree if the value of the ngSwitch directive does not meet any ngSwitchCase statement.

Let's see the directive in action:

```
<div [ngSwitch]="hero.team">
  <div *ngSwitchCase="'avengers'">{{hero.name}} is avenger</
  div>
  <div *ngSwitchCase="'villains'">{{hero.name}} is villain</
  div>
  <div *ngSwitchDefault>{{hero.name}}</div>
</div>
```

The ngSwitch directive evaluates the team property of a hero object. When it finds a match, it activates the appropriate ngSwitchCase statement, avengers, or villains. If the team value does not match any ngSwitchCase statement, the ngSwitchDefault statement is activated.

Directives transform HTML elements by affecting their structure, behavior, and display. On the other hand, pipes transform data and template bindings.

Manipulating data with pipes

Pipes allow us to filter and funnel the outcome of our expressions on a view level. They take data as input, transform it into the desired format, and display the output in the template. To better understand it, think of it like transforming a donkey into a unicorn:

Figure 4.2 – Conceptualized pipe transformation

The donkey may look like a unicorn, but it is always a donkey. That is, the transformation is applied only on a view level; the underlying data remains intact in its original form.

The syntax of a pipe is pretty simple, basically consisting of the pipe name following the expression that we want to transform, separated by a pipe symbol (hence the name). Pipes are usually used with interpolation in Angular templates and can be chained to each other. Angular has a wide range of pipe types already baked in:

- The `uppercase`/`lowercase` pipes transform a `string` into a particular case. The following snippet displays the phrase *hello angular 10* in uppercase and lowercase letters, respectively:

```
<p>{{'hello angular 10' | uppercase}}</p>
<p>{{'HELLO ANGULAR 10' | lowercase}}</p>
```

- The `percent` pipe formats a `number` as a percentage. For example, the output of `<p>{{0.1234 | percent}}</p>` is **12%**.
- The `currency` pipe formats a `number` as a local currency. We can override our local settings and change the symbol of the currency, passing the currency code as a parameter to the pipe. The following snippet displays **$100** and **€100**, respectively:

```
<p>{{100 | currency}}</p>
<p>{{100 | currency:'EUR'}}</p>
```

- The `slice` pipe subtracts a subset (slice) of a collection or `string`. It accepts a starting index, where it will begin slicing the input data, and optionally an end index as parameters. If the end index is omitted, it falls back to the last index of the data. The following snippet displays the second and the third hero from an array of `heroes`:

```
<p>{{heroes | slice:1:3}}</p>
```

> **Important Note**
>
> The `slice` pipe transforms immutable data. The transformed list is always a copy of the original data even when it returns all items.

- The `date` pipe formats a date or a `string` to a particular date format. The time zone of the formatted output is in the local time zone of the end user's machine. The following snippet displays the component property `today` as a date:

```
<p>{{today | date}}</p>
```

- The `today` property is an object that has been initialized using the `Date constructor`:

```
today = new Date();
```

- The default usage of the pipe displays the date in the format MMMM d, Y, but we can pass additional formats that Angular has already baked in as a parameter. For example, to display the date in full date format, we write the following snippet:

```
<p>{{today | date:'fullDate'}}</p>
```

> **Important Note**
>
> You can find more details about predefined date formats at `https://angular.io/api/common/DatePipe#pre-defined-format-options`.

- The `json` pipe is probably the most straightforward in its definition; it takes an object as an input and outputs it in **JSON** format:

```
<p>{{hero | json}}</p>
```

It takes a `hero` object as input:

```
hero = {
  names: {
    name: 'Boothstomper',
    realName: 'Alfie Best'
  },
  planet: 'Earth',
  color: 'cyan'
};
```

It then displays its properties in JSON format, replacing single quotes with double quotes:

{ "names": { "name": "Boothstomper", "realName": "Alfie Best" }, "planet": "Earth", "color": "Cyan" }

So, why do we need this? The main reason is debugging; it's an excellent way to see what a complex object contains and have it nicely printed on the screen. The `hero` object contains some simple properties but also the complicated `names` property. The deeper the object is, the more helpful it is to have the JSON pipe.

> **Important Note**
>
> Remember to always use the `json` pipe when interpolating an object. If you fail to do so, you will see the famous **[object Object]** on the screen when trying to use it.

- The `async` pipe is a special-purpose pipe. It is used when we manage data that is handled asynchronously by our component `class`, and we need to ensure that our views promptly reflect the changes. We will learn more about this pipe later in *Chapter 6, Enrich Components with Asynchronous Data Services*, where we will use it to fetch and display data asynchronously.

Built-in pipes and directives are sufficient for most use cases. There are other cases, though, in which we need to apply complex transformations to our data or templates. The Angular framework provides us with a mechanism to create unique customized pipes and directives. We'll learn how to generate such artifacts in the following sections.

Building custom pipes

We have already seen what pipes are and what their purpose is in the overall Angular ecosystem. Now we are going to dive deeper into how we can build a pipe to provide custom transformations to data bindings. In the following section, we will create a pipe that sorts a list of objects according to a property of the object.

Sorting data using pipes

To create a new pipe, we use the `generate` command of the Angular CLI, passing the word `pipe` followed by its name as parameters:

```
ng generate pipe sort
```

The Angular CLI creates the pipe file, `sort.pipe.ts`, along with the accompanying unit test file, `sort.pipe.spec.ts`, and registers it with the main application module, `AppModule`. On the contrary to the component, pipe files are not created inside a dedicated folder but rather inside the folder that we run the `generate` command in:

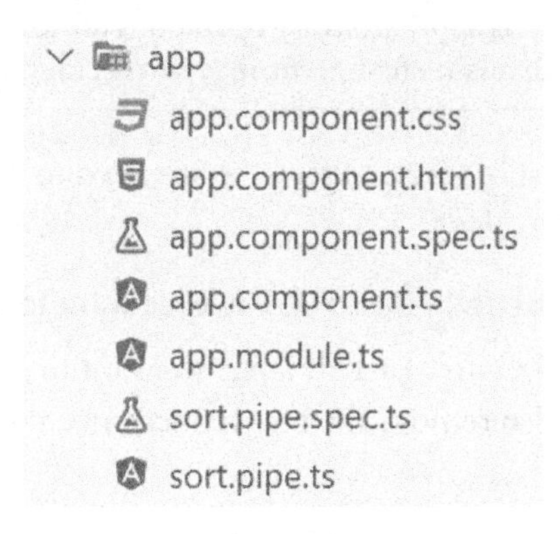

Figure 4.3 – Application folder structure

A pipe is a TypeScript `class` marked with the `@Pipe` decorator that implements the `PipeTransform interface`. The only required property in the decorator is the name of the pipe:

```
@Pipe({
  name: 'sort'
})
```

A pipe must implement the `transform` method of the `PipeTransform interface` to perform a transformation:

```
transform(value: unknown, ...args: unknown[]): unknown {
  return null;
}
```

The first parameter, `value`, is the input that we want to transform. The second parameter, `args`, is an optional list of arguments that we can provide to the transformation method, each one separated by a colon. The Angular CLI helped us by scaffolding an empty `transform` method. We now need to modify it to satisfy our business needs. The first thing that we need to do is to add types to the method.

> **Important Note**
>
> Angular has configured the `transform` method to use a particular type called `unknown`, which works similarly to the `any` type. A variable of the `unknown` type can have a value of any type. The main difference is that TypeScript will not let us apply arbitrary operations on `unknown` values, such as calling a method, unless we first perform type-checking.

The pipe will operate on a list of `Hero` objects, so we need to make the necessary adjustments in the types provided:

1. Change the type of `value` to `Hero[]` since we want to sort a list of `Hero` objects.
2. Change the type of `args` to `string` since we want to sort by a `string` property each time. We must also remove the rest syntax since the pipe will accept a single parameter only.
3. Change the return type of the method to `Hero[]` since the sorted list will also contain `Hero` objects.

We are now ready to implement the sorting algorithm of our method. We use the native `sort` method of the array prototype that sorts items alphabetically, by default. We provide a custom comparator `function` to the `sort` method that overrides the default functionality and performs the sorting logic that we want to achieve:

```
transform(value: Hero[], args: string): Hero[] {
  if (value) {
    return value.sort((a: Hero, b: Hero) => {
      if (a[args] < b[args]) {
        return -1;
```

```
        } else if (b[args] < a[args]) {
            return 1;
        }

        return 0;
    });
  }

  return [];
}
```

It is worth noting that the `transform` method checks whether there is a `value` first before proceeding to the sorting process. Otherwise, it returns an empty array. It mitigates against cases where the collection is set asynchronously, or the component that consumes the pipe does not set the collection at all.

> **Important Note**
> For more information about the `Array.prototype.sort` method refer to `https://developer.mozilla.org/en-US/docs/Web/JavaScript/Reference/Global_Objects/Array/sort`.

That's it! We have successfully created our first pipe. We only need to call it from our component template to see it in action:

```
<ul>
  <li *ngFor="let hero of heroes | sort:'name'">
    {{hero.name}}
  </li>
</ul>
```

We use the `sort` pipe in combination with the `ngFor` directive to display a list of `Hero` objects sorted by `name`. We should mention that when using pipes with other properties of the `ngFor` directive, such as `index` or `first/last`, the pipe must be located *after* the declaration of the array:

```
<ul>
  <li *ngFor="let hero of heroes | sort:'name'; index as
  myIndex">
  </li>
</ul>
```

The `@Pipe` decorator contains another significant property that we can set, which is directly related to the way that pipes react in the change detection mechanism of the framework.

Change detection with pipes

There are two categories of pipes: **pure** and **impure**. All pipes are pure by default unless we set them to `false` explicitly using the `pure` property in the `@Pipe` decorator:

```
@Pipe({
  name: 'sort',
  pure: false
})
```

Why would we do that in the first place? Well, there are situations where this might be necessary. Angular executes pure pipes when there is a change to the reference of the input variable. For example, if the `heroes` array is assigned to a new value, the pipe will correctly reflect the change. However, if we add a new hero in the array, the pipe will not be triggered at all.

Another example is when we have created a pure pipe that operates on a single object. Similarly, if the reference of the value changes, the pipe executes correctly. If a property of the object changes, the pipe is not able to detect the change.

A word of caution, however. This means that the `transform` method is called every time the change detection cycle is triggered. So, this might be bad for performance. Alternatively, you could leave the `pure` property unset and try to cache the value or work with reducers and immutable data to solve this in a better way:

```
this.heroes = [
  ...this.heroes,
  { id: 6, name: 'New hero', team: '' }
];
```

Creating a custom pipe allows us to transform our data in a particular way according to our needs. If we also want to transform template elements, we need to create custom directives.

Building custom directives

Custom directives encompass a vast world of possibilities and use cases, and we would need an entire book to showcase all the intricacies and possibilities they offer. In a nutshell, they allow you to attach advanced behaviors to elements in the DOM or modify their appearance.

If a directive has a template attached, then it becomes a component. In other words, components are Angular directives with a view. This rule becomes handy when we want to decide whether we should create a component or a directive for our needs. If we need a template, we create a component; otherwise, make it a directive.

As we have already learned, directives fall into two categories: structural and attribute. In the following sections, we showcase how to create a directive of each category from scratch.

Displaying dynamic data

We have all found ourselves in a situation where we want to add copyright information to our applications. Ideally, we want to use this information in various parts of our application, on a dashboard, or on an about page. The content of the information should also be dynamic. That is, the year or range of years (it depends on how you want to use it) should update dynamically according to the current year. Our first intention is to create a component, but what about making it a directive instead? In this way, we could attach the directive to any element we want and not bother with a particular template. So let's begin!

Use the `generate` command of the Angular CLI to create a copyright directive. We pass the word `directive` followed by the name of the directive as parameters:

```
ng generate directive copyright
```

The Angular CLI creates the directive file, `copyright.directive.ts`, along with the accompanying unit test file, `copyright.directive.spec.ts`, and registers it with the main application module, `AppModule`. All related directive files are created inside the folder that we run the `generate` command in:

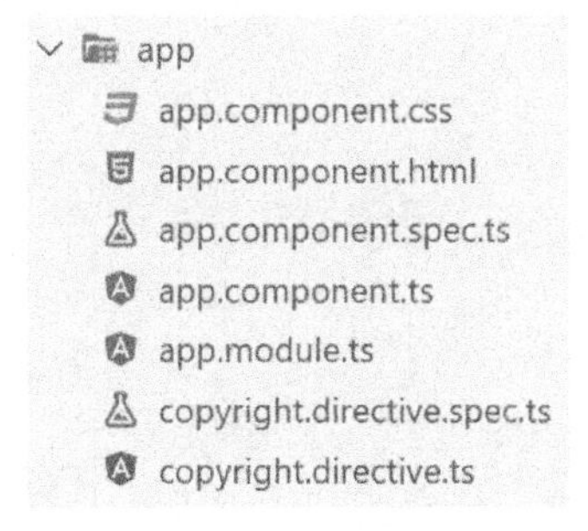

Figure 4.4 – Application folder structure

A directive is a TypeScript `class` marked with the `@Directive` decorator. The only required property in the decorator is the `selector` of the directive:

```
@Directive({
  selector: '[appCopyright]'
})
```

The `selector` can be any valid CSS selector and is similar to that of a component. It contains the prefix of the Angular application, `app` in this case, and is used to identify the directive in a template uniquely. The only difference is that we surround it in square brackets. Be aware though that we use it without them in a template:

```
<p appCopyright></p>
```

> **Important Note**
>
> We use a custom prefix in attribute directives to minimize the risk of conflict with an HTML native attribute or another directive from a third-party library. As we learned in *Chapter 3, Component Interaction and Inter-Communication*, the prefix can be customized when creating the Angular application.

The custom logic of our directive is summarized inside the `constructor`:

```
constructor(el: ElementRef, renderer: Renderer2) {
  renderer.addClass(el.nativeElement, 'copyright');
  renderer.setProperty(
    el.nativeElement,
    'textContent',
    `Copyright ©${new Date().getFullYear()} All Rights
    Reserved.`
  );
}
```

We use two classes, `ElementRef` and `Renderer2`, to manipulate the underlying element. We could use native HTML methods on `nativeElement` directly or on the global `document` object. It is discouraged as this approach is not cross-platform and might break when using server-side rendering or interacting with service workers. Instead, we do all manipulations using an instance of `Renderer2`. It provides a rich set of methods that we can use to manipulate an HTML element. In this case, we use two of them:

- `addClass` adds the `copyright` class to the specified `nativeElement`. The class is defined in the `styles.css` file that exists in the `app` folder. In this file, we place CSS styles that affect our application globally:

```
.copyright {
  background-color: lightgray;
  padding: 10px;
  font-family: Verdana, Geneva, Tahoma, sans-serif;
}
```

- `setProperty` sets the `textContent` property of the specified `nativeElement` to the actual copyright information text.

`ElementRef` and `Renderer2` are Angular built-in **services.** To use a service in a component or a directive, we need to inject it in the `constructor`, as we will learn in *Chapter 6, Enrich Components with Asynchronous Data Services.*

The primary mindset to have when creating directives is to think reusable functionality that doesn't necessarily relate to a particular feature. The topic chosen previously was copyright information, but we could build other functionalities such as tooltips and collapsible or infinite scrolling features with relative ease. In the following section, we build another attribute directive that explores available options further.

Property binding and responding to events

The Angular framework provides two helpful decorators that we can use in our directives to enhance their functionality:

- `@HostBinding` binds a value to the property of the native host element.
- `@HostListener` binds to an event of the native host element.

The native host element is the element where our directive takes action. These decorators are similar to the property and event binding that we learned in *Chapter 3, Component Interaction and Inter-Communication*.

The native HTML `input` element supports different types, such as `text`, `radio`, and `numeric`. When we use the `numeric` type, the `input` adds two arrows inline, up and down, to control its value. It is this feature of the `input` element that makes it look incomplete. If we type a non-numeric character, the `input` renders it correctly. To solve this problem, we will create an attribute directive that rejects non-numeric values. Let's scaffold a new directive named `numeric`:

```
ng generate directive numeric
```

It contains a `currentClass` property that binds to the `class` property of the `input` element and an `onKeyPress` method that binds to the `keypress` native event of the `input` element:

```
import { Directive, HostBinding, HostListener } from '@angular/
core';

@Directive({
  selector: '[appNumeric]'
})
export class NumericDirective {

  @HostBinding('class')
  currentClass: string;

  @HostListener('keypress', ['$event'])
  onKeyPress(event: KeyboardEvent) {}

  constructor() { }

}
```

When the user presses a key inside the `input` element, Angular knows to call the `onKeyPress` method because we have registered it with the `@HostListener` decorator. We need to add the business logic that will prevent non-numeric values inside this method. The `@HostListener` decorator accepts two parameters:

- **eventName** is the name of the triggered event.
- **args** is a list of arguments to pass in the appropriate method upon triggering the event.

In our case, we pass the `keypress` event name and the `$event` argument. `$event` is the current event object that triggered the event, which is of type `KeyboardEvent` and contains the keystrokes entered by the user. All that is missing now is the actual implementation of the method:

```
onKeyPress(event: KeyboardEvent) {
  const charCode = event.key.charCodeAt(0);
  if (charCode > 31 && (charCode < 48 || charCode > 57)) {
    this.currentClass = 'invalid';
    event.preventDefault();
  } else {
    this.currentClass = 'valid';
  }
}
```

Every time the user presses a key, we extract it from the `$event` object, convert it into a Unicode character using the `charCodeAt` method of the `string` prototype and check it against non-numeric code. If the character is non-numeric, we call the `preventDefault` method of the `$event` object to cancel the user action and roll back the `input` element to its previous state. At the same time, we set the respective `class` to the `input` element, `valid` if the key is numeric, and `invalid` if it is not. CSS classes are defined in the global `styles.css` and apply a color to the bottom line of the `input`, either `green` or `red`:

```
.valid {
  border-bottom: solid green;
}

.invalid {
  border-bottom: solid red;
}
```

Everything is now in place, and our directive looks and works great! We can type only numeric values, and we also indicate the validity of each value. Let's summarize this section by creating a structural directive.

Toggling templates dynamically

A typical scenario in enterprise Angular applications is that users should have access to certain parts of the application according to their role. You may think that we could use the `ngIf` built-in directive for this. It would be valid for a simple case, but usually, checking a role involves calling some service to get the current user and extract their role. We'll learn about services in *Chapter 6, Enrich Components with Asynchronous Data Services*. For now, we could create a more straightforward structural directive:

```
ng generate directive permission
```

Similarly to components, we can use an `@Input` decorator in a directive, in cases where we want to pass data to our directive. Thus, we use this decorator to pass the list of available roles that are eligible to access the host element. The role of the current user is hardcoded inside the directive for the sake of simplicity:

```
@Input() appPermission: string[];

private currentRole = 'agent';
```

The name of the input property must have the same name as the `selector` of the directive so that it can be used as follows:

```
<div *appPermission="['admin', 'agent']"></div>
```

Notice the use of the asterisk in front of the directive. If you omit it, the Angular framework throws an error. If we want to add another input property, we should name it differently. The `@Input` decorator accepts an optional parameter that is the name with which the property is exposed to the public API:

```
@Input('anotherProperty') propertyName;
```

The directive should use `propertyName` for internal purposes, whereas components that use the directive should use `anotherProperty`.

We are halfway there. We now need to add the business logic that adds or removes the embedded view of the host element in the DOM according to the roles that we pass in the input property. We use two classes to help us:

- `TemplateRef`: The Angular generated `ng-template` element of the embedded view.
- `ViewContainerRef`: The container used to insert the embedded view, which is adjacent to the host element.

We can get an instance of each one by injecting them into the `constructor` of the directive:

```
constructor(private tmplRef: TemplateRef<any>, private vc:
ViewContainerRef) { }
```

We can then add the business logic to the `ngOnInit` method of the directive:

```
ngOnInit() {
  if (this.appPermission.indexOf(this.currentRole) === -1) {
    this.vc.clear();
  } else {
    this.vc.createEmbeddedView(this.tmplRef);
  }
}
```

The `ngOnInit` method, it first checks whether the `currentRole` belongs to the list of roles that we pass as an input parameter. If it does not, it calls the `clear` method of `ViewContainerRef` to remove the host element from the DOM. Otherwise, it creates an embedded view of the host element inside the view container and adds it to the DOM.

> **Important Note**
>
> In a real-world scenario, we would not hardcode the current role in the directive but use an Angular service to fetch it. The service would probably access the local storage of the browser or call an API method to a backend.

You can now test it out yourself by toggling the current role and watch how the directive performs when adding/removing elements from the DOM.

Summary

Now that we have reached this point, it is fair to say that you know almost everything it takes to build Angular components, which are indeed the wheels and the engine of all Angular applications. In the forthcoming chapters, we will see how we can design our application architecture better, and therefore manage dependency injection throughout our components tree, consume data services, and leverage the new Angular router to show and hide components when required.

Nevertheless, this chapter is the backbone of Angular development, and we hope that you enjoyed it as much as we did when writing about pipes and directives. Now, get ready to assume new challenges—we are about to move from learning how to write components to discovering how we can use them to build larger applications while enforcing good practices and rational architectures. We will see all this in the next chapter.

5
Structure an Angular App

We have reached a point in our journey where we can successfully develop more complex applications by nesting components within other components, in a sort of component tree. However, bundling all our business logic into a single component is not the way to go. Our application might become unmaintainable very soon. Later in this chapter, we'll investigate the advantages that Angular's dependency management mechanism can bring to the game to overcome such problems.

In this chapter, we will learn how to build application architectures based on trees of components and organize them into modules. We will also learn about the new Angular dependency injection mechanism, which helps us to declare and consume our dependencies across the application with minimum effort and optimal results. By the end of this chapter, you will be able to create an Angular application that is correctly structured to enforce separation of concerns using modules and services.

We will cover the following topics:

- Organizing components into modules
- Organizing our Angular project using the Angular CLI folder structure
- Different approaches to dependency injection
- Injecting dependencies into our components
- Overriding global dependencies throughout the component tree

Let's get started!

Technical requirements

The source code for this chapter is available at the following GitHub link:

`https://github.com/PacktPublishing/Learning-Angular--Third-Edition/tree/master/ch05.`

Organizing components into modules

As we learned in *Chapter 3*, *Component Interaction and Inter-Communication*, Angular 10 applications are represented as a tree of components. The top main component (usually dropped somewhere in the main HTML index file) acts as a global placeholder where child components turn into hosts for other nested child components, and so on. Modern web applications based on web component architectures often conform to this sort of tree hierarchy.

There are distinct advantages to this approach. On the one hand, reusability does not get compromised, and we can reuse components throughout the component tree with little effort. Secondly, the resulting granularity reduces the burden required for envisioning, designing, and maintaining larger applications. We can simply focus on a single piece of UI and then wrap its functionality around new layers of abstraction until we wrap up a full-blown application from the ground up.

Alternatively, we can approach our web application the other way around and group our components into blocks of cohesive functionality called **modules**. We start from a more generic functionality just to end up breaking the app into smaller pieces, which become our web components:

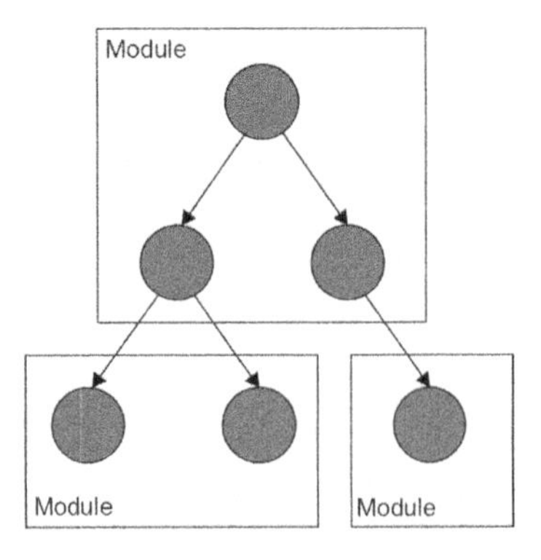

Figure 5.1 – Grouping components into modules

The latter has become the most common approach when building component-based architectures. The module-based approach scales better and is easier to test. If we think of a module as a separate feature of an application, it allows us to develop a particular piece of functionality independently of the others. It dramatically enhances team management in large organizations where each development team can work in a separate feature. Features can gradually be deployed, ensuring the seamless operation of our app.

Introducing Angular modules

We have already tackled a good number of the most common concerns that modern web developers confront when building web applications nowadays. Therefore, it makes sense to define an architecture that separates them into manageable units.

Angular's approach to this is the concept of an Angular module. An Angular module is a container for a particular block of code that adheres to the same functionality. The functionality of an Angular module is dedicated to an application domain, such as orders or customers, or a specific workflow, such as user registration. Generally, it addresses a particular set of capabilities that an application can have. As we have learned in previous chapters, an Angular application has, at the very least, a main module, `AppModule`. We can also create other modules, usually called *feature modules*. These represent the main features of the application.

Creating your first module

To create a new module in an Angular app, use the `generate` command of the Angular CLI while passing the name of the module as a parameter:

```
ng generate module heroes
```

The preceding command creates a `heroes` folder inside the `app` folder. This is the physical container for Angular artifacts with the same `heroes` functionality:

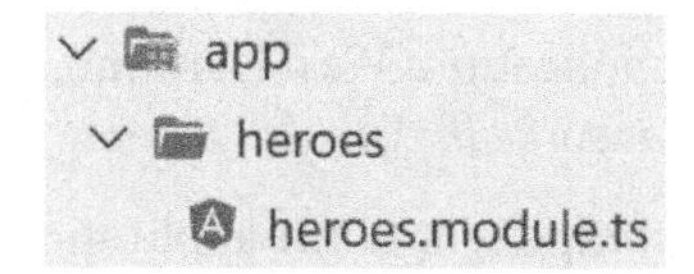

Figure 5.2 – Heroes folder structure

It also creates a TypeScript file for the Angular module that is responsible for registering these artifacts:

```
import { NgModule } from '@angular/core';
import { CommonModule } from '@angular/common';

@NgModule({
  declarations: [],
  imports: [
    CommonModule
  ]
})
export class HeroesModule { }
```

An Angular module is a TypeScript `class` marked with the `@NgModule` decorator, which defines the following properties:

- `declarations`: The components, directives, and pipes that are registered with the module.
- `imports`: Other modules that contain declarations to be used by this module. The Angular CLI defines `CommonModule` automatically for us in this property. It is a module that is always used in Angular applications because it contains all the built-in directives and pipes that we usually would like to use. Be careful not to get caught in circular references when you import a module that already imports yours.
- `exports`: Angular artifacts that are defined in `declarations` and are available for other modules to use. This is the public API of the module. It defines what is publicly accessible or not. Everything else that's not explicitly exported would be considered private or internal to the module.
- `providers`: Services that are provided from the module and are accessible from any module of the application. We'll learn more about providers in the *How dependency injection works in Angular* section.
- `bootstrap`: The main component of the application that will be rendered when the application starts up. This property is set only once in the main application module, `AppModule`, and is usually `AppComponent`. Typically, you should not change it unless there is a particular reason to do so.

> **Important Note**
>
> The main application module, `AppModule`, does not need to import `CommonModule`. Instead, it imports `BrowserModule`, which is used to run Angular applications in a browser platform that exports `CommonModule` by itself.

When creating a new Angular application, the first step is to define the different features our application needs. We should keep in mind that each one should make sense on its own in isolation from the others. Once we've defined the set of features required, we will create a module for each one. Each module will then be filled with the components, directives, pipes, and services that shape the feature it represents. Always remember the principles of encapsulation and reusability when defining your feature set. The second step is to start creating components that will be used to visualize the features on the screen.

Registering components with a module

There are two ways to register a component with a module when using the `generate` command of the Angular CLI: either implicitly by running the command inside the folder of the respective module or explicitly by using one of its available options. We saw the first option in *Chapter 3, Component Interaction and Inter-Communication,* so we'll focus on the latter one here. We can create a component and register it at the same time using the following Angular CLI command:

```
ng generate component heroes/heroList --module=heroes
```

The `--module` parameter denotes the module that the component is registered with. It can also be used when generating directives and pipes. The Angular CLI is pretty smart in finding the correct Angular module to use. In this case, it looks for a `heroes.module.ts` file inside the `heroes` folder relative to the current path. Alternatively, we could pass the whole path of the Angular module file:

```
ng generate component heroes/heroList --module=heroes/heroes.
module.ts
```

Did you notice that the name of the component is `heroes/heroList`? It is an alternative syntax where we can pass the name of the folder where we want to create an Angular artifact. It is a good practice to create artifacts of a module inside the module's folder. It helps you visualize the functionality of a module at a glance and concentrate on that specific module during development. It is also helpful when you decide to make a refactor to your code and must move the whole module. When creating the component, you may have noticed that the folder of the component, along with the necessary files, is not `heroList` but instead `hero-list`. This is a feature of the Angular CLI that converts camel case into kebab case when it comes to folder and file creation. It also converts the selector of the component into kebab case format.

In real-world applications, feature modules are not standalone modules but share their encapsulated functionality (components, directives, and pipes) with other modules too.

Exposing module features

In the previous section, we created our `HeroListComponent` in a separate module. It is now time to display this component in our Angular application. We already know that the component that is first displayed in an Angular application is `AppComponent`. So, we need to find a way to declare `HeroListComponent` in this component so that it will be displayed too. In *Chapter 3, Component Interaction and Inter-Communication*, we learned about the selector of the component and how it provides a way of defining a component in HTML. Just like `index.html`, where we use the selector of `AppComponent`, we can use the selector of `HeroListComponent` in the template of `AppComponent`:

```
<app-hero-list></app-hero-list>
```

If we try to run our Angular application using `ng serve`, we'll get the following error:

```
ERROR in src/app/app.component.html:1:1 - error NG8001: 'app-hero-list' is not a known element:
1. If 'app-hero-list' is an Angular component, then verify that it is part of this module.
2. If 'app-hero-list' is a Web Component then add 'CUSTOM_ELEMENTS_SCHEMA' to the '@NgModule.schemas' of this component to suppress this message.

<app-hero-list></app-hero-list>

  src/app/app.component.ts:5:16
      templateUrl: './app.component.html',

    Error occurs in the template of component AppComponent.
```

Figure 5.3 – Angular compiler error

The Angular compiler does not recognize the `app-hero-list` selector because it is declared in a different Angular module. `AppComponent` is defined in the `declarations` property of `AppModule`. `HeroListComponent` is defined in `declarations` of the heroes module. If you are using VSCode and have the Angular Language Service extension installed, you'll get the error long before you start building the application:

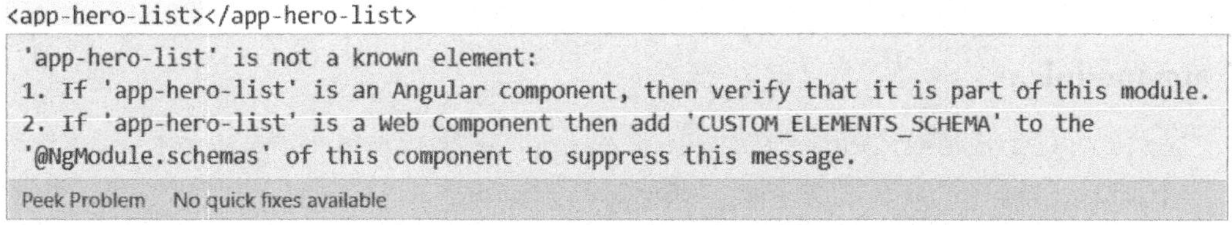

```
<app-hero-list></app-hero-list>
'app-hero-list' is not a known element:
1. If 'app-hero-list' is an Angular component, then verify that it is part of this module.
2. If 'app-hero-list' is a Web Component then add 'CUSTOM_ELEMENTS_SCHEMA' to the
'@NgModule.schemas' of this component to suppress this message.
Peek Problem    No quick fixes available
```

Figure 5.4 – Angular Language Service error

You may think that we could define `HeroListComponent` in the `declarations` property of `AppModule`. This approach is discouraged because of the following reasons:

- It goes against the basic principle of Angular modules, where each module contains a set of Angular artifacts with a single form of functionality and responsibility. The purpose of `AppModule` is to orchestrate the entire application and is not tied to a specific feature.
- An Angular component can be declared only in one module. The same rule applies to directives and pipes.

The right way to do this is to use the `imports` and `exports` properties of each module. First, the heroes module must export `HeroListComponent` so that it can be available in Angular modules that need it:

heroes.module.ts

```
import { NgModule } from '@angular/core';
import { CommonModule } from '@angular/common';
import { HeroListComponent } from './hero-list/hero-list.
component';

@NgModule({
  declarations: [HeroListComponent],
  imports: [
    CommonModule
  ],
```

```
  exports: [HeroListComponent]
})
export class HeroesModule { }
```

Any Angular module can now import the `HeroesModule` to gain access to its exported artifacts, including `AppModule`:

app.module.ts

```
import { BrowserModule } from '@angular/platform-browser';
import { NgModule } from '@angular/core';

import { AppComponent } from './app.component';
import { HeroesModule } from './heroes/heroes.module';

@NgModule({
  declarations: [
    AppComponent
  ],
  imports: [
    BrowserModule,
    HeroesModule
  ],
  providers: [],
  bootstrap: [AppComponent]
})
export class AppModule { }
```

> **Important Note**
>
> The `imports` and `exports` properties of an Angular module should not be confused with the `import` statement at the top of the Angular module file, nor the `export` keyword in front of the `class` of an Angular module. These keywords refer to JavaScript modules, not Angular modules.

Always remember that the `exports` property refers to any artifacts that can be placed in the `declarations` property of a module; that is, components, directives, and pipes. On the contrary, the `imports` property defines whole Angular modules. An Angular module does not care about the individual exported artifacts of another module. This is something that concerns the Angular component that finally uses the exported artifact. An Angular module should care about which artifacts it exposes to other modules because it may not want to give access to all of them.

So far, we have seen two types of modules: the main application module, `AppModule`, and feature modules. There are also other types of modules that we can use in Angular applications that serve specific purposes and needs. We'll look at these in the next section.

Extending functionality with modules

Angular modules are used to group similar functionality and provide this functionality to other modules. They can be further organized by the type of functionality and the way an Angular app loads them. We can separate modules according to the feature that they represent:

- **Root module**: This is the main module of an Angular application, and it is named `AppModule` as a convention. It is bootstrapped when the application starts. It aims to orchestrate the application by importing all other modules. An Angular application can only have one root module.
- **Feature modules**: They typically represent the main features of an Angular application. They contain a specific set of functionalities such as orders, products, and customers and help us split our application into particular areas. They also aim to deliver features easier as developers work in isolation from the rest of the application. Feature modules usually do not stand on their own but are imported from `AppModule`.
- **Core module**: This module usually contains application-wide artifacts that do not fit in a specific module. Such artifacts are components that are used once in our application, such as a top bar that contains the main menu of the application, a footer component with copyright information, or a loading spinner. It also contains services that can be shared among modules such as a local cache service or a custom logger. This module should be loaded only once in `AppModule`.

- **Shared module**: This module contains components, directives, and pipes that can be used in feature modules. It may also provide a container for other exported modules that contain reusable artifacts such as `CommonModule` or `ReactiveFormsModule`, a module for working with HTML forms. Shared module is imported from each feature module that wants to use its exported artifacts.

We can also distinguish between modules according to how the Angular framework loads them:

- **Eager loaded modules**: These are modules that are loaded when the application starts. You can distinguish between an eagerly loaded module by whether it is declared in the `imports` property of another module or not.
- **Lazy loaded modules**: These are modules that are loaded on-demand as a result of navigating to the route of our application or user action, such as clicking on a button. Lazy loaded modules are not declared in the `imports` property of a module, but they have their specific way of loading, as we will learn in *Chapter 7, Navigate Through Components with Routing*. The way Angular loads a module is directly related to the final bundle of our application. In *Chapter 12, Bringing an Angular App to Production*, we will see that the way we load our Angular modules affects the build process of our application directly.

Angular modules may not be necessary for small scale Angular applications but are an essential asset when working with large enterprise Angular projects. In the following section, we'll explore the structure of such a project and get a brief overview of the various files that the Angular CLI creates for us.

Configuring the application

As we have learned in previous chapters, the Angular CLI does most of the work to scaffold a new Angular project for us when running the `ng new` command in the command line. It creates the bare minimum amount of files that are needed to have an initial Angular skeleton application up and running in zero time.

Configuring the workspace

The following command creates an Angular CLI workspace with an Angular application at its root level, named `my-app`:

```
ng new my-app
```

The workspace contains various configuration files that the Angular CLI needs in order to build, test, and publish our Angular application:

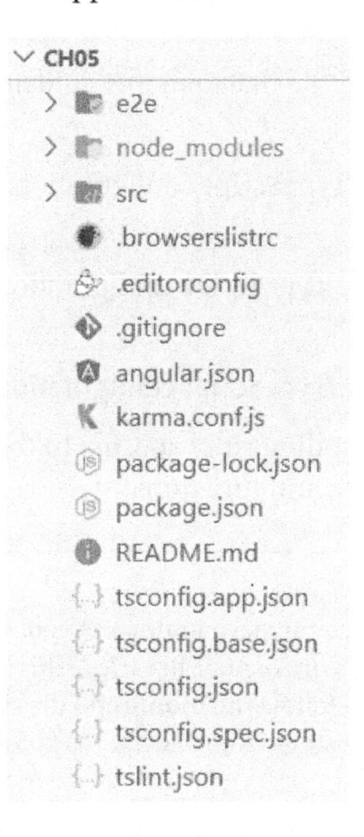

Figure 5.5 – Angular CLI 10 workspace

The following is a brief overview of each one:

- `e2e`: Contains end-to-end tests and configuration files to run them.
- `node_modules`: Includes npm packages that are needed for development and running the Angular app.
- `src`: Contains all the source files that the Angular app requires.
- `.browserslistrc`: Defines which browsers and versions the Angular app supports.
- `.editorconfig`: Defines coding styles for your editor.
- `.gitignore`: Specifies files and folders that should not be tracked by Git.
- `angular.json`: The main configuration file of the Angular CLI workspace.
- `karma.conf.js`: The main configuration file for running unit tests.

- `package.json` and `package-lock.json`: Provide definitions of npm packages, along with their exact versions, which are needed to develop, test, and run the Angular app.
- `README.md`: A README file that contains guidelines on how to start the Angular app.
- `tsconfig.app.json`: TypeScript configuration that is specific to the Angular app.
- `tsconfig.base.json`: TypeScript configuration that is specific to the Angular CLI workspace.
- `tsconfig.spec.json`: TypeScript configuration that is specific to unit tests.
- `tslint.json`: Defines coding rules specific to the workspace to enforce readability, maintainability, and functionality.

> **Important Note**
> An Angular CLI workspace can have multiple Angular projects, such as other Angular applications or Angular libraries. This approach is suitable for organizations that want to follow the **monorepo** development style, where all Angular projects exist in a single source code repository.

As developers, we should only care about writing the source code that implements features for our application. Nevertheless, having a piece of basic knowledge on how the application is orchestrated and configured helps us better understand the mechanics and means we can intervene if necessary.

Developing the application

When we develop an Angular application, it's likely that we'll interact with the `src` folder. This is where we write the code and tests of our application. It is also the place where we define the styles of our application and any static assets that we use, such as icons, images, and JSON files:

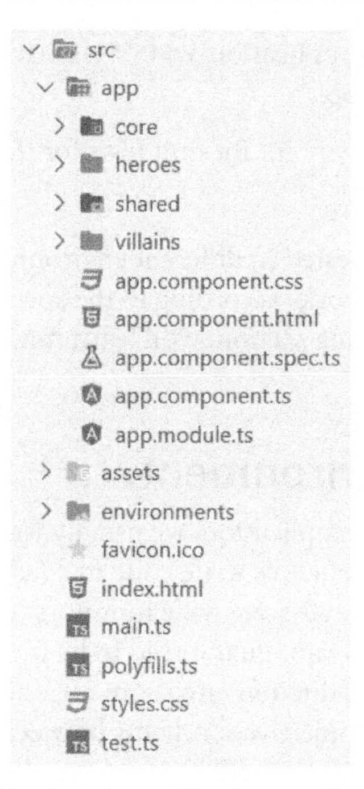

Figure 5.6 – Angular application sample structure

The `src` folder contains the following components:

- `app`: Contains all the Angular-related files of the application. You interact with this folder most of the time during development. In the previous screenshot, we can see that it contains the `shared` module, the `core` module, and the `heroes` and `villains` feature modules.
- `assets`: Contains static assets such as fonts, images, and icons.
- `environments`: Contains environment-specific files according to the target environment used when serving or building the Angular app.
- `favicon.ico`: The icon that is displayed in the tab of your browser, along with the page title.
- `index.html`: The main HTML page of the Angular app.
- `main.ts`: The main entry point of the Angular app.
- `polyfills.ts`: Contains scripts that enable support for specific features on browsers. Not all browsers support all the latest features. For example, there are JavaScript features that are not yet fully supported by all browsers. Angular overcomes this type of limitation by providing polyfills to add support to these browsers.

- `styles.css`: Contains application-wide styles. These are CSS styles that apply globally to the Angular app.
- `test.ts`: The main entry point for unit tests for the Angular app. It is less likely to edit this file.

An Angular application can be tested in different environments before it's deployed to production to ensure that it works according to the specifications provided and with no problems. In the following section, we'll learn how to configure and use such an environment.

Configuring the environment

During the development of our application, we usually work within the boundaries of a specific development environment. We write code in a fast computer with lots of memory and storage space, and we use large-scale wide monitors to preview our application. The development environment is not guaranteed to be the same one that the end user uses. Most bugs occur in the production environment, and they are difficult to track. An organization can also have multiple environments between development and production, such as testing or staging. We must be able to test our application against each one to ensure that it works properly.

The Angular CLI enables us to define different configurations for each environment and serve, build, and test our application with each one. We can run each of these commands while passing the configuration name as a parameter using the following syntax:

```
ng command --configuration=name
```

Here, `command` can be `serve`, `build`, or `test`. The first thing that we need to do when defining a new environment configuration is create the corresponding environment file in the `environments` folder. The Angular CLI creates two environment files by default:

- `environment.ts`: Denotes the development environment
- `environment.prod.ts`: Denotes the production environment

If we want to define an environment for staging, we need to create a file called `environment.staging.ts`. The naming of each file follows the convention of `environment.{env}.ts`, where `{env}` is a distinct name for the environment that we want to add.

Each environment file exports an `environment` object:

environment.ts

```
export const environment = {
  production: false
};
```

The properties of the exported object must be defined in all environment files.
An environment file is a good place to define the URL of your backend API. The `production` property is set by default to distinguish between whether an environment works in production or not. You may have noticed that, in the `main.ts` file of an Angular application, we use it like so:

main.ts

```
import { enableProdMode } from '@angular/core';
import { platformBrowserDynamic } from '@angular/platform-
browser-dynamic';

import { AppModule } from './app/app.module';
import { environment } from './environments/environment';

if (environment.production) {
  enableProdMode();
}

platformBrowserDynamic().bootstrapModule(AppModule)
  .catch(err => console.error(err));
```

`enableProdMode` enables production mode and disables unnecessary assertions and checks of the framework, such as warning messages in the browser console, that may slow down the application.

After creating the environment file, we need to define the appropriate configuration in the `angular.json` configuration file of the workspace. It contains an `architect` property that defines basic CLI commands such as `serve`, `build`, and `test`. Each command contains a configuration for each environment in the `configurations` property. Each configuration contains a `fileReplacements` property that defines the environment file that will replace the development one while executing the specific command:

```
"production": {
  "fileReplacements": [
    {
      "replace": "src/environments/environment.ts",
      "with": "src/environments/environment.prod.ts"
    }
  ]
}
```

When we run the `ng build --configuration=production` command, the Angular CLI replaces the `environment.ts` file with the `environment.prod.ts` file, which is specific for the production target environment. In the case of staging, we need to add a `staging` property and set the `with` property to the relative path of the staging environment file, that is, `src/environments/environment.staging.ts`.

Organizing our components into Angular modules and structuring them inside an Angular CLI workspace is essential when dealing with large enterprise applications. At some point, our modules and their components will need to interact with each other using the **dependency injection (DI)** mechanism, as described in the following section.

How dependency injection works in Angular

Dependency injection is an application design pattern that we also come across in other languages, such as C# and Java. As our applications grow and evolve, each of our code entities will internally require instances of other objects, which are better known as **dependencies**. The action of passing such dependencies to the consumer code entity is known as **injection**, and it also entails the participation of another code entity, called the **injector**. The injector is responsible for instantiating and bootstrapping the required dependencies so that they are ready for use when they've been injected into a consumer. This is essential since the consumer knows nothing about how to instantiate its dependencies and is only aware of the interface they implement to use them.

Angular includes a top-notch dependency injection mechanism to expose required dependencies to any Angular artifact of an Angular application. Before delving deeper into this subject, let's look at the problem that dependency injection in Angular is trying to address.

In *Chapter 4, Enhance Components with Pipes and Directives*, we learned how to display a list of objects using the `ngFor` directive. We used a static list of `Hero` objects that were declared in the `HeroesComponent class`, as shown here:

heroes.component.ts

```
import { Component, OnInit } from '@angular/core';
import { Hero } from '../hero.model';

@Component({
  selector: 'app-heroes',
  templateUrl: './heroes.component.html',
  styleUrls: ['./heroes.component.css']
})
export class HeroesComponent implements OnInit {

  heroes: Hero[] = [
    { id: 1, name: 'Boothstomper', team: 'avengers' },
    { id: 2, name: 'Drogfisher', team: 'avengers' },
    { id: 3, name: 'Bloodyllips', team: 'villains' },
    { id: 4, name: 'Mr Bu Moverse', team: 'villains' },
    { id: 5, name: 'Piranhaelli', team: '' }
  ];

  constructor() { }

  ngOnInit(): void {
  }

  trackByHeroes(index: number, hero: Hero): number {
    return hero.id;
  }

}
```

This approach has two main drawbacks:

- In real-world applications, we rarely work with static data. It usually comes from a backend API or some other service.
- The list of heroes is tightly coupled with the component. Angular components are responsible for the presentation logic and should not be concerned with how to get data, either from a static list or a remote endpoint. They only need to display it in the template. Thus, they delegate business logic to services to handle this type of task.

In the following section, we'll learn how to avoid these obstacles using Angular services. We are going to create an Angular service that will return the list of heroes by itself. Thus, we will effectively delegate business logic tasks away from the component. Remember: **the component should only be concerned with presentation logic**.

Delegating complex tasks to services

To create a new Angular service, we use the `generate` command of the Angular CLI while passing the name of the service as a parameter:

```
ng generate service heroes/hero
```

This creates the Angular service file, `hero.service.ts`, along with the accompanying unit test file, `hero.service.spec.ts`, inside the `heroes` module folder:

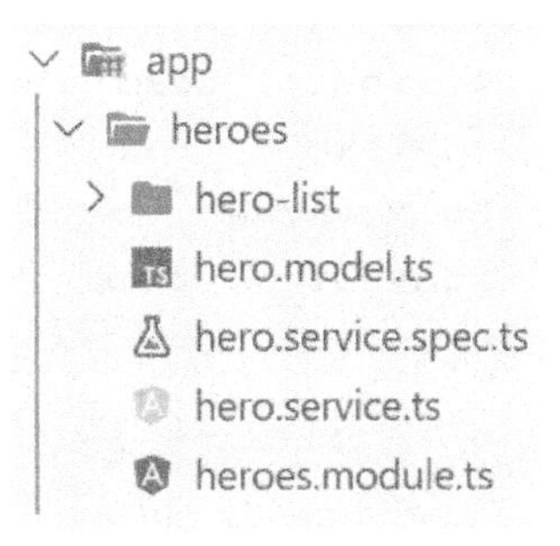

Figure 5.7 – Heroes folder structure

We usually name a service after the functionality that it represents. Every service has a context. When it starts to cross boundaries between different contexts, this is an indication that you should break it into different services.

An Angular service is a TypeScript `class` marked with the `@Injectable` decorator. The decorator identifies `class` as an Angular service that can be injected into an Angular component or another Angular service. It accepts an object as a parameter with a single option, `providedIn`. An Angular service, by default, is not registered with a specific module like components, directives, and pipes are. Instead, it is registered with an injector – the `root` injector of the Angular application – as defined in the `providedIn` option:

```
import { Injectable } from '@angular/core';

@Injectable({
  providedIn: 'root'
})
export class HeroService {

  constructor() { }
}
```

Our service does not contain any implementation. Let's add some logic so that our component can use it:

1. Create a method called `getHeroes`; leave the method body empty for now.
2. The method will return an array of `Hero` objects. Set the return type of the method to `Hero[]`.
3. Copy the contents of the `heroes` property from `HeroesComponent` in the body of the `getHeroes` method. Remove the `team` property from each object.

   Do not forget to add the `return` keyword inside the method. The service should now look like this:

hero.service.ts

```
import { Injectable } from '@angular/core';
import { Hero } from './hero.model';

@Injectable({
  providedIn: 'root'
})
export class HeroService {

```

```
  constructor() { }

  getHeroes(): Hero[] {
    return [
      { id: 1, name: 'Boothstomper' },
      { id: 2, name: 'Drogfisher' },
      { id: 3, name: 'Bloodyllips' },
      { id: 4, name: 'Mr Bu Moverse' },
      { id: 5, name: 'Piranhaelli' }
    ];
  }
}
```

That's it! We have successfully decoupled our component from hero data and extracted its logic into an Angular service! Now, we need to inject it into our component and use it.

4. Declare a `heroes` property in `HeroListComponent`.
5. Create a `private` property called `heroService` and give it a type of `HeroService`:

```
private heroService: HeroService;
```

6. Instantiate the property using the `new` keyword in the component's `constructor`:

```
constructor() {
  this.heroService = new HeroService();
}
```

7. Call the `getHeroes` method of `heroService` inside the `ngOnInit` method and assign the return value to the `heroes` property:

```
ngOnInit(): void {
  this.heroes = this.heroService.getHeroes();
}
```

Run the application using the `ng serve` command to verify that the list of heroes is shown correctly on the page:

My heroes

- Boothstomper
- Drogfisher
- Bloodyllips
- Mr Bu Moverse
- Piranhaelli

Figure 5.8 – List of heroes

Awesome! We have successfully wired up our component with the service, and our application looks great. Well, it seems like this is the case, but it's not. There are some problems with the actual implementation. If the `constructor` component of `HeroService` must change, maybe to accommodate for another dependency, `HeroListComponent` should also change the implementation of its `constructor`. Thus, it is evident that `HeroListComponent` is tightly coupled to the implementation of `HeroService`. This prevents us from altering, overriding, or neatly testing the service if required. It also entails that a new `HeroService` object is created every time we render a `HeroListComponent`, which might not be desired in specific scenarios, such as when we are expecting to use an actual singleton service.

Dependency injection systems try to solve these issues by proposing several patterns, and the constructor injection pattern is the one enforced by Angular. We could refactor the previous snippet to this:

```
import { Component, OnInit } from '@angular/core';
import { Hero } from '../hero.model';
import { HeroService } from '../hero.service';

@Component({
  selector: 'app-hero-list',
  templateUrl: './hero-list.component.html',
  styleUrls: ['./hero-list.component.css']
})
export class HeroListComponent implements OnInit {

  heroes: Hero[];

  constructor(private heroService: HeroService) { }

  ngOnInit(): void {
    this.heroes = this.heroService.getHeroes();
  }

}
```

Now, the component does not need to know how to instantiate the service. On the other hand, it expects such a dependency to be already available before it is instantiated so that it can be injected through its `constructor`. This approach is easier to test as it allows us to override it or mock it up if we wish.

When we create a new Angular service, the Angular CLI registers this service with the root injector of the application by default. In the following section, we'll learn the internals of the dependency injection mechanism and how the root injector works.

Providing dependencies across the application

The Angular framework offers an actual injector that can introspect the tokens used to annotate the parameters in the `constructor` component of an Angular artifact. It returns a singleton instance of the type represented by each dependency so that we can use it straight away in the implementation of our `class`. The injector maintains a list of all dependencies that an Angular application needs. When a component or other artifact wants to use a dependency, the injector first checks to see if it has already created an instance of this dependency. If not, it creates a new one, returns it to the component, and keeps a copy for further use. The next time the same dependency is requested, it returns the copy previously created. But how does the injector know which dependencies an Angular application needs?

When we create an Angular service, we use the `providedIn` property of the `@Injectable` decorator to define how it is provided to the application. That is, we create a **provider** for this service. A provider is a recipe that contains guidelines on how to create a specific service. During application startup, the framework is responsible for configuring the injector with providers of services so that it knows how to create one upon request. An Angular service is configured with the root injector when created with the CLI, by default. The root injector creates singleton services that are globally available through the application. Alternatively, we can pass different values to the `providedIn` property to register the service with a different type of injector:

- Angular module: We can pass the `class` property of an Angular module to make the service available only to this module.
- `any`: Provides a new instance of the service in every Angular artifact that injects it.
- `platform`: Provides the same instance of the service on the same platform. This is especially handy when we have multiple Angular applications on a page.

In the *Organizing components into modules* section, we learned that the `@NgModule` decorator of an Angular module has a `providers` property where we can register services. Registering a service in this way is the same as configuring the service with `providedIn: root` when the Angular module is imported directly from `AppModule`. The main difference between them is that the `providedIn` syntax is tree shakable.

> **Important Note**
>
> Tree shaking is the process of finding dependencies that are not used in an application and removing them from the final bundle. In the context of Angular, the Angular compiler can detect Angular services that are not used by any module and delete them, resulting in a smaller bundle.

When you provide a service using the `@NgModule` decorator, the Angular compiler cannot say if the service is used somewhere in this module. So, it includes the service in the application bundle *a priori*. Thus, it is preferable to use the `@Injectable` decorator over the `@NgModule` one. You should always register services with the root injector unless you want to satisfy a particular case.

The root injector is not the only injector in an Angular application. Lazy loaded modules and components have their own injectors too. The injectors of an Angular application are hierarchical. Whenever an Angular component defines a token in its constructor, the injector searches for a type that matches that token in the pool of registered providers. If no match is found, it delegates the search on the parent component's provider and keeps bubbling the component injector tree. Should the provider lookup finish with no match, it returns to the injector of the component that requested the provider and bubbles up the module injector hierarchy until it reaches the root injector. If no match is found, Angular throws an exception.

The following diagram shows how the Angular DI mechanism works:

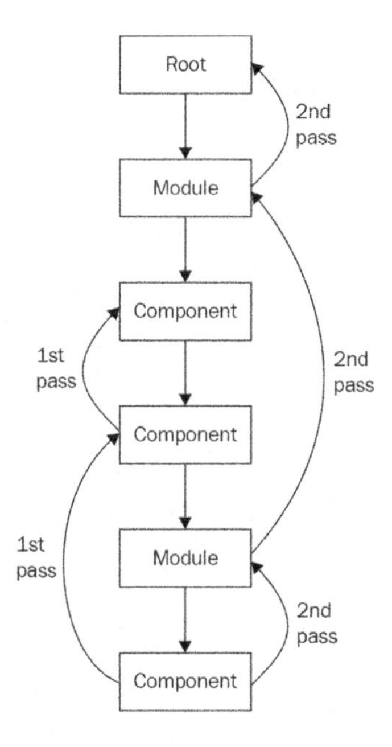

Figure 5.9 – The injector tree

When a component asks for a dependency, the application enters a process that is divided into two phases, known as passes:

- **1st pass**: It searches through the injectors of all the parent components up through the component tree. If it finds the dependency, it stops and returns an instance of it to the component that requested it. Otherwise, it proceeds to the 2nd pass.
- **2nd pass**: It searches through the injectors of all the parent modules, including the root injector of the application. If the dependency is not found, an error is thrown. Otherwise, it returns an instance of the dependency on the component.

Components create their injectors so that they are immediately available to their child components. We'll learn about this in detail in the following section.

Injecting dependencies into the component tree

The `@Component` decorator has a `providers` property that's similar to the `@NgModule` decorator to register services with a component injector. A service that registers with the component injector can serve two purposes:

- It can be shared with the child components of the component that provides the service.
- It can create multiple copies of the service every time the component that provides the service is rendered.

In the following sections, we'll learn how to apply each of the different approaches in more detail.

Sharing dependencies through components

A service provided through the component injector can be shared among the child components of the parent component injector, and it is immediately available for injection at their constructors. Child components reuse the same instance of the service from the parent component. Let's walk our way through an example to understand this better and test some of the learning outcomes from the previous chapter:

1. Create a new component named `favorite-heroes` inside the `heroes` module.
2. Add the newly created component at the end of the `HeroListComponent` template.

The `HeroListComponent` template should look like this:

```
<h3>My heroes</h3>
<ul>
  <li *ngFor="let hero of heroes">
    {{hero.name}}
  </li>
</ul>
<app-favorite-heroes></app-favorite-heroes>
```

3. Open the `hero-list.component.ts` file and add `HeroService` to the `providers` property of the `@Component` decorator.
4. Inject `HeroService` into the `constructor` of `FavoriteHeroesComponent`.
5. Inside the `ngOnInit` method of the component, call the `getHeroes` method of the service and set the returned value to a `heroes` property.
6. Use the `ngFor` directive in the `FavoriteHeroesComponent` template to display the list of heroes.
7. Our favorite heroes will be a subset of the initial list of heroes. Apply the `slice` pipe to the `ngFor` statement to display the first three heroes only.

   The `FavoriteHeroesComponent` template should look like this:

favorite-heroes.component.html

```
<h3>My favorite heroes</h3>
<ul>
  <li *ngFor="let hero of heroes | slice:0:3">
    {{hero.name}}
  </li>
</ul>
```

When running the application using `ng serve`, you should see the following output:

Figure 5.10 – Application output

Let's explain what we did in the previous example in more detail. We injected `HeroService` into the `constructor` of `FavoriteHeroesComponent`, but we did not provide it through its injector. So, how was the component aware of how to create an instance of `HeroService` and use it? It didn't. When we added the component to the `HeroListComponent` template, we made it a direct child of this component, thus giving it access to all its provided services. In a nutshell, `FavoriteHeroesComponent` can use `HeroService` out of the box because it is provided through its parent component, `HeroListComponent`.

So, even if `HeroService` was initially registered with the root injector, we were also able to register it with the injector of `HeroListComponent`. In the next section, we'll investigate how it is possible to achieve such behavior.

Root versus component injector

We have already learned that when we create an Angular service using the Angular CLI, the service is provided in the application's root injector by default. How does this differ when providing a service through the injector of a component?

Services that are provided with the application root injector are available through the whole application. When a component wants to use such a service, it only needs to inject it through its `constructor`, nothing more. Now, if the component provides the same service through its injector, it will get an instance of the service that is entirely different from the one from the root injector. This is a technique called **service scope limiting** because we limit the scope of the service to a specific component tree:

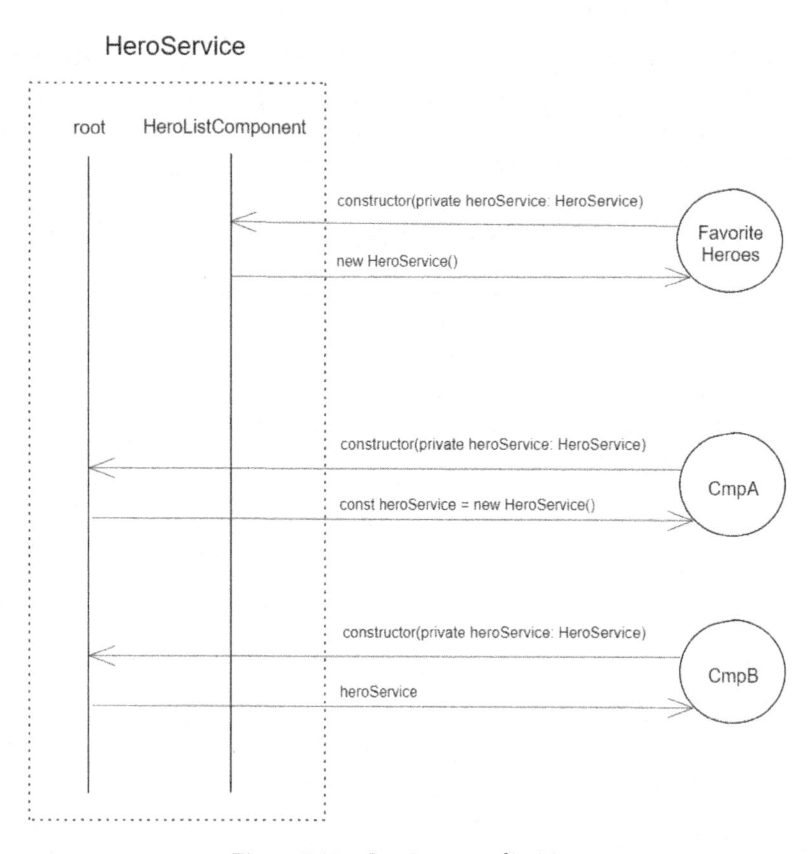

Figure 5.11 – Service scope limiting

As shown in the previous diagram, `HeroService` can be provided through two injectors: the application root injector and the `HeroListComponent` one. `FavoriteHeroesComponent` injects `HeroService` into its `constructor` in order to use it. As we have already seen, `FavoriteHeroesComponent` is a child component of `HeroListComponent`. According to the application injector tree that we saw in the *Providing dependencies across the application* section, it will first ask the injector of its parent component, `HeroListComponent`, about providing the service. `HeroListComponent` indeed provides `HeroService`, so it creates a new instance of the service and returns it to `FavoriteHeroesComponent`.

Now, consider that another component in our application, called `CmpA`, wants to use `HeroService`. Since it is not a child component of `HeroListComponent` and does not contain any parent component that provides the required service, it will finally reach the application root injector. Luckily, `HeroService` is also registered with the root injector. The root injector checks if it has already created an instance for that service. If not, it creates a new one, called `heroService`, and returns it to `CmpA`. It also keeps `heroService` in the local pool of services for later use.

Now, suppose that another component that is similar to `CmpA`, called `CmpB`, also wants to use `HeroService` and asks the application root injector. The root injector knows that it has already created an instance of that service, `heroService`, and it returns it immediately to the `CmpB` component.

Sandboxing components with multiple instances

When we provide a service through the component injector and inject it into the component's `constructor`, a new instance is created every time the component is rendered on the page. This can come in handy in cases such as when we want to have a local cache service for each component.

In our `heroes` module, we're already displaying a list of available heroes in `HeroListComponent`. Let's take this one step further and show the details of a specific hero as a separate component. Follow these steps:

1. Create a new component named `hero-detail` inside the `heroes` module.
2. Add a `@Input` property with the `number` type to the component so that we can pass the ID of the hero that we want to display.
3. Create a service named `hero-detail` inside the folder of the component. The location that we create a service in is not related to the injector that provides it. This is just a visual representation so that we can quickly identify where it is used. If we had created the service in the folder of the `heroes` module, we might have deduced that it is available to the whole module.
4. Inject `HeroService` into the `constructor` component of `HeroDetailService`. This technique is called **service in a service**.
5. Create a method in `HeroDetailService` named `getHero` that takes the ID of a hero as a parameter, calls the `getHeroes` method of `HeroService`, and searches through the results for the given hero ID.
6. Remove the `providedIn` property from the `@Injectable` decorator as we will be providing the service in `HeroDetailComponent`.

`HeroDetailService` should look like this:

hero-detail.service.ts

```
import { Injectable } from '@angular/core';
import { Hero } from '../hero.model';
import { HeroService } from '../hero.service';

@Injectable()
export class HeroDetailService {

  private hero: Hero;

  constructor(private heroService: HeroService) { }

  getHero(id: number): Hero {
    const heroes = this.heroService.getHeroes();
    if (!this.hero) {
      this.hero = heroes.find(hero => hero.id === id);
    }
    return this.hero;
  }
}
```

7. Add `HeroDetailService` to the `providers` array of `HeroDetailComponent` and create a property named `hero` to store the details of the specific hero.
8. Inject `HeroDetailService` into the component's `constructor`.
9. Call the `getHero` method of `HeroDetailService` inside the `ngOnInit` method of the component. Pass the input property, `id`, as a parameter and assign the returned value to the `hero` property.
10. Finally, display the `id` and `name` components of the `hero` property in the template of the component:

The final `HeroDetailComponent` should look like this:

hero-detail.component.ts

```
import { Component, OnInit, Input } from '@angular/core';
import { HeroDetailService } from './hero-detail.
service';
import { Hero } from '../hero.model';

@Component({
  selector: 'app-hero-detail',
  templateUrl: './hero-detail.component.html',
  styleUrls: ['./hero-detail.component.css'],
  providers: [HeroDetailService]
})
export class HeroDetailComponent implements OnInit {

  hero: Hero;
  @Input() id: number;

  constructor(private heroDetailService:
  HeroDetailService) { }

  ngOnInit(): void {
    this.hero = this.heroDetailService.getHero(this.id);
  }

}
```

To display the final output of the application, edit the `hero-list.component.html` file and change the contents of the `li` tag element so that it uses the `HeroDetailComponent` selector:

```
<h3>My heroes</h3>
<ul>
  <li *ngFor="let hero of heroes">
    <app-hero-detail [id]="hero.id"></app-hero-detail>
  </li>
</ul>
```

The final output of the page should be as follows:

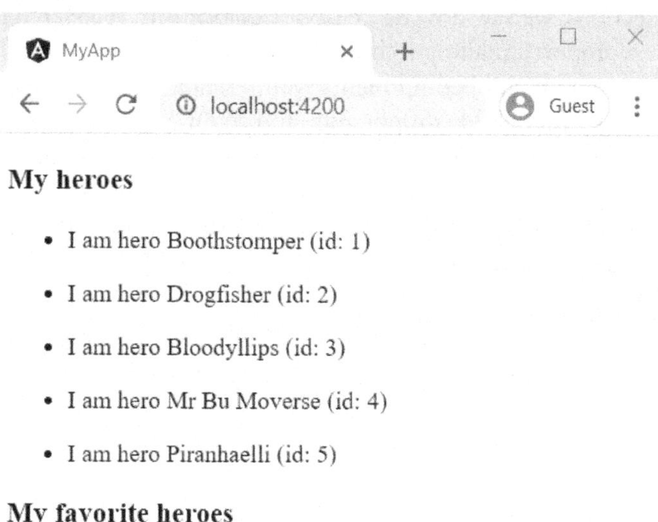

Figure 5.12 – Application output

Each `HeroDetailComponent` that is rendered using the `ngFor` method of `HeroListComponent` creates a dedicated `HeroDetailService` instance for its purposes. This cannot be shared by any other instance of the component and cannot be changed, except by the component that provides it. Try to provide `HeroDetailService` in `HeroListComponent` instead of `HeroDetailComponent`; you will see that only the first hero is rendered multiple times. In this case, there is only one instance of the service that is shared among the child components.

With that, we learned how dependencies are injected into the component hierarchy and how provider lookup is performed by bubbling the request upward in the component tree. However, what if we want to constrain such injection or lookup actions? We'll see how to do so in the next section.

Restricting dependency injection down the component tree

In the previous sections, we saw how `HeroListComponent` registered `HeroService` in its `providers` property, making it immediately available to all the child components. A component may contain child components at different levels. That is, its child components can have other child components, and so on. Sometimes, we might need to constrain the injection of dependencies so that we reach only those that are immediately next to a specific component in the hierarchy. We can do that by registering the service in the `viewProviders` property of the `@Component` decorator. In the previous example, we can restrain the downward injection of `HeroService` to one level only, as shown in the following code:

```
@Component({
  selector: 'app-hero-list',
  templateUrl: './hero-list.component.html',
  styleUrls: ['./hero-list.component.css'],
  viewProviders: [HeroService]
})
```

Here, we define that `HeroService` should only be accessible by the injectors of the components located in the `HeroListComponent` view, not by children of such components. The use of this technique is exclusive to components since they only feature views.

Restricting provider lookup

Just like we can restrict dependency injection, we can constrain dependency lookup to the next upper level only. To do so, we just need to apply the `@Host` decorator to those dependency parameters whose provider lookup we want to restrict:

```
import { Component, OnInit, Host } from '@angular/core';
import { HeroService } from '../hero.service';
import { Hero } from '../hero.model';

@Component({
  selector: 'app-favorite-heroes',
  templateUrl: './favorite-heroes.component.html',
  styleUrls: ['./favorite-heroes.component.css']
})
```

```
export class FavoriteHeroesComponent implements OnInit {

  heroes: Hero[];

  constructor(@Host() private heroService: HeroService) { }

  ngOnInit(): void {
    this.heroes = this.heroService.getHeroes();
  }

}
```

According to the preceding example, the `FavoriteHeroesComponent` injector will look up a `HeroService` type at its parent component's providers. If `HeroListComponent` does not provide the service, it will not bubble up the injector hierarchy; instead, it will stop there and throw an exception. We can configure the injector so that it does not throw an error if we decorate the service with the `@Optional` decorator:

```
constructor(@Host() @
Optional() private heroService: HeroService) { }
```

The `@Host` and `@Optional` decorators define at what level the injector searches for dependencies. There are two other decorators additional to them, called `@Self` and `@SkipSelf`. When using the `@Self` decorator, the injector looks for dependencies in the injector of the current component. On the contrary, the `@SkipSelf` decorator instructs the injector to skip the local injector and search further up in the injector hierarchy.

So far, we have learned how Angular's DI framework uses classes as dependency tokens to introspect the type required and return it from any of the providers available along the injector hierarchy. However, there are cases where we might need to override the instance of `class` or provide types that are not actual classes, such as primitive types.

Overriding providers in the injector hierarchy

We have already learned how to use the class provider syntax, that is, `providers: [HeroService]`. This is shorthand for the `provide` object literal:

```
providers: [{provide: HeroService, useClass: HeroService}]
```

It contains two properties:

- `provide`: This is the token that's used to configure the injector. It is the `class` that consumers of the dependency inject into their constructors.
- The second one is the actual implementation that the injector will provide to the consumers. This can be a `class`, a value, or a factory `function`.

Let's have a look at some examples to get an overview of how to use this type of syntax.

We've already learned that a component could share its dependencies with the child components, as in the case of `FavoriteHeroesComponent`. What if it needs to get data through a trimmed version of `HeroService` and not directly from the service instance of `HeroListComponent`? We could create a new service that would extend `HeroService` and filter out data using the `slice` array method instead of the pipe:

hero-favorite.service.ts

```
import { Injectable } from '@angular/core';
import { HeroService } from './hero.service';
import { Hero } from './hero.model';

@Injectable({
  providedIn: 'root'
})
export class HeroFavoriteService extends HeroService {

  constructor() {
    super();
  }

  getHeroes(): Hero[] {
    return super.getHeroes().slice(0, 3);
  }
}
```

We could then add it to the `providers` property of `FavoriteHeroesComponent` using the `useClass` syntax:

```
@Component({
  selector: 'app-favorite-heroes',
```

```
  templateUrl: './favorite-heroes.component.html',
  styleUrls: ['./favorite-heroes.component.css'],
  providers: [{
    provide: HeroService,
    useClass: HeroFavoriteService
  }]
})
```

The `useClass` property essentially overwrites the initial implementation of `HeroService` for `FavoriteHeroesComponent`.

Alternatively, we can go the extra mile and use a `function` to return the specific object instance we need, depending on other requirements. In the previous example, we could create a factory and return either `HeroFavoriteService` or `HeroService`, depending on a `boolean` condition:

hero-squad.ts

```
import { HeroFavoriteService } from './hero-favorite.service';
import { HeroService } from './hero.service';

export function heroSquadFactory(isFavorite: boolean) {
  return () => {
    if (isFavorite) {
      return new HeroFavoriteService();
    }

    return new HeroService();
  };
}
```

We could then modify the `providers` property of `FavoriteHeroesComponent` so that it looks like this:

```
providers: [{
  provide: HeroService,
  useFactory: heroSquadFactory(true)
}]
```

It is also worth noting that if the two services also injected other dependencies into their `constructor`, the previous syntax would not suffice. For example, if both services were dependent on the `HttpClient` service from the built-in Angular HTTP client that we will learn in the next chapter, we should add it to the `deps` property of the `provide` object literal:

```
providers: [{
  provide: HeroService,
  useFactory: heroSquadFactory(true),
  deps: [HttpClient]
}]
```

Then, we need to inject it into `heroSquadFactory`:

```
export function heroSquadFactory(isFavorite: boolean) {
  return (http: HttpClient) => {
    if (isFavorite) {
      return new HeroFavoriteService();
    }

    return new HeroService();
  };
}
```

What if the dependency we want to provide is not a `class` but a value such as a `string` or an `object`? We can use the `useValue` syntax to accomplish this task. In real-world applications, it is common to keep application settings in a constant object. How could we use the `useValue` syntax to provide these settings in our components? Suppose that our application settings are as follows:

```
export interface AppConfig {
  title: string;
  version: number;
}

export const appSettings: AppConfig = {
  title: 'My app',
  version: 1.0
};
```

You may think that we could provide these settings as `{ provide: AppConfig, useValue: appSettings }`, but this will throw an error because `AppConfig` is an `interface`, not a `class`. Interfaces are syntactic sugar in TypeScript that are thrown away during compilation. Instead, we should provide an `InjectionToken` object:

```
export const APP_CONFIG = new InjectionToken<AppConfig>('app.
config');
```

We could then use it in the `provide` literal object, along with the `@Inject` decorator, to inject it into our component:

app.component.ts

```
import { Component, Inject } from '@angular/core';
import { APP_CONFIG, appSettings, AppConfig } from './app.
config';

@Component({
  selector: 'app-root',
  templateUrl: './app.component.html',
  styleUrls: ['./app.component.css'],
  providers: [{
    provide: APP_CONFIG,
    useValue: appSettings
  }]
})
export class AppComponent {
  title: string;
  version: number;

  constructor(@Inject(APP_CONFIG) config: AppConfig) {
    this.title = config.title;
    this.version = config.version;
  }
}
```

Note that although the `AppConfig interface` did not have a significant role in the injection process, we need it to provide typing on the configuration object.

The Angular DI is a powerful and robust mechanism that allows us to manage the dependencies of our applications efficiently. The Angular team has put a lot of effort into making it simple to use and removed the bargain from the developer's side. As we have seen, the combinations are plentiful, and the ones we use depend on the use case of how we are going to leverage them.

Summary

This chapter has set the foundation for all great applications that you will be building on top of Angular. The Angular dependency management implementation is, in fact, one of the gems of this framework and a time saver. Application architectures based on component trees and modules improve the development workflow and help us design application features. The Angular CLI does a great job of setting up a convenient workspace for working with large-scale Angular applications.

This chapter concludes our trip through the core of Angular and its application architecture, and has set the standards that we will follow from now on while building applications on top of this new and exciting framework.

In the next chapter, we will focus on concrete tools and modules that we can use to solve everyday problems when crafting our web projects. We will learn how to develop better HTTP networking clients with Angular.

6
Enrich Components with Asynchronous Data Services

Connecting to data services and APIs and handling asynchronous information is a common task in our everyday lives as developers. In this sense, Angular provides an unparalleled toolset to help us when it comes to consuming, digesting, and transforming all kinds of information fetched from data services. Observable streams and HTTP data access are at the forefront of this toolset, giving developers a rich set of capabilities when creating Angular apps.

There are many possibilities to describe what you can do to connect to APIs through HTTP or to consume information from the filesystem asynchronously. In this book, we will only scratch the surface. Still, the insights covered in this chapter will give you all that you need to connect your Angular applications to HTTP services in no time, leaving all that you can do with them up to your creativity.

In this chapter, we will do the following:

- Look at the different strategies for handling asynchronous data
- Introduce the observer software design pattern
- Discuss functional reactive programming and **RxJS**
- Learn about the built-in HTTP client in Angular and its API
- Have a look at how to intercept an HTTP request and set additional HTTP headers
- Learn about the Angular **in-memory web API** and how to connect it to your Angular app

Technical requirements

Here is the corresponding GitHub link: `https://github.com/PacktPublishing/Learning-Angular--Third-Edition/tree/master/ch06`.

Strategies for handling asynchronous information

Consuming information from an API is a typical operation in our daily development workflow. We consume data over HTTP all the time, such as when authenticating users by sending out credentials to an authentication service. We also use HTTP when fetching the latest tweets in our favorite Twitter widget. Modern mobile devices have introduced a unique way of consuming remote services. They defer requests and response consumption until mobile connectivity is available. Responsivity and availability have become a big deal. Although internet connections are high-speed nowadays, there is always a response time involved when serving such information. Thus, as we will see in the following sections, we put in place mechanisms to handle states in our applications in a transparent way for the end user.

Shifting from callback hell to promises

Sometimes, we might need to build functionalities in our application that change its state asynchronously once some time has elapsed. To handle this deferred change in the application state, we need to introduce code patterns such as the **callback pattern**.

In a callback, the `function` that triggers asynchronous action accepts another `function` as a parameter, which is called when the asynchronous operation is completed. Let's see how to use a callback through an example:

1. First, create a new Angular application with the name `my-app`.
2. Open the `app.component.ts` file and create a `setTitle` property to change the `title` property of the component. Notice that it returns an arrow `function` because we are going to use it as a callback to another method:

```
private setTitle = () => {
  this.title = 'Hello Angular 10';
}
```

3. Next, create a `changeTitle` method that calls another method, named, by convention, `callback`, after 2 seconds:

```
private changeTitle(callback) {
  setTimeout(() => {
    callback();
  }, 2000);
}
```

4. Finally, call the `changeTitle` method inside the `constructor` of the component, passing the `setTitle` property as a parameter:

```
constructor() {
  this.changeTitle(this.setTitle);
}
```

If we run the Angular application, we see that the `title` property does indeed change after 2 seconds. Notice how the `changeTitle` method uses `setTitle` without parentheses. When we use callbacks, we pass `function` signatures, not actual `function` calls.

The problem with this pattern is that code can become quite confusing and cumbersome as we introduce more and more nested callbacks. Consider the following scenario where we need to drill down a folder hierarchy to access photos in a device:

```
getRootFolder(folder => {
  getAssetsFolder(folder, assets => {
    getPhotos(assets, photos => {
```

```
        });
    });
});
```

We are dependent on the previous asynchronous call and the data it brings back before we can do the next call. We must execute a method inside a callback, that executes another method with a callback, and so on. The code quickly ends up looking horrible and complicated, which leads to a situation known as **callback hell**.

We can avoid callback hell using **promises**. Promises introduce a new way of envisioning asynchronous data management by conforming to a neater and more solid interface. Different asynchronous operations can be chained at the same level and even be split and returned from other functions. To better understand how promises work, let's refactor our previous callback example:

1. Create a new method named `onComplete` that returns a `Promise` object. A `Promise` object accepts two parameters; a `resolve` method to indicate that the promise completed successfully and optionally return a result, and a `reject` method to indicate that an error occurred during execution and optionally return the cause of the error:

```
private onComplete() {
  return new Promise((resolve, reject) => {

  });
}
```

2. Introduce a timeout of 2 seconds in the promise so that it resolves after this time has elapsed. Notice the absence of the `reject` method in the promise body. The `reject` method is optional to use:

```

return new Promise((resolve, reject) => {
  setTimeout(() => {
    resolve();
  }, 2000);
});
```

3. Now, replace the `changeTitle` call in the `constructor` with the promise-based method. To execute a method that returns a promise, we invoke the method and chain it with the `then` method:

```
constructor() {
  this.onComplete().then(this.setTitle);
}
```

If we rerun the Angular application, we do not notice any significant difference. The real value of promises lies in the simplicity and readability afforded to our code. We could now refactor the previous example of folder hierarchy accordingly:

```
getRootFolder()
  .then(getAssetsFolder)
  .then(getPhotos);
```

The chaining of the `then` method called in the preceding code shows how we can line up one asynchronous call after another. Each previous asynchronous call passes its result in the upcoming asynchronous method.

Promises are compelling, but why do we need another paradigm? Well, sometimes we might need to produce a response output that follows a more complex digest process or even cancel the whole process. We cannot accomplish such behavior with promises, because they are triggered as soon as they're being instantiated. In other words, promises are not lazy. On the other hand, the possibility of tearing down an asynchronous operation after it has been fired but not completed yet can become quite handy in specific scenarios. Promises allow us to resolve or reject an asynchronous operation, but sometimes we might want to abort everything before getting to that point.

On top of that, promises behave as one-time operations. Once they are resolved, we cannot expect to receive any further information or state change notification unless we rerun everything from scratch. Moreover, we sometimes need a more proactive implementation of asynchronous data handling, which is where **observables** come into the picture. To summarize the limitations of promises, note the following:

- They cannot be canceled.
- They are immediately executed.
- They are one-time operations only; there is no easy way to retry them.
- They respond with only one value.

Observables in a nutshell

An observable is an object that maintains a list of dependents, called **observers**, and informs them about state and data changes by emitting events asynchronously. To do so, the observable implements all of the machinery that it needs to produce and emit such events. It can be fired and canceled any time, regardless of whether it has emitted the expected data already.

Observers need to subscribe to an observable so that they can be notified and react to reflect the change of state. This pattern, also known as the **observer pattern**, allows concurrent operations and more advanced logic. These observers, also known as subscribers, keep listening to whatever happens in the observable until it is disposed of.

We can probably see all this with more transparency in an actual example:

1. Refactor the `onComplete` method we covered previously by replacing `setTimeout` with `setInterval`:

```
private onComplete() {
  return new Promise((resolve, reject) => {
    setInterval(() => {
      resolve();
    }, 2000);
  });
}
```

2. Modify the `setTitle` property to append the current timestamp in the `title` property of the component:

```
private setTitle = () => {
  const timestamp = new Date().getMilliseconds();
  this.title = `Hello Angular 10 (${timestamp})`;
}
```

3. Run the Angular application, and you will notice that the timestamp is set only once after 2 seconds and is never changed again. The promise resolves itself, and the entire asynchronous event terminates at that very moment. Let's fix this behavior using observables!

4. Create a component property named `title$` that creates an `Observable` object. We call the `next` method of `observer` every 2 seconds to indicate a data or application state change:

```
title$ = new Observable(observer => {
  setInterval(() => {
    observer.next();
  }, 2000);
});
```

5. Modify the `constructor` of the component to use the newly created `title$` property. We use the `subscribe` method to register to an observable and get notified of any changes. If we do not call this method, `setInterval` never executes:

```
constructor() {
  this.title$.subscribe(this.setTitle);
}
```

> **Important Note**
> When we define an observable variable, we tend to append the $ sign to the name of the variable. This is a convention that we follow so that we can identify observables in our code efficiently and quickly.

If you run the application, you will notice that the timestamp now changes every 2 seconds. Congratulations! You have entered the world of observables and reactive functional programming!

Observables return a stream of events, and our subscribers receive prompt notification of those events so that they can act accordingly. They do not perform an asynchronous operation and die (although we can configure them to do so), but start a stream of continuous events on which we can subscribe.

That's not all, however. This stream can be a combination of many operations before they hit observers subscribed to it. Just as we can manipulate arrays with methods such as `map` or `filter` to transform them, we can do the same with the stream of events that are emitted by observables. This is known as reactive functional programming, and Angular makes the most of this paradigm to handle asynchronous information.

Reactive functional programming in Angular

The observer pattern stands at the core of what we know as reactive functional programming. The most basic implementation of a reactive functional script encompasses several concepts that we need to become familiar with:

- An observable
- An observer
- A timeline
- A stream of events
- A set of composable operators

Sound daunting? It really isn't. The big challenge here is to change our mindset and learn to think reactively, and that is the primary goal of this section.

To put it simply, we can just say that reactive programming entails applying asynchronous subscriptions and transformations to observable streams of events. Let's explain it through a more descriptive example.

Think about an interaction device such as a keyboard. It has keys that the user presses. Each one of those keystrokes triggers a specific keyboard event, such as **keyUp**. That event features a wide range of metadata, including—but not limited to—the numeric code of the specific key the user pressed at a given moment. As the user continues hitting keys, more keyUp events are triggered and piped through an imaginary timeline that should look like the following diagram:

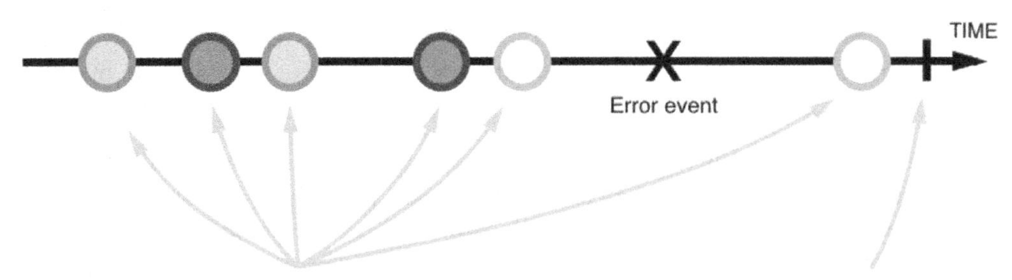

Figure 6.1 – Timeline of keystroke events

The timeline is a continuous stream of data where the keyUp event can happen at any time; after all, the user decides when to press those keys. Recall the example with observables from the previous section. That code was able to notify an observer that every 2 seconds, another value was emitted. What's the difference between that code and our keyUp events? Nothing. Well, we know how often a timer interval is triggered. In the case of keyUp events, we don't know because it is not under our control. But that is the only difference, which means keyUp events can be thought of as an observable as well. Let's try to explain it further by implementing a key logger in our app:

1. Create a new Angular component with the name `key-logger`.
2. Add an `input` element to the template of the newly created component and attach a template reference variable to it. A template reference variable can be added to any HTML element, not just to components, as we learned in *Chapter 3, Component Interaction and Inter-Communication*:

```
<input type="text" #keyContainer>
```

3. Create a new component property, named `input`, to read the template reference variable that we have just created. Create also a second property, named `keys`, to keep all the keys that the user has pressed:

```
keys = '';
@ViewChild('keyContainer', {static: true}) input:
ElementRef;
```

Template reference variables can be queried not only in the template, but also in the `class` component, using the `@ViewChild` decorator. The `@ViewChild` decorator accepts two parameters: the name of the template reference variable and an object with a `static` property. The `static` property indicates whether the element that we want to query will be available during component initialization. There are cases, however, where its value is `false`, such as when using an HTML element with an `ngIf` directive. In this case, we can omit the property entirely, as this is the default behavior.

The result of querying the `keyContainer` template reference variable is an `ElementRef` object. To use `ViewChild` and `ElementRef` in our component, we first need to import them from the `@angular/core` npm package:

```
import { Component, OnInit, ViewChild, ElementRef } from
'@angular/core';
```

4. Use the `keys` property that we created earlier for persisting the pressed keyboard keys in order to display them on the template using interpolation:

```
<input type="text" #keyContainer>
You pressed: {{keys}}
```

5. The RxJS library has a variety of helpful operators that we can use with observables. One of them is the `fromEvent` operator, which creates an observable from the DOM event of a native HTML element. We use this operator in the `ngOnInit` method of the component to listen for `keyup` events in the `input` element:

```
ngOnInit(): void {
  const logger = fromEvent(this.input.nativeElement,
  'keyup');
  logger.subscribe((evt: KeyboardEvent) => {
    this.keys += evt.key;
  });
}
```

Notice that we get access to the native HTML `input` element through the `nativeElement` property of the template reference variable. The result of using the `@ViewChild` decorator is an `ElementRef` object, which is a wrapper over the actual HTML element.

6. For the sake of simplicity, remove all content of the `AppComponent` template and leave only the `title` interpolation:

```
<span>{{ title }} app is running!</span>
```

7. Add the `KeyLoggerComponent` to the template of `AppComponent`.
8. Run the application and start pressing keys to verify the use of the key logger that you have just created.

An essential aspect of observables is the ability to use special functions called operators and chain observables together, enabling **rich composition**. Observables look like arrays as far as operators are concerned. For example, there is a `map` operator for observables that is used in a similar manner to the `map` method of an array. In the following section, we will learn about the RxJS library, which provides these operators, and learn some of them through examples.

The RxJS library

As mentioned previously, Angular comes with a peer dependency on RxJS, the JavaScript flavor of the ReactiveX library that allows us to create observables out of a large variety of scenarios, including the following:

- Interaction events
- Promises
- Callback functions
- Events

In this sense, reactive programming does not aim to replace asynchronous patterns, such as promises or callbacks. All the way around, it can leverage them as well to create observable sequences.

RxJS comes with built-in support for a wide range of composable operators to transform, filter, and combine the resulting event streams. Its API provides convenient methods for observers to subscribe to these streams so that our components can respond accordingly to state changes or input interaction. Let's see some of these operators in action.

Creating observables

We have already learned how to create an observable from a DOM event using the `fromEvent` operator. Two other popular operators that are concerned with observable creation are the `of` and `from` operators.

The `of` operator is used to create an observable from values such as numbers:

```
const values = of(1, 2, 3);
values.subscribe(value => console.log(value));
```

The previous snippet will print the numbers `1`, `2`, and `3` in the console window *in sequence*. Operators that are used to create observables must be imported from the `rxjs` npm package in order to use them:

```
import { of } from 'rxjs';
```

The `from` operator is used to convert an array or a promise to an observable:

```
const values = from([1, 2, 3]);
values.subscribe(value => console.log(value));
```

The previous snippet may look the same as the one used with the `of` operator, but it is not. If you look closely, you will notice that we are passing an array of numbers as a parameter. If we run the snippet, it will print the whole array *at once* in the console window.

The `from` operator is also very useful when we want to convert promises or callbacks to observables. We could wrap the `onComplete` method of the `AppComponent` using this operator as follows:

```
const obsComplete = from(this.onComplete());
obsComplete.subscribe(this.setTitle);
```

> **Important Note**
>
> The `from` operator is an excellent way to start migrating from promises to observables in your Angular application if you have not done so already!

Except for creating observables, the RxJS library also contains a couple of handy operators to manipulate and transform data emitted from observables.

Transforming observables

We have already learned how to create a numeric-only directive in *Chapter 4, Enhance Components with Pipes and Directives*. We will now use RxJS operators to accomplish the same thing in our key logger:

1. Open the `key-logger.component.ts` file and refactor the `logger` observable so that it uses the `pipe` operator:

```
ngOnInit(): void {
  const logger = fromEvent(this.input.nativeElement,
  'keyup');
  logger.pipe(
    tap((evt: KeyboardEvent) => this.keys += evt.key)
  ).subscribe();
}
```

The `pipe` operator is used to link and combine multiple operators separated by commas. We can think of it as a recipe that defines the set of operators that should be applied to an observable. One of them is the `tap` operator, which is used when we want to do something with the data emitted without modifying it.

2. If you run the application, you will not notice any difference in its behavior. However, we have already set the basis for manipulating the emitted data from the observable. It is worth noting that all RxJS operators that are applied on existing observables are imported from the `rxjs/operators` namespace:

```
import { tap } from 'rxjs/operators';
```

3. We want to exclude non-numeric values that the `logger` observable emits. We already get the actual `key` pressed from the `evt` property, but it returns alphanumeric values. It would not be efficient to list all non-numeric values and exclude them manually. What we will do instead is use the `map` operator to get the actual Unicode value of the key. It behaves similar to the `map` method of an array as it returns an observable with a modified version of the initial data. Add the following snippet above the `tap` operator:

```
map((evt: KeyboardEvent) => evt.key.charCodeAt(0))
```

4. We can now add the `filter` operator that operates in a similar manner to the `filter` method of an array, so as to exclude non-numeric values:

```
filter(code => {
  if (this.numeric) {
    return !(code > 31 && (code < 48 || code > 57));
  }
  return true;
})
```

5. Finally, we need to refactor the `tap` operator so that it converts Unicode characters back to actual keyboard codes:

```
tap(digit => this.keys += String.fromCharCode(digit))
```

6. As a final touch, add an input binding in the component to toggle the numeric-only feature on and off, conditionally. You should also refactor the `filter` operator to accommodate the input binding.

   The `ngOnInit` method should finally look like the following:

```
ngOnInit(): void {
  const logger = fromEvent(this.input.nativeElement,
  'keyup');
  logger.pipe(
```

```
        map((evt: KeyboardEvent) => evt.key.charCodeAt(0)),
        filter(code => {
          if (this.numeric) {
            return !(code > 31 && (code < 48 || code > 57));
          }
          return true;
        }),
        tap(digit => this.keys += String.fromCharCode(digit))
      ).subscribe();
  }
```

> **Important Note**
>
> Do not forget to call `subscribe` after the `pipe` operator. Otherwise, the `logger` observable will never be called.

You are probably wondering how we can apply this pattern to an asynchronous scenario, such as consuming information from an HTTP service. You have so far become used to submitting asynchronous requests to AJAX services and then delegating the response to a callback or a promise. Now, we will handle the call by returning an observable. The observable will emit the server response as an event in the context of a stream, which can be funneled through RxJS operators to digest the response better.

In a real-world scenario, you will most likely interact with a real backend API service through HTTP. For the sake of simplicity, we will use a library created by the Angular team that is called the **in-memory web API**. This will act as our backend server and handle all HTTP requests. In the following section, we will learn more details about how to configure it.

Creating a backend API-the Angular way

A web application usually connects to a server and uses an HTTP backend API to perform operations on data. It fetches existing data and updates it, creates a new one, or deletes it. This sequence of actions is also known in software development as **Create Read Update Delete (CRUD)** operations.

There are cases, though, where we do not have access to a real backend API:

- We may work remotely, and the server is only accessible through a VPN connection in which we do not have access.
- We want to set up a quick prototype for demo purposes.
- Available HTTP endpoints are not yet ready for consumption from the backend development team. This is a common problem when working inside a large team of different types of developers.

To overcome all the previous obstacles during development, we can use a fake server such as the Angular in-memory web API. This can mimic all CRUD operations of an HTTP REST API and much more besides, such as introducing a delay in responses and setting custom headers. We can access it using standard HTTP methods as we would for a real backend server, except that our data resides locally to our application.

A word of caution, however. It has limited capabilities, and it is not intended for production use. This book uses it extensively through examples as a replacement for a full-blown production API for the following reasons:

- It is easy to set up and configure.
- Readers should not concern themselves with learning how to set up a backend API.
- The book is intended for frontend development.

In the following steps, we learn how to configure and start using it:

1. We first need to install it from the `npm` package registry:

```
npm install angular-in-memory-web-api --save-dev
```

> **Important Note**
>
> We can install an npm package in our Angular app, either as a runtime dependency or as a development dependency. A runtime dependency is required in order for our application to run, whereas a development one is only needed during development. We denote that a package should be used only for development using the `--save-dev` option during installation. Angular packages, such as `@angular/core` and `@angular/common`, are runtime dependencies. `angular-in-memory-web-api` is only needed during development. We are going to use it as long as the real backend API is not accessible.

2. Our backend API is an actual Angular service that implements the `InMemoryDbService` interface:

```
import { Injectable } from '@angular/core';
import { InMemoryDbService } from 'angular-in-memory-web-api';

@Injectable({
  providedIn: 'root'
})
export class DataService implements InMemoryDbService {

  constructor() { }
}
```

3. The Angular service must implement the `createDb` method of the `InMemoryDbService interface`. The `createDb` method creates an object in memory that represents our database. Each key of the object represents an entity of our application, such as `heroes`. Each value represents a list of entity objects:

```
export class DataService implements InMemoryDbService {

  constructor() { }

  createDb() {
    return {
      heroes: []
    };
  }
}
```

4. The Angular in-memory web API exports `HttpClientInMemoryWebApiModule`, an Angular module that we need to import into our Angular app. As we have learned in *Chapter 5, Structure an Angular App*, we need to import a module in order to use its features:

```
import { BrowserModule } from '@angular/platform-browser';
import { NgModule } from '@angular/core';

```

```
import { AppComponent } from './app.component';
import { KeyLoggerComponent } from './key-logger/
key-logger.component';
import { HttpClientInMemoryWebApiModule } from 'angular-
in-memory-web-api';
import { DataService } from './data.service';

@NgModule({
  declarations: [
    AppComponent,
    KeyLoggerComponent
  ],
  imports: [
    BrowserModule,
    HttpClientInMemoryWebApiModule.forRoot(DataService)
  ],
  providers: [],
  bootstrap: [AppComponent]
})
export class AppModule { }
```

Notice how we import `HttpClientInMemoryWebApiModule`. We don't import it like an ordinary module, such as `BrowserModule`. Instead, we call its `forRoot` method, passing the service that we created earlier as a parameter.

The `forRoot` pattern is used when a module defines services and other declarable artifacts such as components and pipes. If we try to import it normally, we will end up with multiple instances of the same service, thereby violating the singleton pattern. It works similar to when we provide a service to the root injector of the application, as we learned in *Chapter 5, Structure an Angular App*.

> **Important Note**
>
> We could use environment files, as we learned in *Chapter 5, Structure an Angular App*, in order to switch from the in-memory web API back to the real one in production. We should then change the way that we import the module as `(environment.production ? HttpClientInMemoryWebApiModule.forRoot(DataService) : [])`.

That's it for now! We have successfully structured a backend API for our Angular app without using any server infrastructure at all. We are now ready to start leveraging its full capabilities and integrate it with our components. In the following sections, we learn how to use the Angular built-in HTTP client and its methods to communicate with our backend API.

Communicating data over HTTP

Before we dive deeper into describing what the Angular built-in HTTP client is and how to use it to communicate with servers, let's talk about native implementations of HTTP first. Currently, if we want to communicate with a server over HTTP using JavaScript, we can use the `XMLHttpRequest` object. This contains all the necessary methods to establish a connection with a server and start exchanging data. You can see an example of how to fetch data in the following code:

```
const request = new XMLHttpRequest();
request.addEventListener("load", () => {
  if (request.readyState === 4 && request.status === 200) {
    console.log(request.responseText);
  } else {
    console.log('An error has occurred');
  }
});
request.open("GET", url);
request.send();
```

It is worth noting that the request is successful when the `readyState` property has a value of `4` and a `status` property of `200`.

> **Important Note**
>
> To learn more details about `XmlHttpRequest`, check out the official documentation at `https://developer.mozilla.org/en-US/docs/Web/API/XMLHttpRequest`.

Let's try now to convert it to an observable. We use the `constructor` of the `Observable class` that we have learned to wrap into an observable stream. We replace the `log` method of the `console` with the appropriate `observer` object methods:

```
const request$ = new Observable(observer => {
  const request = new XMLHttpRequest();
  request.addEventListener("load", () => {
    if (request.readyState === 4 && request.status === 200) {
      observer.next(request.responseText);
      observer.complete();
    } else {
      observer.error('An error has occured');
    }
  });
  request.open("GET", url);
  request.send();
});
```

The `next` method emits response data back to subscribers as soon they arrive, and the `complete` method notifies them that there will be no other data available in the stream. In the case of an error, the `error` method alerts subscribers that an error has occurred.

That's it! You have now built your custom HTTP client. Of course, this isn't much. There are many cases we are not handling, such as POST, PUT, DELETE, and caching. It was, however, essential to realize all the heavy lifting the HTTP client in Angular was doing for us since it also uses `XmlHttpRequest` under the hood for HTTP communication. Another important lesson is how easy it is to take any kind of asynchronous API and turn that into an observable that fits in nicely with the rest of our asynchronous concepts. So, let's continue with Angular's implementation of an HTTP service.

Introducing the Angular HTTP client

The built-in HTTP client of the Angular framework is a separate Angular library that resides in the `@angular/common` npm package under the `http` namespace. The Angular CLI installs this package by default when creating a new Angular project. To start using it, we need to import `HttpClientModule` in the main application module, `AppModule`:

```
import { BrowserModule } from '@angular/platform-browser';
import { NgModule } from '@angular/core';

```

```
import { AppComponent } from './app.component';
import { KeyLoggerComponent } from './key-logger/key-logger.component';
import { HttpClientInMemoryWebApiModule } from 'angular-in-memory-web-api';
import { DataService } from './data.service';
import { HttpClientModule } from '@angular/common/http';

@NgModule({
  declarations: [
    AppComponent,
    KeyLoggerComponent
  ],
  imports: [
    BrowserModule,
    HttpClientModule,
    HttpClientInMemoryWebApiModule.forRoot(DataService)
  ],
  providers: [],
  bootstrap: [AppComponent]
})
export class AppModule { }
```

> **Important Note**
>
> We must import `HttpClientModule` before `HttpClientInMemoryWebApiModule` so that the in-memory web API overwrites the default behavior of the HTTP client in the Angular framework.

`HttpClientModule` provides a variety of Angular services that we can use to handle asynchronous HTTP communication. The most basic among them is the `HttpClient` service, which provides a robust API and abstracts all operations required to handle asynchronous connections through a variety of HTTP methods. Its implementation was considered with much care to ensure that developers feel at ease while developing solutions that take advantage of this class.

In a nutshell, instances of the `HttpClient` service have access to a variety of methods to perform common request operations, such as GET, POST, PUT, and every existing HTTP verb. In this book, we are interested in the most basic ones, which also constitute the primary CRUD operations:

- `get`: This performs a GET operation to fetch data from the backend.
- `post`: This performs a POST operation to add new data.
- `put`: This performs a PUT operation to update existing data.
- `delete`: This performs a DELETE operation to remove existing data.

All the previous methods return an observable stream of data that our components can subscribe to. In the following section, we explore how to use these methods and communicate with the API that we set up earlier.

Handling data with CRUD in Angular

CRUD applications are widespread in the Angular world and particularly in the enterprise sector. You will hardly find any web app that does not follow this pattern. Angular does a great job supporting this type of application by providing the `HttpClient` service. In the rest of this section, we will walk through an example to understand better how all this fits together. Let's get started by getting some boilerplate code from *Chapter 5, Structure an Angular App*:

1. Copy the `heroes` folder and paste it under the app subfolder of the current Angular project.
2. Refactor the `heroes` folder so that it looks like the following:

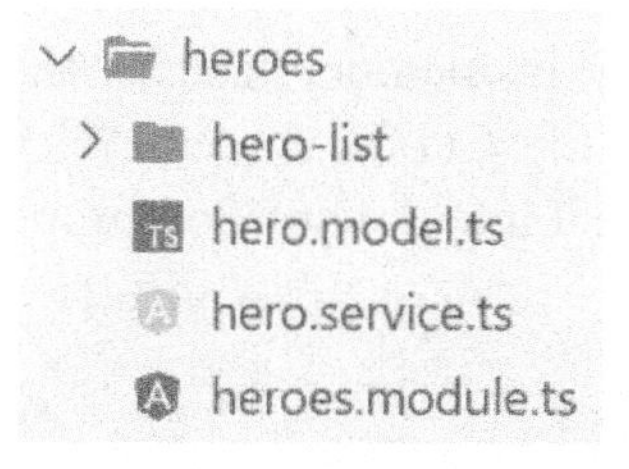

Figure 6.2 – Heroes folder structure

3. Replace the use of the `app-hero-detail` component in the template of `HeroListComponent` with the actual content of `HeroDetailComponent`:

```
<h3>My heroes</h3>
<ul>
  <li *ngFor="let hero of heroes">
    <p>I am hero {{hero.name}} (id: {{hero.id}})</p>
  </li>
</ul>
```

4. Import `HeroesModule` into `AppModule`.
5. Add `HeroListComponent` to the template of `AppComponent`.
6. Run `ng serve` to start the application and walk your way through fixing some errors that you see in the terminal window. Don't worry. These errors are due to the refactoring that you have just made. The list of heroes should finally appear on the page.

Currently, `HeroListComponent` uses `HeroService` to fetch data. As we have learned in *Chapter 5*, *Structure an Angular App*, components delegate complex tasks to services, so we are not going to change that. Instead, we will refactor `HeroService` so that it uses the Angular built-in HTTP client to fetch data.

Injecting service into a service

We have already learned how to use the DI mechanism in Angular to inject an Angular service into a component. In this section, we learn how to inject an Angular service, `HttpClient`, into other services as well:

1. First, we need to set up the in-memory database that we created previously in the `data.service.ts` file. Cut the contents of the `getHeroes` method from `HeroService` and paste it into the `heroes` property of the `createDb` method:

```
createDb() {
  return {
    heroes: [
      { id: 1, name: 'Boothstomper' },
      { id: 2, name: 'Drogfisher' },
      { id: 3, name: 'Bloodyllips' },
      { id: 4, name: 'Mr Bu Moverse' },
      { id: 5, name: 'Piranhaelli' }
```

```
    ]
  };
}
```

2. Now, inject `HttpClient` into `HeroService` to start using it:

```
import { Injectable } from '@angular/core';
import { Hero } from './hero.model';
import { HttpClient } from '@angular/common/http';

@Injectable({
  providedIn: 'root'
})
export class HeroService {

  constructor(private http: HttpClient) { }

  getHeroes(): Hero[] {
    return [];
  }
}
```

3. Modify the `getHeroes` method so that it uses the `HttpClient` service to get the list of heroes. The `get` method of `HttpClient` accepts the URL of an API endpoint as a parameter. For the in-memory database that we use, the URL always starts with the word `api`, followed by the entity that we want to access. In our case, the entity is `heroes`, as defined in the `createDb` method of `DataService`:

```
getHeroes(): Observable<Hero[]> {
  return this.http.get<Hero[]>('api/heroes');
}
```

It is worth noting that the `getHeroes` method no longer returns a list of `Hero` objects, but an `Observable` of them. You may also notice that we pass the `Hero[]` type in the `get` method to get a response of the specific type from the server. We are denoting that the type of data returned from the server will be a list of `Hero` objects indeed.

We have so far converted our Angular service to use the newly introduced `HttpClient`. But what happens with our component? Well, we must also modify it accordingly since the related method of the service returns an observable stream instead of raw data. In the following section, we learn how to accomplish this task.

Subscribing in components

We have already learned that observables emit data when we subscribe to them. So, our component must subscribe to the particular method in `HeroService` that returns an observable:

1. Open the `hero-list.component.ts` file and create a new `private` method named `getHeroes`.
2. The new method should subscribe to the `getHeroes` method of `HeroService` and set the result to the `heroes` property of the component:

```
private getHeroes() {
  this.heroService.getHeroes().subscribe(heroes => this.
  heroes = heroes);
}
```

3. Replace the simple assignment in the `ngOnInit` life cycle hook of the component with a call to the newly created method:

```
ngOnInit(): void {
  this.getHeroes();
}
```

4. Do not forget to remove the `providers` property of the `@Component` decorator since we are going to use the `HeroService` instance provided from the root injector.

Run `ng serve` to start the Angular application, and you should see the list of heroes rendered on the screen with a slight delay. The in-memory web API does a great job of faking a backend server so that it introduces a delay between making a request and getting back a response. You can modify its value by setting the `delay` property in the optional configuration object of the `forRoot` method of `HttpClientInMemoryWebApiModule`.

We have already covered the *Read* part of the CRUD operations. In the following section, we cover the remaining ones, which are mainly concerned with modifying data.

Modifying data through HTTP

When we are talking about modifying data in a CRUD application, we refer to adding new data and updating or deleting existing data. To demonstrate how to implement such functionality in an Angular app using `HttpClient`, we will modify `HeroListComponent` slightly. We are going to add three buttons that will perform each of the remaining CRUD operations:

- Add a new hero in the list of heroes.
- Update the name of an existing hero.
- Delete an existing hero and remove it from the list.

We will wire up a separate method on each button that will call a particular method of `HeroService`. Let's get started in a backward fashion by creating the `HeroService` methods first:

1. Add a `private` property at the top of `HeroService` to keep the URL endpoint that we are going to use for all methods:

   ```
   private heroesUrl = 'api/heroes/';
   ```

2. Create a method, `createHero`, that takes the `name` of a hero as a parameter and returns an `Observable` of the `Hero` type:

   ```
   createHero(name: string): Observable<Hero> {
     const hero = { name };
     return this.http.post<Hero>(this.heroesUrl, hero);
   }
   ```

   We use the `post` method of `HttpClient`, which accepts two parameters: the URL endpoint of the entity that we want to create, and the actual entity object.

3. Create another method, `editHero`, which takes the `id` of a hero and a `Hero` object as parameters:

   ```
   editHero(id: number, hero: Hero): Observable<any> {
     return this.http.put(this.heroesUrl + id, hero);
   }
   ```

   We now use the `put` method of `HttpClient`, which accepts two parameters: the URL endpoint of the entity that we want to update, followed by its `id`, and the new details of the actual entity object.

4. Finally, create a method, `deleteHero`, which takes the `id` of the hero as a parameter:

```
deleteHero(id: number): Observable<any> {
  return this.http.delete(this.heroesUrl + id);
}
```

We use the `delete` method of `HttpClient`, which accepts the URL endpoint of the entity that we want to delete, followed by its `id`, as a parameter.

At this point, we should step back and notice some facts relating to the `editHero` and `deleteHero` methods:

- They return an `Observable` object of `any` type. We do not care about the actual type of response. We are only interested in knowing whether these operations have completed successfully. Everything else should be taken care of by the component.
- They append the `id` of the hero that we want to update or delete in the URL endpoint. Why is that? The in-memory web API does its best to behave like a real backend REST API by making a number of assumptions. One of them is that all collections must contain a field with the name `id`, which acts as the primary key of each object in the collection.

Now that we have configured `HeroService` so that it uses `HttpClient` for the remaining CRUD operations, it is time to move on with `HeroListComponent`:

1. Create an `add` method that takes the `name` of a new hero as a parameter. It subscribes to the `createHero` method of `HeroService` and adds the returned `hero` name to the list:

```
add(name: string) {
  this.heroService.createHero(name).subscribe(hero =>
  this.heroes.push(hero));
}
```

2. Create a `rename` method that takes a `Hero` object as a parameter, creates a copy of it, and changes its `name`. It then subscribes to the `editHero` method of `HeroService`. As soon as the subscription completes successfully, it updates the name of the hero on the list as well:

```
rename(hero: Hero) {
  const existingHero = { id: hero.id, name: 'Pricezog' };

```

```
    this.heroService.editHero(hero.id, existingHero).
    subscribe(() => {
      this.heroes.find(hero => hero.id).name = 'Pricezog';
    });
  }
```

3. Finally, create a `remove` method that takes a `Hero` object as a parameter and subscribes to the `deleteHero` method of `HeroService`. It then uses the `filter` method to remove the hero from the list when the subscription completes:

```
  remove(hero: Hero) {
    this.heroService.deleteHero(hero.id).subscribe(() => {
      this.heroes = this.heroes.filter(selected => selected
      !== hero);
    });
  }
```

4. Add three `button` elements to the `hero-list.component.html` file and bind their `click` events to each of the previous methods:

```
<h3>My heroes</h3>
<ul>
  <li *ngFor="let hero of heroes">
    <p>I am hero {{hero.name}} (id: {{hero.id}})</p>
  </li>
</ul>
<div>
  <button (click)="add(<Thudread>)">Add Thudread</button>
</div>
<div>
  <button (click)="rename(heroes[0])">Rename Boothstomper
  to Pricezog</button>
</div>
<div>
  <button (click)="remove(heroes[4])">Delete
  Piranhaelli</button>
</div>
```

Congratulations! You can now run `ng serve` to preview your CRUD application in Angular.

> **Important Note**
> Do not forget that the in-memory web API is a database that holds data in memory. If you refresh or close the browser, any changes that you have made will be lost.

In a real-world enterprise CRUD application, some data can be accessed only by authorized users. Backend servers provide authentication mechanisms to control access to this data. Web applications usually authenticate the backend API using HTTP headers, as we will learn in the following section.

Authenticating with HTTP

Let's consider that we are working with a backend API that expects all requests to include a custom header named `Authorization`. In this case, we should refactor the `HeroService` methods to include this header in each HTTP request. For example, the `getHeroes` method should transform into the following:

```
getHeroes(): Observable<Hero[]> {
  return this.http.get<Hero[]>(this.heroesUrl, {
    headers: new HttpHeaders({'Authorization': 'myAuthToken'})
  });
}
```

For the sake of simplicity, we are using a hardcoded value for the authentication token. In a real-world scenario, we may get it from the local storage of the browser or some other means.

All `HttpClient` methods that we have met so far accept an optional object as a parameter that is used to pass additional options to a request. These options can be a custom header, as in our case, or even query string parameters to the URL. To set a header, we use the `header` key of the option's object and create a new instance of `HttpHeaders` as a value. The `HttpHeaders` object is a key-value pair that defines custom HTTP headers.

Now imagine what is going to happen if we have many requests that require the authentication token. We should go to each one of them and write the same piece of code again and again. Our code could quickly become cluttered and difficult to test. Luckily, the Angular built-in HTTP library has another feature that we can use to help us in such a situation – HTTP interceptors.

An HTTP interceptor is an Angular service that intercepts HTTP requests and responses originating from `HttpClient`. It can be used in the following scenarios:

- When we want to pass custom HTTP headers in every request, such as an authentication token
- When we want to display a loading indicator while we wait for a response from the server
- When we want to provide a logging mechanism for every HTTP communication

We create an interceptor as we would typically create an Angular service. The only differences are the following:

- It must implement the `HttpInterceptor` interface.
- It should not set the `providedIn` property in the `@Injectable` decorator:

```
import { Injectable } from '@angular/core';
import { HttpInterceptor } from '@angular/common/http';

@Injectable()
export class AuthInterceptorService implements
HttpInterceptor {}
```

Alternatively, we can use the `generate` command of the Angular CLI to create an Angular interceptor:

```
ng generate interceptor auth
```

The previous command will create an Angular interceptor, named `auth`, and it will add all the necessary imports and methods.

Angular interceptors must be registered with an Angular module to use them. To register an interceptor with a module, we import the `HTTP_INTERCEPTORS` injection token and use it in conjunction with the `provide` object literal that we learned about in *Chapter 5, Structure an Angular App*:

```
@NgModule({
  declarations: [
    AppComponent,
    KeyLoggerComponent
  ],
  imports: [
```

```
    BrowserModule,
    HttpClientModule,
    HttpClientInMemoryWebApiModule.forRoot(DataService),
    HeroesModule
  ],
  providers: [
    { provide: HTTP_INTERCEPTORS, useClass:
    AuthInterceptorService, multi: true }
  ],
  bootstrap: [AppComponent]
})
export class AppModule { }
```

> **Important Note**
>
> An HTTP interceptor must be provided in the same Angular module that imports `HttpClientModule`.

The `provide` object literal contains a key named `multi` that takes a `boolean` value. We set it to `true`, to indicate that the current injection token, `HTTP_INTERCEPTORS` in our case, can accept multiple service instances. This is the reason that we do not set the `providedIn` property in the decorator of the service in the first place. It also enables us to combine multiple interceptors, each one satisfying a particular need. But how can they cooperate and play nicely altogether?

The `HttpInterceptor` interface contains a method named `intercept` that our interceptor must implement:

```
intercept(req: HttpRequest<any>, next: HttpHandler) {
  return next.handle(req);
}
```

It accepts two parameters: an `HttpRequest` object that indicates the current request, and an `HttpHandler` object that denotes the next interceptor in the chain. The purest form of an interceptor is to delegate the request to the next interceptor using the `handle` method. Thus, it is evident that the order in which we import interceptors matters. Here you can see how interceptors process HTTP requests and responses according to their order:

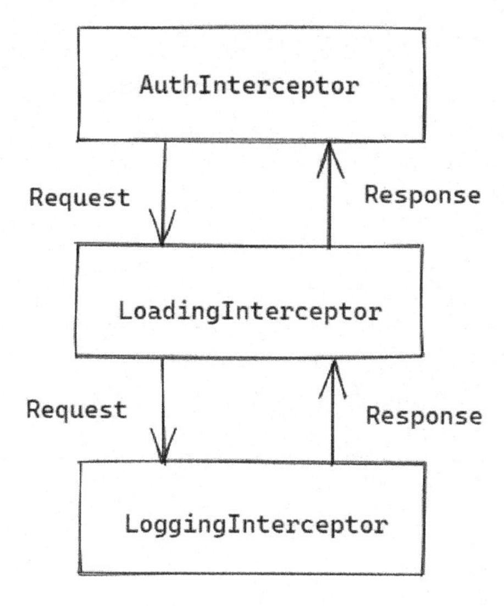

Figure 6.3 – Execution order of Angular interceptors

By default, the last interceptor before sending the request to the server is a particular service named `HttpBackend`.

You may not realize it, but you have already come across an HTTP interceptor before! The in-memory web API is an HTTP interceptor. It listens for HTTP requests that would typically go to a real backend server and redirects them to a data store that is kept in memory. The in-memory web API overrides `HttpBackend` so that it prevents all HTTP requests from being sent to a real server.

Now that we have covered some of the basics of interceptors, let's use the one that we created earlier to set the authentication header:

auth-interceptor.service.ts

```
import { Injectable } from '@angular/core';
import { HttpInterceptor, HttpRequest, HttpHandler } from
'@angular/common/http';

@Injectable()
export class AuthInterceptorService implements HttpInterceptor
{

  constructor() { }

```

```
  intercept(req: HttpRequest<any>, next: HttpHandler) {
    const authReq = req.clone({ setHeaders: { Authorization:
    'myAuthToken' } });
    return next.handle(authReq);
  }
}
```

`HttpRequest` objects are immutable. If we need to modify them, we need to use their `clone` method. The `HttpHeaders` object is also immutable. We can't just create a new instance of headers. Instead, we use the shorthand `setHeaders` method to update them.

> **Important Note**
>
> There are cases where you may need to access `HttpClient` in an interceptor. For example, you may want to refresh your authentication token before sending a new HTTP request. While it is tempting to inject the `HttpClient` service into the interceptor, it generally should be avoided unless you know what you are doing. You should be very careful because you may end up with cyclic dependencies.

HTTP requests might not reach the destination server, or the server may return an error response. In the following section, we learn how to handle such errors with the Angular built-in HTTP client.

Handling HTTP errors

Handling errors in HTTP requests would typically require an inspection of the information returned in the error response object manually. RxJS provides the `catchError` operator to simplify that. In conjunction with the `pipe` operator, it can catch potential errors that may occur when initiating an HTTP request:

```
getHeroes(): Observable<Hero[]> {
  return this.http.get<Hero[]>(this.heroesUrl).pipe(
    catchError((error: HttpErrorResponse) => {
      console.error(error);
      return throwError(error);
    })
  );
}
```

The signature of the `catchError` method contains the actual `HttpErrorResponse` object that is returned from the server. After catching the error, we use another operator, named `throwError`, which re-throws the error as an observable. In this way, we make sure that the stream will not crash, which would result in a potential memory leak, but will complete gracefully.

In a real-world scenario, we would probably create a helper method that would involve logging the error in a more solid tracking system and return something meaningful or add some retry logic. There is an RxJS operator for nearly everything, even one for retrying HTTP requests. It accepts the number of retries where the particular request has to be executed until it completes successfully:

```
getHeroes(): Observable<Hero[]> {
  return this.http.get<Hero[]>(this.heroesUrl).pipe(
    retry(2),
    catchError((error: HttpErrorResponse) => {
      console.error(error);
      return throwError(error);
    })
  );
}
```

The point is that with the `catchError` operator, we have a way of capturing the error; how we handle it depends on the scenario.

When we create observables, we are immune to potential memory leaks if we do not clean them up on time. In the following section, we learn about different ways of how to accomplish that.

Unsubscribing from observables

There are some known techniques to use when we are concerned with cleaning up resources from observables:

- Unsubscribe from observables manually.
- Use the `async` pipe.

Let's see both techniques in action in the following sections.

Destroying a component

A component has life cycle events that we can hook on them and perform custom logic, as we learned in *Chapter 3, Component Interaction and Inter-Communication*. One of them is the `ngOnDestroy` event, which is called when the component is destroyed and no longer exists.

Recall `HeroListComponent`, which we used earlier in our examples. It subscribes to the `getHeroes` method of `HeroService` upon component initialization. When the component is destroyed, the reference of the subscription seems to stay active, which may lead to unpredictable behavior.

> **Important Note**
>
> Luckily for us, it is not. The `getHeroes` method is handled internally by `HttpClient`, which takes care of all cleanup tasks for us, such as unsubscribing from observables by itself.

It is good practice, though, to clean up subscriptions manually by ourselves as an extra precaution measure:

1. Create a `private` property of the `Subscription` type in the component. `Subscription` can be imported from the `rxjs` npm package:

```
private heroSub: Subscription;
```

2. Assign the `heroSub` property to the subscription of the `getHeroes` method call of `HeroService`:

```
private getHeroes() {
  this.heroSub = this.heroService.getHeroes().
  subscribe(heroes => this.heroes = heroes);
}
```

3. Add the `OnDestroy` interface to the component.
4. Implement the `ngOnDestroy` method and call the `unsubscribe` method of the `heroSub` property:

```
ngOnDestroy() {
  this.heroSub.unsubscribe();
}
```

That's a lot of boilerplate code just to unsubscribe from a single subscription. It may quickly become unreadable and unmaintainable if we have many subscriptions. Can we do better than this? Yes, we can!

We can use a particular type of observable called `Subject`, which extends an `Observable` object as it is both an observer and an observable. It can multicast values to multiple observers, whereas an `Observable` object is unicast. We have already met such an object before in *Chapter 3, Component Interaction and Inter-Communication*. The `EventEmitter` that we used in the output binding of a component is a `Subject`. Other cases that can be used are the following:

- An alternative way for components to pass data between each other.
- Implement a mechanism with *search as you type* features.

Let's convert the `Subscription` of `HeroListComponent` to a `Subject` instead:

1. Initialize the `heroSub` property as a `Subject` object. The `Subject` object can also be imported from the `rxjs` npm package:

```
private heroSub = new Subject();
```

2. Use the `pipe` and `takeUntil` operators to subscribe to the `getHeroes` observable of `HeroService`. The `takeUntil` operator indicates that the observer keeps listening for emitted values until `heroSub` completes:

```
private getHeroes() {
  this.heroService.getHeroes().pipe(
    map(heroes => this.heroes = heroes),
    takeUntil(this.heroSub)
  ).subscribe();
}
```

3. Modify the `ngOnDestroy` method so that `heroSub` emits one value and then completes:

```
ngOnDestroy() {
  this.heroSub.next();
  this.heroSub.complete();
}
```

We have now converted our subscription to a more declarative way that is more readable. But the problem of maintainability still exists. We can solve that using a special-purpose Angular pipe, the `async` pipe.

Using the async pipe

The `async` pipe is an Angular pipe that is used in conjunction with observables, and its role is two-fold. It helps us to type less code, and it saves us the whole rigmarole of having to set up and tear down a subscription. Let's use it to simplify the code of `HeroListComponent`:

1. Create a component property of `Observable` type. The observable will emit the values of an array of `Hero` objects:

```
heroes$: Observable<Hero[]>;
```

2. Assign the property that you have just created in the `getHeroes` method call of `HeroService`. Notice that you *should not* subscribe to it:

```
private getHeroes() {
  this.heroes$ = this.heroService.getHeroes();
}
```

3. Modify the template of the component to use the `async` pipe in the `ngFor` directive:

```
<ul>
  <li *ngFor="let hero of heroes$ | async">
    <p>I am hero {{hero.name}} (id: {{hero.id}})</p>
  </li>
</ul>
```

That's it! We do not need to either subscribe or unsubscribe from the observable! The `async` pipe does everything for us in three steps only. Ideally, we would also need to make changes to the rest of the CRUD methods because we operate on observables, but that is beyond the scope of this chapter.

Summary

It takes much more than a single chapter to cover in detail all the great things that we can do with the Angular HTTP library. The good news is that we have covered pretty much all the tools and classes we need. We learned what reactive functional programming is and how it can be used in Angular. We saw how to apply reactive techniques such as observables to communicate with a backend HTTP API. We also investigated various approaches in HTTP as far as authentication and error handling are concerned.

The rest is just left to your imagination, so feel free to go the extra mile and put all of this knowledge into practice in your Angular applications. The possibilities are endless, and you have assorted strategies to choose from, ranging from promises to observables. You can leverage the incredible functionalities of the reactive operators and the powerful `HttpClient` to communicate with backend servers. If you are preparing a prototype of your favorite application or the backend API is just not ready, you can create a fake one using the Angular in memory web API.

As we have already highlighted, the sky's the limit. However, we still have a long and exciting road ahead. Now that we know how to consume asynchronous data in our components, let's discover how we can provide a broader user experience in our applications by routing users into different components. We will cover this in the next chapter.

Section 3: User Experience and Testability

This section explains how to use the Angular router and integrate with HTML forms to provide a unique experience to the user, how to style your application using Google Material Design and animations to components, and how to write unit tests to ensure that your components do not break.

This part comprises the following chapters:

- *Chapter 7, Navigate through Components with Routing*
- *Chapter 8, Orchestrating Validation Experiences in Forms*
- *Chapter 9, Introduction to Angular Material*
- *Chapter 10, Give Motion to Components with Animations*
- *Chapter 11, Unit test an Angular App*

7
Navigate through Components with Routing

In previous chapters, we did a great job of separating concerns and adding different layers of abstraction to increase the maintainability of an Angular 10 app. However, we have barely concerned ourselves with the user experience that we provide through the app.

Currently, our user interface is bloated with components scattered across a single screen. We need to provide a better navigational experience and a logical way to change the application's view intuitively. Now is the right time to incorporate routing and split the different areas of interest into different pages that are interconnected by a grid of links and URLs.

So, how do we deploy a navigation scheme between components of an Angular 10 app? We use the Angular router that was built with componentization in mind and create custom links to make our components react to them.

In this chapter, we will do the following:

- Discover how to define routes to switch components on and off, and redirect them to other routes.
- Learn how to trigger routes and load components in our views, depending on the requested route.
- Uncover how to pass and handle parameters to our components using the router.
- Learn how to secure our routes.
- Investigate how to improve the response time and the bundle size of our Angular app.

Technical requirements

GitHub link: `https://github.com/PacktPublishing/Learning-Angular--Third-Edition/tree/master/ch07`.

Introducing the Angular router

In traditional web applications, when we wanted to change from one view to another, we needed to request a new page from the server. The browser would create a URL for the view and send it to the server. As soon as a response was received from the server, the browser would reload the page. This was a process that resulted in round trip time delays and a bad user experience for our applications:

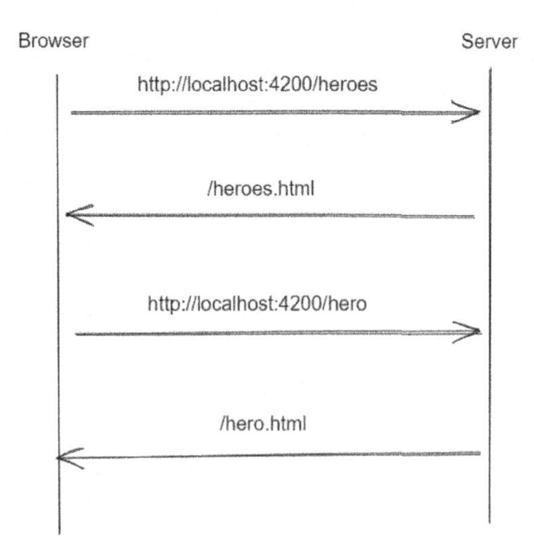

Figure 7.1 – Traditional web applications

Modern web applications that use a JavaScript framework such as Angular follow a different approach. They handle changes between views or components on the client side without bothering the server. They contact the server only once during bootstrapping to get the main `index.html` file. Any subsequent URL changes are intercepted and handled by the router on the client. These types of applications are called **Single-Page Applications** (**SPA**) because they do not cause a full reload of a page:

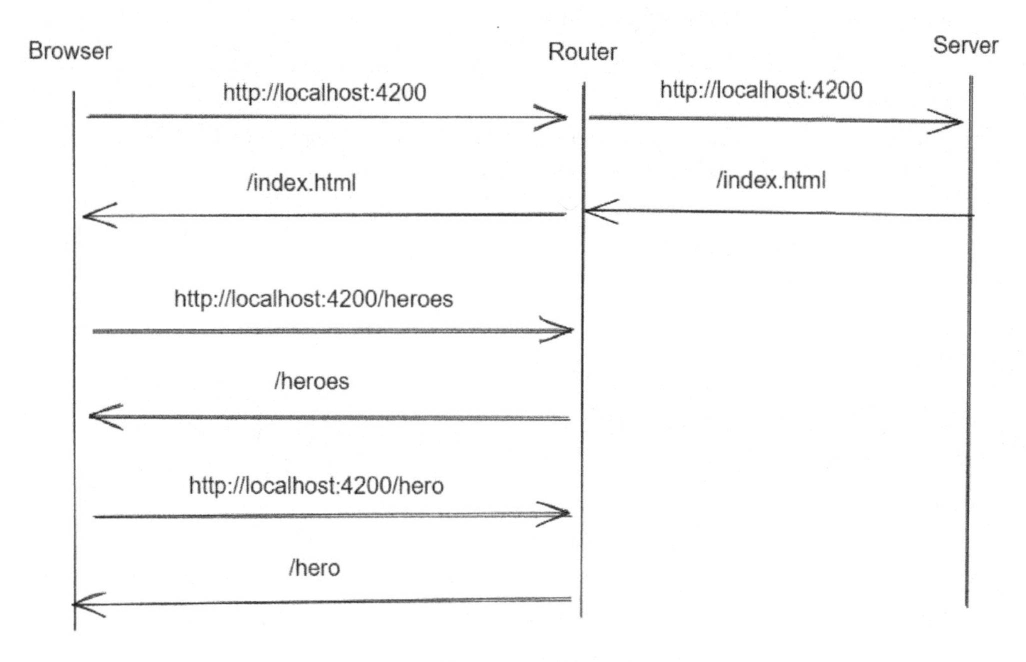

Figure 7.2 – SPA

The Angular framework provides the `@angular/router` npm package, which we can use to navigate between different components in an Angular 10 app. Adding routing in an Angular app involves the following steps:

1. Specify the base path for the Angular app.
2. Use an appropriate Angular module from the `@angular/router` package.
3. Configure different routes for the Angular app.
4. Decide where to render components upon navigation.

In the following sections, we will learn the basics of Angular routing before diving deeper into hands-on examples.

Specifying a base path

As we have already seen, modern and traditional web applications react differently when a URL changes inside the app. The architecture of each browser plays an essential part in this behavior. Older browsers initiate a new request to the server when the URL changes. Modern browsers, also known as **HTML5 browsers**, can change the URL and the history of the browser, when navigating in different views, without sending a request to the server using a technique called **HTML5 pushState**.

> **Important Note**
> HTML5 pushState allows in-app navigation without causing a full reload of the page and is supported by all modern browsers.

An Angular application must set the `base` HTML tag in the `index.html` file to enable pushState routing:

index.html

```
<!doctype html>
<html lang="en">
<head>
  <meta charset="utf-8">
  <title>MyApp</title>
  <base href="/">
  <meta name="viewport" content="width=device-width,
  initial-scale=1">
  <link rel="icon" type="image/x-icon" href="favicon.ico">
</head>
<body>
  <app-root></app-root>
</body>
</html>
```

The `href` attribute informs the browser about the path it should follow when attempting to load external resources, such as media or CSS files, once it goes deeper into the URL hierarchy.

The Angular CLI adds the `base` tag by default when creating a new Angular app and sets the `href` value to the application root, `/`. If your app resides in a different folder than the app, you should change it according to the name of that folder.

Importing the router module

The Angular router library contains `RouterModule`, an Angular module that we need to import into our application to start using the routing features:

```
import { RouterModule } from '@angular/router';
```

We import `RouterModule` in the main application module, `AppModule`, using the `forRoot` pattern that we have already seen in *Chapter 6, Enrich Components with Asynchronous Data Services*:

```
@NgModule({
  imports: [
    RouterModule.forRoot(routes)
  ]
})
```

The `forRoot` method of `RouterModule` returns an Angular module that contains a set of Angular artifacts related to routing:

- Services to perform common routing tasks such as navigation
- Directives that we can use in our components to enrich them with navigation logic

It accepts a single parameter, which is the route configuration of the application.

Configuring the router

The `routes` variable that we pass in the `forRoot` method is a list of `Routes` objects that specify what routes exist in the application and what components should respond to a specific route. It can look like the following:

```
const routes: Routes = [
  { path: 'heroes', component: HeroListComponent },
  { path: '**', component: PageNotFoundComponent }
];
```

Each route definition object contains a `path` property, which is the URL path of the route, and a `component` property that defines which component will be loaded when the application navigates to that path. Note that the value of the `path` property does not contain a leading `/`.

Navigation in an Angular 10 app can occur either by changing the URL of the browser or by instructing the router to navigate along a route path in the application code. In the first case, when the browser URL contains the `/heroes` path, the router creates an instance of `HeroListComponent` and displays its template on the page. On the contrary, when the application navigates to `/heroes` by code, the router follows the same procedure, and additionally, it updates the URL of the browser.

If the user tries to navigate to a URL that does not match any route, Angular activates a custom type of route called the **wildcard route**. The wildcard route has a `path` property with two asterisks and matches any URL. The `component` property is usually an application-specific `PageNotFoundComponent` or the main component of the application.

Rendering components

One of the directives that the router library exports using the `forRoot` method is `router-outlet`. It is used as an Angular component, and it acts as a placeholder for components that are activated with routing.

Typically, the `AppComponent` of an Angular 10 app is used only for providing the main layout of the application and orchestrating all other components. We should write it once and forget it, and not modify it when we want to add a new feature to our app. So, a typical example of `AppComponent` is the following:

```
<app-header></app-header>
<router-outlet></router-outlet>
<app-footer></app-footer>
```

`app-header` and `app-footer` are layout components, and `router-outlet` is the place where all other components are rendered using routing. In reality, these components are rendered as a sibling element of the `router-outlet` directive.

We have already covered the basics and provided a minimal setup of the router. In the next section, we will look at a more realistic example and further expand our knowledge of the routing module and how it can help us.

Creating an Angular app with routing

Whenever we have created a new Angular app through the course of this book so far, the Angular CLI has asked us whether we wanted to add routing, and we have always replied *no*. Well, it is time to respond positively and enable routing to our Angular app! In the following sections, we will put into practice all the basics that we have learned about routing:

- Scaffolding an Angular 10 app with routing
- Adding route configuration to our Angular app
- Navigating to application routes

At the end of this section, we will have built a simple Angular 10 app with complete routing capabilities.

Scaffolding an Angular app with routing

We are going to use the Angular CLI to create a new Angular 10 app from scratch:

1. Execute the `ng new` Angular CLI command to create an Angular app named `my-app`.
2. Type `y` (yes) to the question asking whether we would like to add routing to our app, and then press *Enter*.
3. Accept the default `CSS` choice for styling and press *Enter*.

The Angular CLI creates the following structure in the `app` folder:

Figure 7.3 – The Angular app folder structure

It generates roughly the same files as usual but with one exception, the `app-routing.module.ts` file:

```
import { NgModule } from '@angular/core';
import { Routes, RouterModule } from '@angular/router';

const routes: Routes = [];

@NgModule({
  imports: [RouterModule.forRoot(routes)],
  exports: [RouterModule]
})
export class AppRoutingModule { }
```

This is an Angular module that is used to configure and enable the router in our application. It imports `RouterModule` using the `forRoot` method, as we have already learned in the previous section. It also re-exports `RouterModule` so that components of other modules that import `AppRoutingModule` have access to router services and directives. By default, `AppModule` imports `AppRoutingModule`, so all the components of our application are enabled with routing capabilities:

```
import { BrowserModule } from '@angular/platform-browser';
import { NgModule } from '@angular/core';

import { AppRoutingModule } from './app-routing.module';
import { AppComponent } from './app.component';

@NgModule({
  declarations: [
    AppComponent
  ],
  imports: [
    BrowserModule,
    AppRoutingModule
  ],
  providers: [],
  bootstrap: [AppComponent]
})
export class AppModule { }
```

We mentioned in the previous section that `AppModule` imports `RouterModule` directly. We could have followed that approach for a minimal route configuration, but we suggest creating a separate routing module for the following reasons:

- We can change the route configuration of the application anytime, independent of the Angular module that imports it.
- We can easily test the Angular module without enabling routing. Routing is difficult to manage in unit tests.
- We can quickly understand, from the existence of a routing module, that an Angular module supports routing.

Routing modules are used not only in the main application module, `AppModule`, but also in feature modules, as we will learn later in this chapter.

Adding route configuration to our Angular app

The main module of our application does not have a route configuration yet. The `routes` variable in `AppRoutingModule` is an empty array. Let's start filling it with values:

1. Create two Angular components, one named `hero-list` and another named `hero-detail`.

> **Important Note**
>
> Since these components are going to be activated with routing, we can safely remove their `selector` property from the `@Component` decorator. However, it is helpful to leave them unchanged for debugging purposes because we can quickly identify components later in the DOM tree.

2. Add two route definition objects in the `routes` variable, one for each component. The `heroes` route will activate `HeroListComponent`, and the `hero` route will activate `HeroDetailComponent`:

```
const routes: Routes = [
  { path: 'heroes', component: HeroListComponent },
  { path: 'hero', component: HeroDetailComponent }
];
```

Now that we have set up the routing configuration of our app, we just need to learn how to navigate to a specific route.

Navigating to application routes

We are going to use two router directives to perform navigation in our app, the `router-outlet` directive that we have already seen and `routerLink`. We apply the `routerLink` directive to anchor HTML elements, and we assign the route path in which we want to navigate as a value. Notice that the path starts with / as opposed to the `path` property in the route definition object. Let's begin:

1. Open the `app.component.html` file and replace all the contents with a `router-outlet` directive.
2. Add a `nav` HTML element that contains two anchor tags, one for each component.
3. Add the `routerLink` directive to each tag and assign the respective paths from the route configuration that we created earlier:

```
<nav>
  <a routerLink="/heroes">Heroes</a>
  <a routerLink="/hero">Hero</a>
</nav>
<router-outlet></router-outlet>
```

We are now ready to preview our Angular app. Run `ng serve` and click on the **Heroes** link. The application should display the template of `HeroListComponent` underneath the `nav` element. It should also update the URL of the browser to match the path of the route. Now try to do the opposite. Navigate to the root path, `http://localhost:4200`, and append the `/heroes` path at the end of the URL. The application should behave the same as before, and we should get something like the following screenshot:

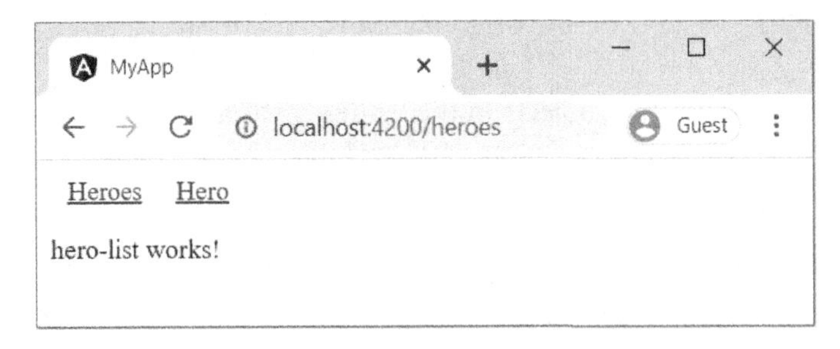

Figure 7.4 – Heroes route

Congratulations! Your Angular app now supports in-app navigation. We have barely scratched the surface of routing in Angular. Many router features are waiting for us to investigate in the following sections. For now, let's try to move our components to a separate feature module so that we can manage it independently of the main application module.

Separating our app into feature routing modules

At this point, we have set up the route configuration so that routing works the way it should. However, this approach doesn't scale so well. As our application grows, more and more routes may be added to `AppRoutingModule`. Thus, we should create a separate feature module for our components that will also have a dedicated routing module.

We have already learned how to create a new Angular module in *Chapter 5, Structure an Angular App*. We will use the same `generate` Angular CLI command, but we will pass a different option to create the routing module as well:

```
ng generate module heroes --routing
```

The `--routing` parameter instructs the Angular CLI to create a routing module along with the `heroes` feature module:

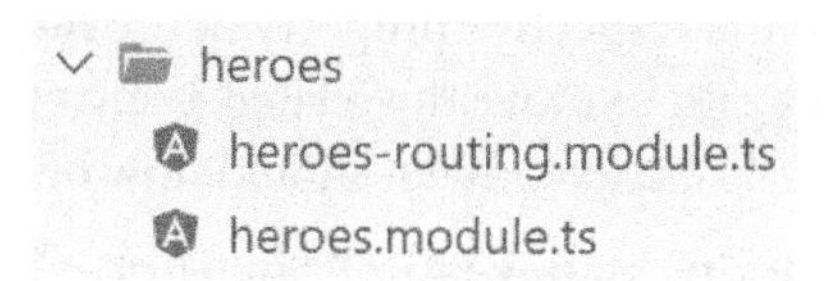

Figure 7.5 – The heroes folder structure

The Angular CLI names the routing module file after the name of the actual feature module, appending the `-routing` suffix. This is a convention that helps us to quickly identify whether a feature module has routing enabled and which one is the routing module of the respective feature module. The name of the TypeScript `class` of the routing module also follows a similar convention:

```
import { NgModule } from '@angular/core';
import { Routes, RouterModule } from '@angular/router';

const routes: Routes = [];

@NgModule({
```

```
  imports: [RouterModule.forChild(routes)],
  exports: [RouterModule]
})
export class HeroesRoutingModule { }
```

In the previous snippet, you may have noticed that we do not import `RouterModule` using the `forRoot` method as we did before. Instead, we use the `forChild` method for that. The `forChild` method is used when we want to register routes in a feature module. You should call the `forRoot` method **only** in the routing module of the main application module, `AppRoutingModule`.

Now that we have created our feature module and the related routing module, we should move all feature-related artifacts from `AppModule` into `HeroesModule`. Begin by moving components first and then proceed with the route configuration:

1. Move the `hero-list` and `hero-detail` folders into the `heroes` folder.
2. Remove the `HeroListComponent` and `HeroDetailComponent` declarations of `AppModule` and add them to the `declarations` property of `HeroesModule`. Do not forget to move their `import` statements at the top of the file.
3. Take the contents of the `routes` variable from the `app-routing.module.ts` file and move them to the respective property of the `heroes-routing.module.ts` file. Do not forget again to move the related `import` statements. The route configuration of `AppRoutingModule` should now be an empty array.
4. Finally, add `HeroesModule` **above** `AppRoutingModule` in the `imports` property of `AppModule`.

> **Important Note**
>
> The order that we import routing modules in does matter. The router selects a route with a *first match wins* strategy. We place feature routing modules that contain more specific routes before the main application routing module that contains more generic routes, such as a wildcard route. Thus, we want to force the router to first search through our specific route paths and then fall back to an application-specific one.

If we now run the Angular application using `ng serve`, we will see that it is working as before. We have not introduced any new features or done anything fancy, but we have paved the way to separating our route configurations effectively. The router combines the routes of our feature module, `HeroesModule`, with those of the main application module, `AppModule`. Thus, we can continue to work with routing in our feature module without modifying the main route configuration.

Currently, the route configuration of our app is pretty straightforward. There are some scenarios that we need to take into account when working with routing in a web application, such as the following:

- Do we want to display a specific view when we bootstrap our application?
- What is going to happen if we try to navigate to a non-existing route path?

In the following section, we will explore how to handle the last case so that we do not break our app.

Handling unknown route paths

We have already come across the concept of unknown routes in the *Introducing the Angular router* section. We set up a wildcard route to display a `PageNotFoundComponent` when our application tries to navigate to a route path that does not exist. Now it is time to add that component for real:

1. Use the Angular CLI to create a new component named `page-not-found`. Our app will display the newly generated component when we navigate to an unknown route path. Make sure that you give it meaningful content in the template:

```
<h3>Ooops!</h3>
<p>The requested page was not found</p>
```

2. Open the `app-routing.module.ts` file and add a new route definition object in the `routes` variable. Set the `path` property to double asterisks and the `component` property to the new component that you created:

```
const routes: Routes = [
  { path: '**', component: PageNotFoundComponent }
];
```

> **Important Note**
> It is better to define a wildcard route along with the related component in `AppRoutingModule`. The wildcard route applies to the whole application, and thus it is not tied to a specific feature.

If we run `ng serve` and point the browser to `http://localhost:4200/angular`, we see that the `page-not-found` component is displayed on the screen because our app does not have an `angular` route:

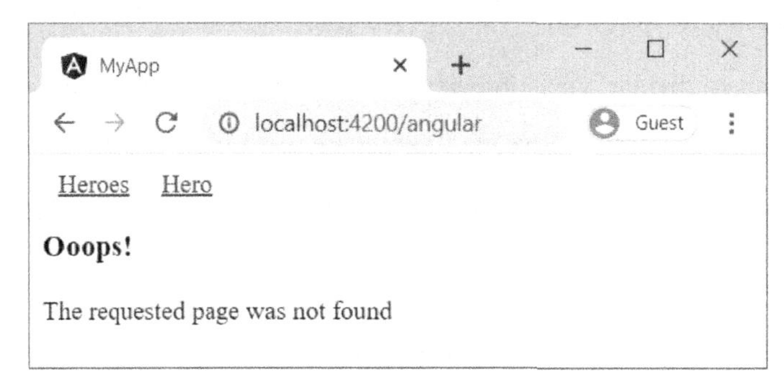

Figure 7.6 – Page not found route

> **Important Note**
> When the router encounters an unknown route, it navigates to the wildcard route, but the browser still points to the invalid URL.

Try to navigate to the root path of our application, `http://localhost:4200`, and you will notice that the `page-not-found` component is still visible on the screen. We have accidentally broken our application! Why did this happen?

The `href` attribute of the `base` tag is the location at which an Angular application starts, as we learned in the *Introducing the Angular router* section. The Angular CLI sets the value of `href` to / by default when creating a new Angular app. We have also learned that a route does not contain / in its `path` property. So, when our application bootstraps, it loads in the `''` empty route path. According to our route configurations, we have not defined such a path. Thus, the router falls back to the wildcard route and displays the `page-not-found` component on the screen.

We need to define a default route for our Angular app, which brings us to the first scenario that we described: how to define a default route path when our application bootstraps.

Setting a default path

We set the `path` property of a route to an empty string to indicate that the route is the default one for an Angular app. In our case, we want the default route path to display `HeroListComponent`:

1. Open the `heroes-routing.module.ts` file and add a new route definition object **below** the existing routes.
2. Set the `path` property to an empty string, `''`, and the `component` property to `HeroListComponent`.
3. Run the application, and you will notice that when the browser URL points to the root path of our application, the `hero-list` component is displayed on the screen.

However, we could have done better than defining a new route path for `HeroListComponent`. Let's introduce another term of routing, `redirect`. Replace the default route definition object with the following:

```
{ path: '', redirectTo: '/heroes', pathMatch: 'full' }
```

We tell the router to redirect to the `/heroes` path when the application navigates to the default route. The `pathMatch` property tells the router how to match the URL to the route `path` property. In this case, the router redirects to the `/heroes` path only when the URL matches the default route.

It is worth noting that we added the empty route path after all other routes because, as we have already learned, the order of the routes is important. We want more specific routes before less specific ones. In the following diagram, you can see the order in which the router resolves paths in our application:

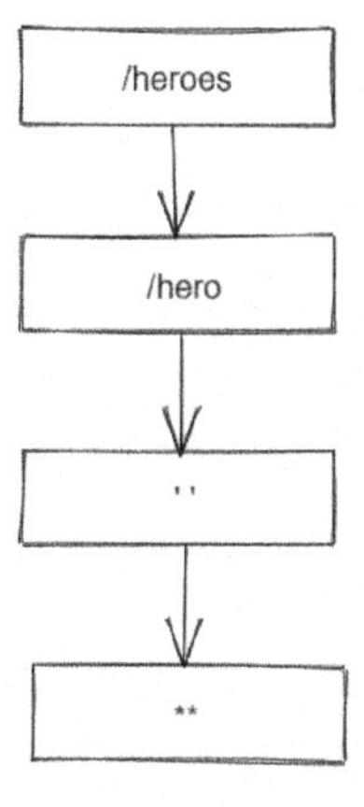

Figure 7.7 – Route path resolve process

We have already learned how to navigate in our app using the `routerLink` directive. This is the preferred way when using anchor elements in a template. However, in a real-world application, we also use buttons for navigation. In the following section, we will learn how to navigate to a route path imperatively using a `button` element.

Navigating imperatively to a route

When we navigate to a wildcard route, the template of the `component` property is displayed on the screen. However, as we have seen, the address bar of the browser stays on the invalid URL. So, we need to provide a way for the user to escape from this route:

1. Open the `page-not-found.component.html` file and add a `button` HTML element.
2. Add an event binding to the native `click` DOM event of the `button` element. Set the template statement of the binding to a `goHome` component method, which does not exist yet. We have already learned about event bindings in *Chapter 3, Component Interaction and Inter-Communication*:

```
<button (click)="goHome()">Home</button>
```

3. Open the `page-not-found.component.ts` file and create the `goHome` method.
4. `RouterModule` exports the `Router` service that we can use in our components for performing imperative navigation, in code. Inject the service into the constructor of `PageNotFoundComponent`.
5. Call the `navigate` method of the `Router` service in the `goHome` method to navigate into the root path of the application. It accepts a **link parameters array** that contains two items – the destination route path and any route parameters, as we will learn later in the chapter:

page-not-found.component.ts

```
import { Component } from '@angular/core';
import { Router } from '@angular/router';

@Component({
  selector: 'app-page-not-found',
  templateUrl: './page-not-found.component.html',
  styleUrls: ['./page-not-found.component.css']
})
```

```
export class PageNotFoundComponent {

  constructor(private router: Router) { }

  goHome() {
    this.router.navigate(['/']);
  }

}
```

It is worth noting that the link parameters array can also be used in the `routerLink` directive. For example, we could have written the anchor element for the heroes route as follows:

```
<a [routerLink]="['/heroes']">Heroes</a>
```

> **Important Note**
> We could use imperative navigation with an anchor element, as well as a `routerLink` directive with a `button` element. That is perfectly fine. However, it is more semantically correct to use them as suggested in this book. The `routerLink` directive modifies the behavior of the target element and adds an `href` attribute, which targets anchor elements.

Until now, we have relied on the address bar of the browser to indicate which route path is active at any given time. We could improve the user experience by using CSS styling to do that.

Decorating router links with styling

`RouterModule` exports the `routerLinkActive` directive, which we can use to change the style of an active route. It works similarly to the class binding that we learned about in *Chapter 3, Component Interaction and Inter-Communication*. It accepts a list of class names or a single class that is added when the link is active and is removed when inactive:

1. Open the `app.component.css` file and define an `active` class that sets the background color to a value of your choice:

   ```
   .active {
     background-color: lightgray;
   }
   ```

2. Add the `routerLinkActive` directive to both links in `app.component.html` and set it to the `active` class name:

```
<a routerLink="/heroes" routerLinkActive="active">Heroes</
a>
<a routerLink="/hero" routerLinkActive="active">Hero</a>
```

Now, when we click in a link in our app, its background color turns to the color that we chose.

We have already learned that we can navigate to a route with a static path value. In the next section, we will learn how to do this when the path changes dynamically passing route parameters.

Passing parameters to routes

A common scenario in enterprise web applications is to have a list of items, and when you click on one of them, the page changes the current view and displays details of the selected item. This resembles a master-detail browsing functionality, where each generated URL living in the master page contains the identifiers required to load each item in the detail page.

We can represent the previous scenario with two routes that navigate to different components. One component is the list of items and the other is the details of an item. So, we need to find a way to create and pass dynamic item-specific data from one route to the other.

We are tackling double trouble here: creating URLs with dynamic parameters at runtime and parsing the value of these parameters. No problem: the Angular router has got our back, and we will see how using a real example.

Building a detail page using route parameters

We need to refactor the Angular CLI project that we are working on so that we reproduce the previous scenario. The flow of our application should be the following:

1. `HeroListComponent` displays a list of heroes from a backend API.
2. The user clicks on a hero from the list.
3. The application redirects the user to the `HeroDetailComponent` component, which is responsible for fetching the details of the selected hero from the backend API.

Let's get started by reusing some content from *Chapter 6, Enrich Components with Asynchronous Data Services*:

1. Copy the `data.service.ts` file into the app folder of the Angular CLI project.
2. Copy the `hero.model.ts` and `hero.service.ts` files into the `heroes` folder of the Angular CLI project.
3. Import `HttpClientModule` into `AppModule`.
4. Install the Angular in-memory web API library and import `HttpClientInMemoryWebApiModule` into `AppModule`.
5. Replace the `hero-list` folder with the same folder from the code of the previous chapter.

Up to this point, our Angular app should display the following when run with `ng serve`:

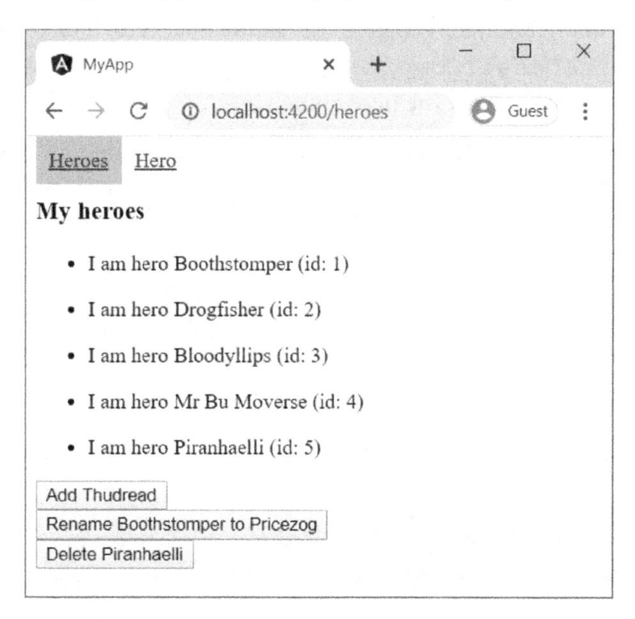

Figure 7.8 – Application output

The user should be able to click on each hero from the list and navigate to the details of the selected hero. We need to define our route configuration accordingly and modify the list of heroes so that each hero is clickable:

1. Open the `heroes-routing.module.ts` file and append the `/:id` suffix onto the `path` property of the hero route:

```
{ path: 'hero/:id', component: HeroDetailComponent }
```

The colon character denotes that `id` is a route parameter. If a route has more than one parameter, we separate them with `/`. The name of the parameter, `id`, is important when we want to consume its value in our components, as we will learn later.

2. Open the `hero-list.component.html` file and convert each paragraph element into an anchor element that displays the `name` property of a hero. Add the `routerLink` directive to each anchor element and use property binding to set its value in a link parameters array. Set the second item of the array to the `id` property of the `hero` template reference variable:

```
<a [routerLink]="['/hero', hero.id]">{{hero.name}}</a>
```

The `routerLink` directive requires property binding when dealing with dynamic routes. It will create an `href` attribute that contains the `/hero` path, followed by the value of its `id` property.

If we run the application and click on the name of a hero, it does nothing more than navigate to `HeroDetailComponent` as before. We have not taken advantage of the new route parameter of the hero route yet.

`HeroDetailComponent` should get the value of the `id` parameter and make an HTTP request to the backend API to fetch the hero with that particular id. Finally, it should set the returned hero in a component property so that we can display its details in the template of the component:

1. Remove the anchor element that points to the hero route from the template of `AppComponent`.
2. Add a `getHero` method to `HeroService` that uses the HTTP client to get details about a particular hero. The method should return an `Observable` of the `Hero` type:

```
getHero(id: number): Observable<Hero> {
  return this.http.get<Hero>(this.heroesUrl + id);
}
```

3. `RouterModule` exports the `ActivatedRoute` service, which we can use to retrieve information about the currently active route, including any parameters. Inject the `ActivatedRoute` service into the constructor of `HeroDetailComponent`:

```
constructor(private route: ActivatedRoute) { }
```

4. Create a `hero` property in the component and use interpolation to display its `name` property in the template of the component:

```
<p>{{hero?.name}} works!</p>
```

The `?` character that we have added to the `hero` property is called a **safe navigation operator**. It is used to guard our component against `null` or `undefined` values of the `hero` property. If we do not use this operator, the delay that we experience because of the HTTP request will break our template. The template will try to display the `name` property of a `hero` object that has not been set yet and will throw an error. Alternatively, we could have used the `ngIf` directive in the paragraph element to prevent this type of error.

The `ActivatedRoute` service contains the `paramMap` observable, which we can subscribe to get route parameter values. `HeroDetailComponent` needs to get the `id` parameter value from the `paramMap` observable and make a call to the `getHero` method of `HeroService`, which is also an observable. So, how can we accomplish this task?

We introduce another RxJS operator, `switchMap`, to switch from one observable to the other. We also take advantage of the `map` operator to set the returned hero from the backend API to the local `hero` component property:

```
ngOnInit(): void {
  this.getHeroObs();
}

private getHeroObs() {
  this.route.paramMap.pipe(
    switchMap((params: ParamMap) => {
      const id = +params.get('id');
      return this.heroService.getHero(id);
    }),
    map(hero => this.hero = hero)
  ).subscribe();
}
```

The benefit of using the `switchMap` operator is that it can cancel any pending HTTP requests. That is, if the user renavigates to the same route path with a different id, and the previous HTTP request has not completed yet, it discards the old request and proceeds with the new one.

In the previous snippet, it is worth noting the following:

- The `paramMap` observable returns an object of the `ParamMap` type. We can use the `get` method of the `ParamMap` object and pass the name of the parameter that we defined in the route configuration to access its value.
- We add the plus sign in front of the `id` parameter to convert it from a `string` into a `number`.

Run the application using `ng serve` and click on the name of a hero from the list. The application navigates to `HeroDetailComponent` and displays the name of the selected hero. We have successfully integrated routing and HTTP into our Angular 10 app. Awesome!

In the previous example, we used `paramMap` to get route parameters as an observable. So, ideally, our component could be notified with new values during its lifetime. But the component is destroyed each time we want to select a different hero from the list, and so is the subscription to the `paramMap` observable. So, what's the point of using it after all?

The router can reuse the instance of a component as soon as it remains rendered on the screen during consecutive navigations. We can achieve this behavior using child routes.

Reusing components using child routes

We use child routes when we want to define a container component for a feature module that will act as the routing orchestrator for components of that module. It contains a `router-outlet` element in which child routes will be loaded. Suppose that we wanted to define the layout of our Angular app like the following:

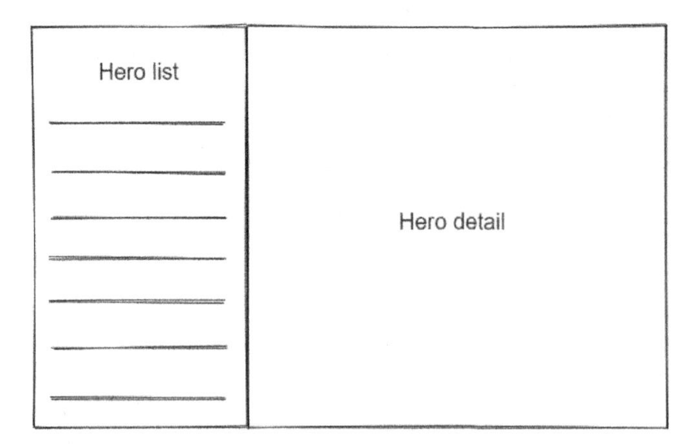

Figure 7.9 – Layout of the Angular app

`HeroListComponent` should contain existing contents along with a `router-outlet` element. The additional `router-outlet` element is used to render `HeroDetailComponent` when the related route is activated.

> **Important Note**
> The template of `HeroDetailComponent` is rendered in the `router-outlet` element of `HeroListComponent` and not in the `router-outlet` element of `AppComponent`.

`HeroDetailComponent` is not destroyed when we navigate from one hero to another. Instead, it remains in the DOM tree, and the `ngOnInit` method is called once, the first time that we select a hero. When we select a new hero from the list, the `paramMap` observable emits the id of the new hero. `HeroService` fetches the requested hero, and the template of the component is refreshed to reflect the new changes.

The route configuration of our Angular app, in this case, would be as follows:

```
const routes: Routes = [
  {
    path: 'heroes',
    component: HeroListComponent,
    children: [
      { path: ':id', component: HeroDetailComponent },
    ]
  },
  { path: '', redirectTo: '/heroes', pathMatch: 'full' }
];
```

We use the `children` property of a route configuration object to define child routes, which contains a list of route configuration objects. Notice also that we removed the word `hero` from the `path` property of the `hero` route. We wanted to make it clear that it is a child of the `heroes` route, and it should be accessed using the `/heroes/:id` path.

We should also change the `routerLink` directive of the anchor elements in the `hero-list.component.html` file so that our application works correctly:

```
<a [routerLink]="['./', hero.id]">{{hero.name}}</a>
```

Notice that we replaced `/hero` with `./`. What is this strange syntax? It is called **relative navigation** and tells the router to navigate to a specific route relative to the current activated route. It is the opposite of the current syntax that we have used so far, which is called **absolute navigation**. For example, the `./` path indicates to navigate relative to the current level, which is `/heroes`, in our case. If the route that we wanted to navigate to was one level above the `heroes` route, we would have used `../` as a path. You can think of it as navigating between folders using the command line. The same syntax applies to imperative navigation also:

```
this.router.navigate(['./', hero.id], { relativeTo: this.route
});
```

In this case, we pass an additional `NavigationExtras` object after the link parameters array that defines the `relativeTo` property that points to the current activated route.

> **Important Note**
>
> Relative navigation is considered a better choice over absolute navigation because it is easier to refactor. It decouples hardcoded links by defining paths relative to the current route. Imagine moving a bunch of components around, and suddenly all your hardcoded paths are wrong. Navigation inside a feature module works as expected, even if you decide to change the parent route.

We have learned how we can take advantage of the `paramMap` observable in Angular routing. It clearly does not provide any benefit to our Angular app. In the following section, we will discuss an alternative approach using route snapshots.

Taking a snapshot of route parameters

Currently, when we select a hero from the list, `HeroListComponent` is removed from the DOM tree and `HeroDetailComponent` is added. To select a different hero, either we click the **Heroes** link or the back button of our browser. Consequently, `HeroDetailComponent` is removed from the DOM, and `HeroListComponent` is added. So, we are in a situation where only one component is displayed on the screen at a time.

When `HeroDetailComponent` is destroyed, so is the `ngOnInit` method and the subscription to the `paramMap` observable. So, we do not gain any benefits by using observables at this point. Alternatively, we could use the `snapshot` property of the `ActivatedRoute` service to get values for route parameters:

```
private getHeroSnap() {
  const id = this.route.snapshot.params['id'];
  this.heroService.getHero(id).subscribe(hero => this.
  hero = hero);
}
```

The `snapshot` property always contains the current value of a route parameter, which happens also to be the initial value. It contains the `params` property, which is an object of the `Params` type. A `Params` object contains route parameter key-value pairs, which we can access as we would access a standard object in TypeScript.

> **Important Note**
>
> If you are sure that your component is not going to be reused, you should go with the snapshot approach since it is also more readable.

So far, we have been dealing with routing parameters in the form `heroes/:id`. We use these types of parameters when we want to route to a component that requires the parameter to work correctly. In our case, `HeroDetailComponent` requires the `id` parameter so that it can get details of a specific hero. However, there is another type of parameter that is considered optional, as we will learn in the following section.

Filtering data using query parameters

Query parameters are considered optional parameters because they aim to either sort data or narrow down the size of a dataset. Some examples are as follows:

- `/heroes?sortOrder=asc`: Sorts a list of heroes in ascending order
- `/heroes?page=3&pageSize=10`: Splits a list of heroes in pages of 10 records and gets the third page

Query parameters are recognized in a route by the `?` character. We can combine multiple query parameters by chaining them with an ampersand (`&`) character. The `ActivatedRoute` service contains a `queryParamMap` observable that we can subscribe to get query parameter values. It returns a `ParamMap` object, similar to the `paramMap` observable, which we can query to get parameter values. For example, to retrieve the value of a `sortOrder` query parameter, we would use it as follows:

```
constructor(private route: ActivatedRoute) { }

ngOnInit(): void {
  this.route.queryParamMap.subscribe(params => {
    console.log(params.get('sortOrder'));
  });
}
```

A `queryParamMap` property is also available when working with snapshot routing to get query parameter values.

Now that we have learned how to pass parameters during navigation, we have pretty much covered all the essential information that we need to start building Angular apps with routing. In the following sections, we will focus on some advanced practices that are going to enhance the user experience when using in-app navigation in our Angular apps.

Enhancing navigation with advanced features

So far, we have covered basic routing, with route parameters as well as query parameters. The Angular router is quite capable, though, and able to do much more, such as the following:

- Controlling access to a route
- Preventing navigation away from a route
- Preloading data to improve the UX
- Lazy loading routes to speed up the response time
- Providing artifacts to easily enable the debugging of the router behavior in an Angular 10 app

In the following sections, we will learn about all these techniques in more detail.

Controlling route access

When we want to prevent unauthorized access to a particular route, we use a specific Angular service called a **guard**. To create a guard, we use the `generate` command of the Angular CLI, passing the word `guard` and its name as parameters:

```
ng generate guard auth
```

When we execute the previous command, the Angular CLI asks which interfaces we would like our guard to implement:

```
? Which interfaces would you like to implement? (Press <space> to select, <a> to toggle all, <i> to invert selection)
>(*) CanActivate
 ( ) CanActivateChild
 ( ) CanDeactivate
 ( ) CanLoad
```

Figure 7.10 – Choosing the interface

There are multiple types of guards that we can create according to the functionality that they provide. Each guard implements a different interface:

- **CanActivate**: Controls whether a route can be activated.
- **CanActivateChild**: Controls access to child routes of a route.
- **CanDeactivate**: Controls whether a route can be deactivated. Deactivation happens when we navigate away from a route.
- **CanLoad**: Controls access to a route that loads a lazy-loaded module.

For now, let's accept the default value, `CanActivate`, and press *Enter*:

```
import { Injectable } from '@angular/core';
import { CanActivate, ActivatedRouteSnapshot,
RouterStateSnapshot, UrlTree } from '@angular/router';
import { Observable } from 'rxjs';

@Injectable({
  providedIn: 'root'
})
export class AuthGuard implements CanActivate {
  canActivate(
```

```
    next: ActivatedRouteSnapshot,
    state: RouterStateSnapshot): Observable<boolean |
    UrlTree> | Promise<boolean |
    UrlTree> | boolean | UrlTree {
    return true;
  }

}
```

The guard that we created implements the `canActivate` method of the `CanActivate interface`, which accepts two parameters: an `ActivatedRouteSnapshot` object that denotes the route that will be activated and `RouterStateSnapshot`, which contains the state of the router upon successful navigation. The `canActivate` method can return a `boolean` value, either synchronously or asynchronously. In the latter case, the router will wait for the observable or the promise to resolve before continuing. If the asynchronous event does not complete, the navigation will not continue. The `canActivate` method can also return a `UrlTree` object, which will cause new navigation to a defined route.

Currently, our guard returns `true` immediately, allowing free access to a route. Let's create an `isAuthenticated` property so that we can alter the behavior of our guard more easily:

> **Important Note**
>
> In a real-world application, we would delegate the decision of whether a user is authenticated or not to a separate Angular service. The service would probably check the local storage of the browser or any other means to indicate whether the user has already authenticated or not.

```
export class AuthGuard implements CanActivate {
  private isAuthenticated = true;

  constructor(private router: Router) {}

  canActivate(
    next: ActivatedRouteSnapshot,
    state: RouterStateSnapshot): Observable<boolean | UrlTree>
    | Promise<boolean | UrlTree> | boolean | UrlTree {
```

```
        return this.checkLogin();
    }

    private checkLogin(): boolean {
        if (this.isAuthenticated) { return true };

        this.router.navigate(['/']);
        return false;
    }

}
```

We created a separate `checkLogin` method that handles the logic of whether to allow access to the route or not. The `canActivate` method calls the `checkLogin` method and returns its value. It checks the value of the `isAuthenticated` property, and if it is `true`, the application can navigate to the specified route. Otherwise, it uses the `Router` service to navigate to the root path of the Angular app and returns `false` so that the previous navigation can be canceled.

> **Important Note**
>
> When we perform redirection to another route inside a guard, we need to return a `false` value from the `canActivate` method so that the navigation that is currently in progress can be canceled.

A route configuration object contains the `canActivate` property, which we can use to apply a `CanActivate` guard to a specific route:

```
const routes: Routes = [
    { path: 'heroes', component: HeroListComponent },
    { path: 'hero/:id', component: HeroDetailComponent,
    canActivate: [AuthGuard] },
    { path: '', redirectTo: '/heroes', pathMatch: 'full' }
];
```

Only authenticated users can now access the hero route. Run the application and inspect the outcome using different values for the `isAuthenticated` property of `AuthGuard`.

Preventing navigation away from a route

Similarly, to prevent access to a route, we can also prevent navigating away from a route using the `CanDeactivate<T>` interface. `T` indicates the component `class` from which we want to navigate away. We need to implement the `canDeactivate` method in a guard to start using it:

1. Use the Angular CLI to create a new guard named `confirm`.
2. Select only the **CanDeactivate** option to implement when asked by the Angular CLI.
3. Open the `confirm.guard.ts` file and set the type of the `CanDeactivate interface` to `HeroDetailComponent` because we want to check whether the user navigates away from this component only. In a real-world scenario, you may need to create a more generic guard to support additional components:

```
export class ConfirmGuard implements CanActivate,
CanDeactivate<HeroDetailComponent> {
}
```

4. Also, set the type of the `component` parameter of the `canDeactivate` method to `HeroDetailComponent`.
5. Create a `showConfirm` method that uses the `confirm` method of the global `window` object to display a confirmation dialog before navigating away from `HeroDetailComponent`. Make sure that the method returns an observable with a `boolean` value:

```
private showConfirm(): Observable<boolean> {
  const confirmation = window.confirm('Are you sure?');
  return of(confirmation);
}
```

6. The `canDeactivate` method can return a `boolean` or `UrlTree` value synchronously or asynchronously, similar to the `canActivate` method. Call the `showConfirm` method in the `canDeactivate` method:

```
canDeactivate(
  component: HeroDetailComponent,
  currentRoute: ActivatedRouteSnapshot,
  currentState: RouterStateSnapshot,
```

```
    nextState?: RouterStateSnapshot): Observable<boolean |
    UrlTree> | Promise<boolean | UrlTree> | boolean |
    UrlTree
  {
    return this.showConfirm();
  }
```

7. A route configuration object contains a `canDeactivate` property similar to `canActivate`. Open the `heroes-routing.module.ts` file and set it accordingly to use `ConfirmGuard`:

```
  {
    path: 'hero/:id',
    component: HeroDetailComponent,
    canActivate: [AuthGuard],
    canDeactivate: [ConfirmGuard]
  }
```

Run the application using `ng serve` and select a hero from the list. Click on the **Heroes** link or press the browser's back button and a confirmation dialog should be displayed:

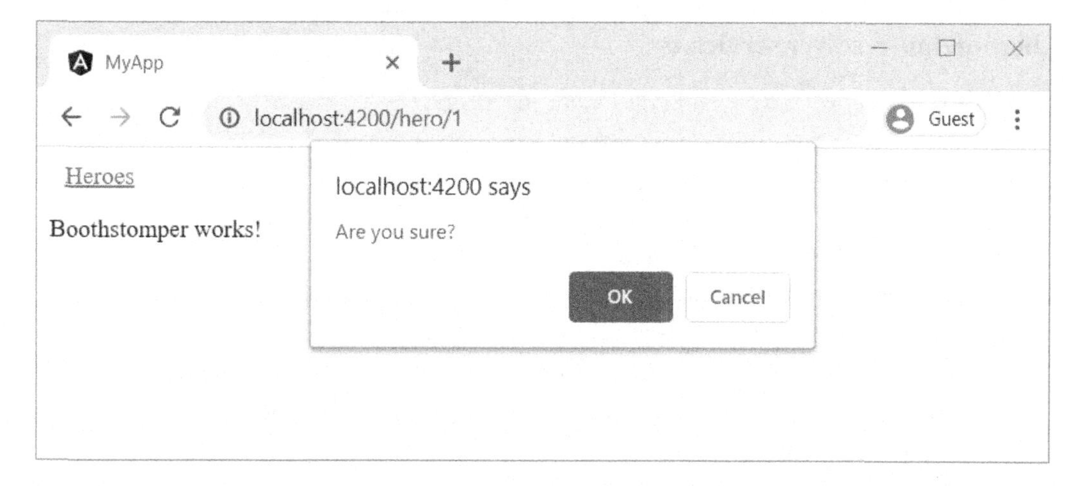

Figure 7.11 – Navigating away from a route

If you select **Cancel**, the navigation is canceled, and the application remains in the current state. If you select **OK**, you will be redirected to the root path of the application.

Preloading route data

You may have noticed that when you select a hero from the list and navigate to `HeroDetailComponent`, there is a delay in displaying the hero details. This is reasonable since we are making an HTTP request to the backend API. However, there is flickering in the user interface, which is bad for the user experience. Thankfully, the Angular router can help us to fix that. We can use a **resolver** to pre-fetch the details of a hero so that they are available when activating the route and displaying the component.

> **Important Note**
>
> A resolver can be handy when we want to handle possible errors before activating a route. It would be more appropriate not to navigate to `HeroDetailComponent` if the id that we pass as a route parameter does not exist in the backend.

A resolver is an Angular service that implements the `Resolve<T> interface`, where `T` is the type of data that is resolved. The service needs to implement the `resolve` method of that `interface` explicitly. It returns resolved data either synchronously or asynchronously. In our case, since we are communicating with a backend API using the HTTP client, it returns an observable of a `Hero` object:

hero-detail-resolver.service.ts

```
import { Injectable } from '@angular/core';
import { Resolve, ActivatedRouteSnapshot, RouterStateSnapshot
} from '@angular/router';
import { Hero } from './hero.model';
import { HeroService } from './hero.service';
import { take, mergeMap } from 'rxjs/operators';
import { of, Observable } from 'rxjs';

@Injectable({
  providedIn: 'root'
})
export class HeroDetailResolverService implements
Resolve<Hero> {

  constructor(private heroService: HeroService) { }

```

```
  resolve(route: ActivatedRouteSnapshot, state:
  RouterStateSnapshot): Observable<Hero> {
    const id = +route.paramMap.get('id');

    return this.heroService.getHero(id).pipe(
      take(1),
      mergeMap(hero => of(hero))
    );
  }
}
```

There are various steps involved in the previous `resolve` method:

1. First, we get the value of the `id` route parameter and convert it into a `number` using the plus sign.
2. We then call the `getHero` method of `HeroService`, and we pass the `id` as a parameter.
3. We use the `pipe` operator to process the returned observable with two other RxJS operators.
4. The `take` operator ensures that the observable completes after emitting the first value.
5. The `mergeMap` operator is used to flatten the observable returned from the `getHero` method.

A route configuration object contains a `resolve` property that we can use to register the resolver we have just created:

```
{
  path: 'hero/:id',
  component: HeroDetailComponent,
  canActivate: [AuthGuard],
  canDeactivate: [ConfirmGuard],
  resolve: {
    hero: HeroDetailResolverService
  }
}
```

The `resolve` property is an object that contains a unique name as a key and the TypeScript class of the resolver as a value. The name of the key is important because we will use that in our components to access the resolved data:

```
ngOnInit(): void {
  this.hero = this.route.snapshot.data.hero;
}
```

Data from a resolver is available in the `data` property of the `snapshot` object. Alternatively, you can subscribe to it directly from the `ActivatedRoute` service:

```
ngOnInit(): void {
  this.route.data.subscribe((data: { hero: Hero }) => {
    this.hero = data.hero;
  });
}
```

Notice that in either case, resolved data is accessed from the `hero` property of the `data` object. It is the name of the key that we defined in the `resolve` property of the route configuration object.

If you run the application now, you will notice that there is no flickering when navigating to `HeroDetailComponent`, and details of the hero are displayed at once. However, you may notice a slight delay upon selecting the hero from the list. This is the delay introduced by the HTTP request to the backend API that originates from the resolver.

Lazy loading routes

At some point, our application may grow in size, and the amount of data we put into it may also grow. The result of this is that the application may take a long time to start initially, or certain parts can take a long time to start. To overcome these problems, we can use a technique called **lazy loading**.

Lazy loading means that we don't load all parts of our app initially. When we refer to parts, we mean Angular modules. Application modules can be separated into chunks that are only loaded when needed. There are many advantages of lazy loading a module in an Angular app:

- Feature modules can be loaded upon request from the user.
- Users that visit certain areas of your application can significantly benefit from this technique.

- We can add more features in a lazy-loaded module without affecting the overall application bundle size.

To fully unveil the potential of lazy loading, let's add a new component in our Angular app:

1. Create a new module named `about` with routing enabled.
2. Create a component named `about-info` in the newly created module.
3. Open the `about-routing.module.ts` file and add a new route configuration object in the `routes` variable to activate `AboutInfoComponent`. Set the `path` property to an empty string so that `AboutInfoComponent` is activated by default:

```
const routes: Routes = [
  { path: '', component: AboutInfoComponent }
];
```

4. Add a new anchor element to the `app.component.html` file that links to the newly created route:

```
<nav>
  <a routerLink="/heroes" routerLinkActive=
  "active">Heroes</a>
  <a routerLink="/about" routerLinkActive="active">About</
  a>
</nav>
<router-outlet></router-outlet>
```

5. Add a new route configuration object to the `routes` variable of `AppRoutingModule`. Set the `path` property to `about` and use the `loadChildren` property to point to `AboutModule` lazily:

```
const routes: Routes = [
  { path: 'about', loadChildren: () => import('./about/
  about.module').then(m => m.AboutModule)},
  { path: '**', component: PageNotFoundComponent }
];
```

The `loadChildren` property returns an arrow `function` that uses the ES6 dynamic `import` statement to lazy load `AboutModule`. The `import function` accepts the relative path of the module that we want to import and returns a promise object that contains the TypeScript `class` of the Angular module that we want to load.

> **Important Note**
>
> We did not add `AboutModule` to the `imports` array of `AppModule`. If we had done so, `AboutModule` would have been loaded twice: once eagerly from `AppModule` and another time lazily from the **About** link.

Run the application using `ng serve` and open the browser's developer tools. Click the **About** link, and inspect the requests in the **Network** tab:

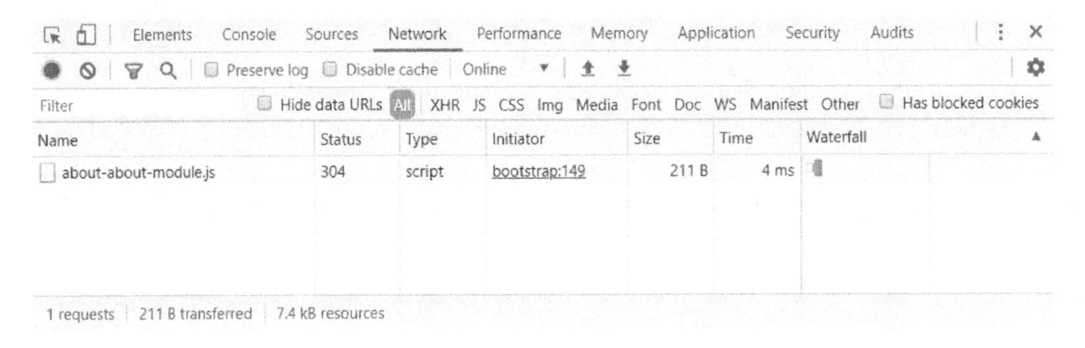

Figure 7.12 – Lazy-loaded route request

The application initiates a new request to the `about-about-module.js` file, which is the bundle of `AboutModule`. The Angular framework creates a new bundle for each module that is lazy-loaded and does not include it in the main application bundle.

If you navigate away and click on the **About** link again, you will notice that the application does not make a new request to load `AboutModule`. As soon as a lazy-loaded module is requested, it is kept in memory and can be used for subsequent requests.

A word of caution, however. As we learned in *Chapter 5, Structure an Angular App*, an Angular service is registered with the root injector of the application using the `providedIn` property of the `@Injectable` decorator. Lazy-loaded modules create a separate injector that is an immediate child of the root application injector. If you use an Angular service registered with the root application injector in a lazy-loaded module, you will end up with a separate instance of the service in both cases. So, we must be cautious as to how we use services in lazy-loaded modules.

Lazy-loaded modules are standard Angular modules, so we can control access to them using guards.

Protecting a lazy-loaded module

We can control unauthorized access to a lazy-loaded module similar to how we can do so in eagerly loaded ones. However, we need to implement a different `interface` for this case, the `CanLoad interface`.

Let's extend `AuthGuard` so that it can also be used for lazy-loaded modules. We need to implement the `canLoad` method from the `CanLoad interface`:

```
canLoad(
  route: Route,
  segments: UrlSegment[]): Observable<boolean> |
  Promise<boolean> | boolean {
  return this.checkLogin();
}
```

As with all previous guards, we must register `AuthGuard` with the lazy-loaded route using the `canLoad` property of the route configuration object:

```
{
  path: 'about',
  loadChildren: () => import('./about/about.module').
  then(m => m.AboutModule),
  canLoad: [AuthGuard]
}
```

If we run the application and change the `isAuthenticated` property of `AuthGuard` to `false`, we will notice that even if we click on the **About** link, our application does not navigate to the route.

Sometimes, we need to preload a lazy-loaded module because we know that it will possibly be accessed by our users at some point. We can achieve this functionality by using a preloading strategy in our modules.

Preloading lazy-loaded modules

A preloading strategy can be applied to lazy-loaded modules only and can be configured using the `forRoot` method of `RouterModule`. We can choose either to preload all the modules or specify a custom strategy as to which module is loaded when. To enable preloading for all the modules, we use the `PreloadAllModules` strategy:

```
@NgModule({
  imports: [RouterModule.forRoot(routes, {preloadingStrategy:
  PreloadAllModules})],
  exports: [RouterModule]
})
```

That might be good enough for a desktop connection; however, if you are on a mobile connection, this might be way too heavy. At this point, we want better, more fine-grained control. What we can do is implement our custom preloading strategy:

1. Create an Angular service that implements the `PreloadingStrategy interface` and particularly its `preload` method.
2. The `preload` method accepts two parameters: a `Route` object, which represents the lazy-loaded route, and a `load` method that is called if the route should be preloaded. Otherwise, it should return an empty observable. We use the `EMPTY` RxJS operator to denote that an observable does not emit any value.
3. Define whether a route should be preloaded by using the `data` property of the `Route` object. The `data` property of a route configuration object can be used for storing arbitrary data associated with the route, such as a page title, breadcrumbs, or other static data.

The Angular service that we created should look like the following:

custom-preloading.service.ts

```
import { Injectable } from '@angular/core';
import { PreloadingStrategy, Route } from '@angular/router';
import { Observable, EMPTY } from 'rxjs';

@Injectable({
  providedIn: 'root'
})
```

```
export class CustomPreloadingService implements
PreloadingStrategy {

  constructor() { }

  preload(route: Route, load: () => Observable<any>):
  Observable<any> {
    if (route.data && route.data['preload']) {
      return load();
    } else {
      return EMPTY;
    }
  }
}
```

We now need to define the newly created preloading strategy in `RouterModule` and set the `data` property of the `about` route:

```
const routes: Routes = [
  {
    path: 'about',
    loadChildren: () => import('./about/about.module').
    then(m => m.AboutModule),
    canLoad: [AuthGuard],
    data: { preload: true }
  },
  { path: '**', component: PageNotFoundComponent }
];

@NgModule({
  imports: [RouterModule.forRoot(routes, {preloadingStrategy:
  CustomPreloadingService})],
  exports: [RouterModule],
})
```

Run the application using `ng serve`, and you should see that the bundle of the `about` route is loaded by default at application bootstrap. However, this is not happening. Why? A preloading strategy preloads every lazy-loaded route, except for the ones guarded by the `canLoad` guard. This makes sense since `canLoad` only loads if we are authenticated or authorized, or based on some other condition that we set up. Try to remove the `canLoad` property from the route, and you will successfully see the `about` route preload correctly.

Debugging route configuration

Why do we want to debug the router? Well, sometimes routing in an Angular app doesn't behave as it should; when that is the case, it is good to know more about how the routing acts and why. To enable debugging, we need to pass a configuration object as the second parameter in the `forRoot` method of `RouterModule`. It contains the `enableTracing` property, which, when set to `true`, logs router events in the console window of the browser:

```
@NgModule({
  imports: [RouterModule.forRoot(routes,
  {enableTracing: true})],
  exports: [RouterModule]
})
```

Another great alternative is to listen for a specific router event and log it. The Angular router emits specific events during each navigation. Navigation events can be accessed by subscribing to the `events` observable of the `Router` service and inspecting the type of the event, as follows:

```
this.router.events.
pipe(filter(event => event instanceof NavigationEnd)).
subscribe();
```

The previous snippet listens only for events of the `NavigationEnd` type. You can find the whole list of supported navigation event types at `https://angular.io/guide/router#router-events`.

Summary

We have now uncovered the power of the Angular router, and we hope you have enjoyed this journey into the intricacies of this library. One of the things that shines in the Angular router is the vast number of options and scenarios we can cover with such a simple but powerful implementation.

We have learned the basics of setting up routing and handling different types of parameters. We have also learned about more advanced features, such as child routing. Furthermore, we have learned how to protect our routes from unauthorized access. Finally, we have shown the full power of asynchronous routing and how you can improve response time with lazy loading and preloading.

In the next chapter, we will beef up our `HeroDetailComponent` to showcase the mechanisms underlying web forms in Angular and the best strategies to grab user input with form controls.

8
Orchestrating Validation Experiences in Forms

Web applications use forms when it comes to collecting data from the user. Use cases vary from allowing a user to log in, filling in payment information, booking a flight, or even performing a search. Form data can later be persisted on local storage or be sent to a server using a backend API. A form usually has the following characteristics that enhance the user experience of a web app:

- Can define different kinds of input fields
- Can set up different kinds of validations and display validation errors to the user
- Can support different strategies for handling data in case the form is in an error state

The Angular framework provides two approaches to handle forms: **template-driven** and **reactive**. Neither approach is considered better than the other; you just have to go with the one that suits your scenario the best. The main difference between the two approaches is how they manage data:

- Template-driven forms are easy to set up and add to an Angular application, but they do not scale well. They operate solely on the template to create elements and configure validation rules, and thus they are not easy to test. They also depend on the change detection mechanism of the framework. Choose this approach if your Angular app contains forms with a few input controls and simple logic.
- Reactive forms are more robust when it comes to scaling and testing, and when they are not interacting with the change detection cycle. They operate in the component `class` to manage input controls and set up validation rules. If you use reactive programming techniques extensively or your Angular app is comprised of many forms, then this technique is for you.

In this chapter, we will focus mainly on reactive forms due to their wide popularity in the Angular community. More specifically, we will cover the following topics:

- Learning how to apply two-way binding with template-driven forms
- Discovering how to design forms using the reactive-oriented approach
- Learning how to bind data with input controls in reactive forms
- Diving into different approaches to input validation
- Building our custom validators
- Learning how to get form data and react when it changes

Let's get started!

Technical requirements

The following is the GitHub link for the code and examples in this chapter: `https://github.com/PacktPublishing/Learning-Angular--Third-Edition/tree/master/ch08`.

Introducing forms to web apps

A form in a web application consists of a `form` HTML element that contains some `input` elements for entering data, and a `button` element for handling that data. The form can retrieve data and either save it locally or send it to a server for further manipulation. The following is a simple form that is used to log a user into a web application:

```
<form>
  <div>>>
    <input type="text" name="username" placeholder="Username">
  </div>
  <div>
    <input type="password" name="password"
    placeholder="Password">
  </div>
  <button type="submit">Login</button>
</form>
```

This form has two `input` elements: one for entering the username and another one for entering the password. The `type` of the password field is set to `password` so that the content of the input control is not visible while typing. The `type` of the `button` element is set to `submit` so that the form can collect data either by clicking on the button or pressing *Enter* on any input control. Optionally, we could have added another `button` element with a `reset` type to clear form data. Notice that an HTML element must reside inside a `form` element so that it can be part of it. The following screenshot shows what the form looks like when rendered on a page:

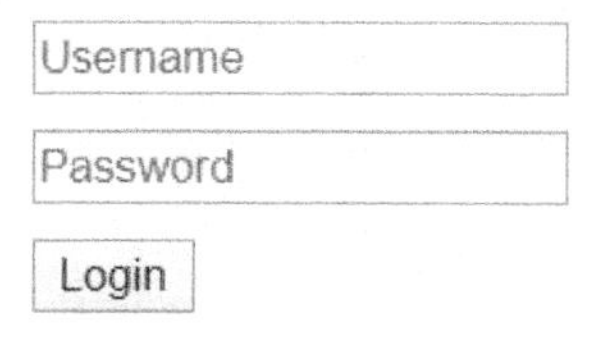

Figure 8.1 – Login form

Web applications can significantly enhance the user experience by using forms that provide features such as autocomplete in input controls or prompting to save sensitive data. Now that we have grasped a basic understanding of what a web form looks like, let's learn how all that fits into the Angular framework.

Data binding with template-driven forms

Template-driven forms are one of two different ways of integrating forms with Angular. It is an approach that is not widely embraced by the Angular community for the reasons described previously. Nevertheless, it can be powerful in cases where we want to create small and simple forms for our Angular app. Template-driven forms can stand out when used with the `ngModel` directive to provide two-way data binding in our components.

We learned about data binding in *Chapter 3, Component Interaction and Inter-Communication*, and how we can use different types to read data from an HTML element or component and write data to it. In this case, binding is either one way or another, which is called **one-way binding**. We can combine both ways and create a **two-way binding** that can read and write data simultaneously. Template-driven forms provide the `ngModel` directive, which we can use in our components to get this behavior. We can add template-driven forms to an Angular 10 app by importing `FormsModule` from the `@angular/forms` npm package. It is `FormsModule` that exports the `ngModel` directive that we want to use:

1. Add `FormsModule` to the `imports` property of `AppModule`:

```
import { BrowserModule } from '@angular/platform-
browser';
import { NgModule } from '@angular/core';
import { FormsModule } from '@angular/forms';

import { AppComponent } from './app.component';
import { LoginComponent } from './login/login.component';

@NgModule({
  declarations: [
    AppComponent,
    LoginComponent
  ],
  imports: [
    BrowserModule,
    FormsModule
  ],
  providers: [],
  bootstrap: [AppComponent]
})
export class AppModule { }
```

2. Create an Angular component named `login` and enter the HTML of the form from the previous section in its template.
3. Open the `login.component.ts` file and add two properties for each input control:

```
export class LoginComponent {
  username: string;
  password: string;
}
```

4. Open the `login.component.html` file and add the `ngModel` directive to each input control. Set the value of the directive to the respective component property that we created earlier:

```
<div>
  <input type="text" name="username"
  placeholder="Username" [(ngModel)]="username">
</div>
<div>
  <input type="password" name="password"
  placeholder="Password" [(ngModel)]="password">
</div>
```

> **Important Note**
>
> The syntax of the `ngModel` directive is known as *a banana in a box*, which is a memory rule for you to be able to remember how to type it. We create it in two steps. First, we create the banana by surrounding `ngModel` in parenthesis `()`. Then, we put the banana in a box by surrounding it in square brackets `[()]`. Remember, it's called banana in a box, not box in a banana.

5. To better understand how two-way binding works, add another `div` element to the template that uses interpolation to display the value of the `username` property:

```
<div>You are trying to login as
<b>{{username}}</b></div>
```

6. Remove the contents of the `app.component.html` file and add the `selector` of the login component to it.

7. Run the application using `ng serve` and start typing inside the **Username** input control. You will notice that the interpolated text updates accordingly as you type. Now, you should understand the magic behind two-way binding and `ngModel`.

8. To simulate a login process, create a `login` method in the component `class` that logs the username and the password in the console window of the browser:

```
login() {
  console.log('User: ' + this.username);
  console.log('Password: ' + this.password);
}
```

9. Finally, connect the `login` method to the form by adding an event binding to the `ngSubmit` event of the `form` element. The `ngSubmit` event is triggered when a form is submitted by any means:

```
<form (ngSubmit)="login()">
  <div>
    <input type="text" name="username"
    placeholder="Username" [(ngModel)]="username">
  </div>
  <div>
    <input type="password" name="password"
    placeholder="Password" [(ngModel)]="password">
  </div>
  <button type="submit">Login</button>
  <div>You are trying to login as <b>{{username}}</b></
  div>
</form>
```

Now, try to enter some data in the **Username** and **Password** fields and either click the **Login** button or press *Enter* in the **Password** field. You should see the login details that you entered in the console window of the browser.

> **Important Note**
>
> The syntax of a banana in a box that we use for the `ngModel` directive is not random at all. Under the hood, `ngModel` is a directive that contains a `@Input` binding named `ngModel` and a `@Output` binding named `ngModelChange`. It implements a particular `interface` called `ControlValueAccessor` that is used to create custom controls for forms. By convention, when a directive or a component contains both bindings that start with the same name, but the output binding ends in `Change`, the property can be used as a two-way binding. You can read more about `ControlValueAccessor` at `https://angular.io/guide/built-in-directives#ngmodel-and-value-accessors`.

We have already seen how template-driven forms can come in handy when creating small and simple forms. In the next section, we dive deeper into the alternate approach offered by the Angular framework: reactive forms.

Using reactive patterns in Angular forms

Reactive forms, as the name implies, provide access to web forms in a reactive manner. They are built with reactivity in mind, where input controls and their values can be manipulated using observable streams. They also maintain an immutable state of form data, making them easier to test because we can be sure that the state of the form can be modified explicitly and consistently.

Reactive forms have a programmatic approach to how we create form elements and set up validation rules. We set everything up in the component `class` and merely point out our created artifacts in the template.

The key classes involved in this approach are as follows:

- `FormControl`: Represents an individual form control, such as an `input` element.
- `FormGroup`: Represents a collection of form controls. The `form` element is the topmost `FormGroup` in the hierarchy of a reactive form.
- `FormArray`: Represents a collection of forms controls, just like `FormGroup`, but can be modified at runtime. For example, we can add or remove `FormControl` objects dynamically as needed.

All these classes are available from the `@angular/forms` npm package. The `FormControl` and `FormGroup` classes inherit from `AbstractControl`, which contains a lot of interesting properties. We can use these properties to render the UI differently based on what status a particular control or group has. For example, we might want to differ UI-wise between a form that we have never interacted with and one that we have. It could also be of interest to know whether we have interacted with a particular control at all. As you can imagine, there are many scenarios where it is interesting to know a specific status. We are going to explore all these properties by using the `FormControl` and `FormGroup` classes.

In the next section, we'll take the template-driven form that we created earlier and recreate it as a reactive one.

Turning a template-driven form into a reactive one

The Angular framework provides `ReactiveFormsModule`, which we can import to start creating reactive forms:

1. Import `ReactiveFormsModule` from the `@angular/forms` npm package and add it to the `imports` property of `AppModule`:

```
import { BrowserModule } from '@angular/platform-
browser';
import { NgModule } from '@angular/core';
import { FormsModule, ReactiveFormsModule } from '@
angular/forms';

import { AppComponent } from './app.component';
import { LoginComponent } from './login/login.component';

@NgModule({
  declarations: [
    AppComponent,
    LoginComponent
  ],
  imports: [
    BrowserModule,
    FormsModule,
    ReactiveFormsModule
  ],
```

```
  providers: [],
  bootstrap: [AppComponent]
})
export class AppModule { }
```

Important Note

`AppModule` imports both `FormsModule` and `ReactiveFormsModule` in the previous example. There is no harm in doing this. You can use them simultaneously in an Angular app, and everything is going to work fine.

2. Create an Angular component named `reactive-login` that will have the same input controls and behavior as the login component that we created previously.
3. Open the `reactive-login.component.ts` file and define a `loginForm` property. Set its value to a new `FormGroup` instance, passing an empty object as a parameter to its `constructor`. The provided parameter will serve as the container used to define input controls later on:

```
loginForm = new FormGroup({});
```

The `constructor` of the `FormGroup class` accepts an object that contains key-value pairs of `FormControl` instances. The key denotes a unique name for the form control that `FormGroup` can use to keep track of it, while the value is an instance of `FormControl`. Create two `FormControl` instances for our case – one for the username and another for the password:

```
loginForm = new FormGroup({
  username: new FormControl(''),
  password: new FormControl('')
});
```

The `constructor` of the `FormControl class` accepts the default value of the input control as a parameter. Since we are building a login form, we're passing an empty string to both controls so that we do not set any value initially.

4. After we have created the form group and its controls, we need to associate them with the respective HTML elements in the template. Copy the contents of the `login.component.html` file into the template of `ReactiveLoginComponent`.

5. `ReactiveFormsModule` exports the `formGroup` directive, which we can use to connect a `FormGroup` instance to a `form` element. Add a property binding between the `formGroup` directive and the `loginForm` property of the component:

```
<form [formGroup]="loginForm"
(ngSubmit)="login()">
```

6. `ReactiveFormsModule` also exports the `formControlName` directive, which we can use to connect a `FormControl` instance to an `input` element. Replace the `ngModel` two-way data binding with the `formControlName` attribute. The value of the `formControlName` directive is set to the name of the `FormControl` instance.

So far, we have managed to recreate the template-driven login form using reactive techniques! Remove the `ngSubmit` event binding and comment out the `div` element that displays the `username` property using interpolation. If you run the application using `ng serve`, you will be able to preview the login form. Currently, it does not contain any logic about reactive forms. Let's change that:

1. Copy the `login` method from `LoginComponent` into the `reactive-login.component.ts` file and modify it accordingly:

```
login() {
  const controls = this.loginForm.controls;
  console.log('User:' + controls.username.value);
  console.log('Password:' + controls.password.value);
}
```

Previously, in the template-driven form, we had access to the `username` and `password` properties of the data model directly. In reactive forms, this is not the case since the form model is the source of truth. So, we need to get input control values from the `FormGroup` or `FormControl` classes. The `FormGroup class` exposes the `controls` property, which we can use to get a specific `FormControl` instance. The `FormControl class` contains various properties, such as the value of the input control associated with it.

> **Important Note**
>
> The `FormGroup class` also contains a `value` property, which we can use to access form control values as a single object. We usually use this property when posting whole entities in a backend API.

2. Now that we know how to get the value of a form control, we can uncomment the `div` element, which displays the value of the `username` property. Modify it accordingly so that it gets the value of the `username` form control from the `loginForm` property. Do not forget to restore the `ngSubmit` event binding on the form element:

```
<div>You are trying to login as
<b>{{loginForm.controls.username.value}}</b></div>
```

3. In real-world applications, forms are not as small and short as the login form that we have already seen. They have many form controls and, in some cases, nested form group hierarchies. They may also need to access a specific form control more than once in the template and the component `class` for checking its status or value. Accessing it directly from the form group can quickly clutter our forms and may become unreadable. Good practice, in this case, is to use a getter method for each such control:

```
get username(): AbstractControl {
  return this.loginForm.controls.username;
}

get password(): AbstractControl {
  return this.loginForm.controls.password;
}
```

4. We can then replace all occurrences of `loginForm.controls.username` and `loginForm.controls.password` in our code with the `username` and `password` getter properties.

If we run the application, we will see that it behaves the same as the template-driven form. Try to click the **Login** button without entering any values in the **Username** or **Password** fields and see what happens in the console window of the browser – here, the application prints out empty values for both form controls. However, this is a situation that we should avoid in a real-world scenario. We should be aware of the status of a form control and take action accordingly.

In the next section, we'll investigate different properties that we can check to get the status of a form control and provide feedback to the user according to that status.

Providing status feedback

The Angular framework sets the following classes automatically in a form control according to its current status:

- `ng-untouched`: Indicates that we have not interacted with the control yet
- `ng-touched`: Indicates that we have interacted with the control
- `ng-dirty`: Indicates that the control has a value
- `ng-pristine`: Indicates that the control does not have a value yet
- `ng-valid`: Indicates that the value of the control is valid
- `ng-invalid`: Indicates that the value of the control is not valid

Each class name has a similar property in the form model. The name of the property is the same as the class name, without the `ng-` prefix. We could try to leverage both and provide a unique experience with our forms.

Suppose that we would like to display a highlighted border in an input control when we interact with that control for the first time. We should define a global CSS style, such as the following:

```
.ng-touched:not(form) {
  border: 3px solid lightblue;
}
```

It is worth noting that the previous CSS rule excludes `form` elements. The same CSS classes that apply to a form control can also be applied to a form group. In our case, we do not want to display the highlighted border in the whole `form` element; we only want to display it in the individual `input` elements.

We can also combine some of the CSS classes according to the needs of our application. Suppose we would like to display a `green` border when an input control has a value and a `red` one when it does not have any at all. The `red` border should be visible only if we have entered a value in the input control initially and deleted it immediately afterward. We should create the following CSS rules:

```
.ng-dirty.ng-valid:not(form) {
  border: 2px solid green;
}

```

```
.ng-dirty.ng-invalid:not(form) {
  border: 2px solid red;
}
```

For the `ng-valid` and `ng-invalid` classes to work, we need to add a validation rule to our `input` elements. There are many built-in validators that we can use, as we will learn later in this chapter, but in this case, we will use the `required` one, which indicates that an input control must have a value to be valid. To apply it, add the `required` attribute to both `input` elements:

```
<div>
  <input type="text" name="username" placeholder="Username"
  formControlName="username" required>
</div>
<div>
  <input type="password" name="password" placeholder="Password"
  formControlName="password" required>
</div>
```

Later, in the *Validating controls in a reactive way* section, we will learn how to apply a validator to a `FormControl` instance directly.

Run the application using `ng serve` and follow these steps to check the applied CSS rules:

1. Click on the **Username** field and then on the **Password** field. The **Username** field should now display a light blue border.
2. Enter some text into the **Password** field and notice that it has a green border.
3. Remove the text from the **Password** field and notice that the border turns red.

We can now understand what happens when the status of an input control changes and notify users visually about that change. In the next section, we'll learn that the status of a form can be spawned across many form controls and groups at different levels.

Creating nesting form hierarchies

We have already seen how to create a login form with two input controls. A login form is a simple form that needs one `FormGroup class` and two `FormControl` classes. There are use cases in enterprise applications that require that we build more advanced forms that involve creating nested hierarchies of form groups. Consider the following form, which you can use to enter hero details:

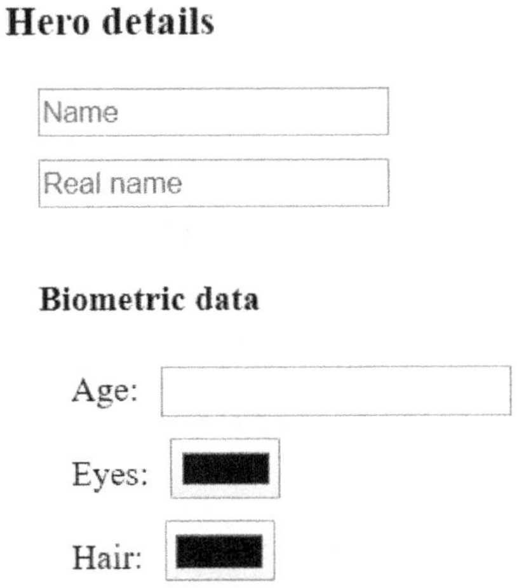

Hero details

Name

Real name

Biometric data

Age:

Eyes:

Hair:

Figure 8.2 – Add hero form

This may look like a single form, but if we take a better look at the component `class`, we will see that it consists of two `FormGroup` instances, one nested inside the other:

```
heroDetails = new FormGroup({
  name: new FormControl(''),
  realName: new FormControl(''),
  biometricData: new FormGroup({
    age: new FormControl(''),
    eyes: new FormControl(''),
    hair: new FormControl('')
  })
})
```

The heroDetails property is the parent form group, while biometricData is its child. A parent form group can have as many children form groups as it wants. If we take a look at the template of the component, we will see that the child form group is defined differently from the parent one:

```
<form formGroupName="biometricData">
  <div>
    <label>Age:</label>
    <input type="number" formControlName="age">
  </div>
  <div>
    <label>Eyes:</label>
    <input type="color" formControlName="eyes">
  </div>
  <div>
    <label>Hair:</label>
    <input type="color" formControlName="hair">
  </div>
</form>
```

We use the formGroupName directive to bind the inner form element to the biometricData property.

> **Important Note**
>
> You may have expected to bind it directly to the heroDetails.biometricData property, but this is not going to work. The Angular framework is pretty smart in that it understands that biometricData is a child form group of heroDetails. It can deduce this information because the form element that is related to biometricData is inside the form element that binds to the heroDetails property.

The status of a child form is shared with its parent in a nested form hierarchy. In our case, when the `biometricData` form becomes invalid, its parent form, `heroDetails`, will also be invalid. The change of status is not the only thing that bubbles up to the parent form. The value of the child form also propagates up the hierarchy, thereby maintaining a consistent form model:

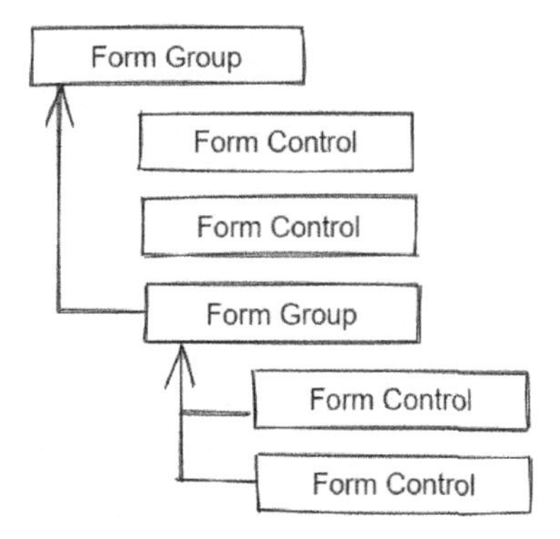

Figure 8.3 – Status and value propagation in a nested form hierarchy

Nested hierarchies add a useful feature for Angular forms to the developer's toolchain when it comes to organizing large form structures. The status, along with the value of each form, propagates through the hierarchy to provide stability to our models.

We have already seen how to define validation rules in a template by triggering a change of status using CSS styling. In the next section, we will learn how to define them in the component `class` and give visual feedback using appropriate messages.

Validating controls in a reactive way

We have already learned how to apply validation to the template of a form. We used the `required` attribute in the *Using reactive patterns in Angular forms* section to indicate that an input control needs to have a value. In reactive forms, the source of truth is our form model, so we need to be able to define validation rules when building the `FormGroup` instance.

To add a validation rule, we will use the second parameter of the `FormControl constructor`:

1. Open the `reactive-login.component.ts` file and add the `Validators.required` method to the `username` and `password` form controls:

```
loginForm = new FormGroup({
  username: new FormControl('', Validators.required),
```

```
    password: new FormControl('', Validators.required)
  });
```

2. The `Validators class` contains almost the same validator rules that are available for template-driven forms, such as the `required` validator. There are other validators, such as `min` and `max`, that are not yet supported by reactive forms. We can combine multiple validators by adding them to an array. For example, we can set the `password` form control to be at least six characters long using the `Validators.minLength` method:

```
password: new FormControl('', [
  Validators.required,
  Validators.minLength(6)
])
```

> **Important Note**
>
> When we add a validator using the `constructor` of `FormControl`, we can remove the respective HTML attribute from the template of the form. However, you could leave it for accessibility purposes so that screen readers can understand how the form control should be validated.

3. We can now use the status of these validation rules and react upon their change. For example, we can disable the `Login button` when the form is not valid:

```
<button type="submit" [disabled]="!loginForm.
valid">Login</button>
```

4. We can also display specific messages to the user upon changing the validity of each control:

```
<div>
  <input type="text" name="username"
  placeholder="Username" formControlName="username"
  required>
  <span class="help-block" *ngIf="username.
  touched && username.invalid">The username is not
  valid</span>
</div>
<div>
```

```
<input type="password" name="password"
placeholder="Password" formControlName="password"
required>
<span class="help-block" *ngIf="password.
touched && password.invalid">The password is not
valid</span>
</div>
```

Notice that we have also created a getter property for the `password` form control so that we can easily refer to it either in the template or the component `class`.

5. It would be nice, though, if we could display different messages, depending on the validation rule. For example, we could display a more specific message when the password is less than six characters long. The `FormControl class` contains the `errors` property, which we can use for this purpose. This is an object where each key is the validation property, such as `required`, and the value is the `boolean` result of the validation:

```
<input type="password" name="password"
placeholder="Password"
formControlName="password" required>
<span class="help-block" *ngIf="password.
touched && password.errors?.
required">The password is required</span>
<span class="help-block" *ngIf="password.
touched && password.errors?.
minlength">The password is too short</span>
```

> **Important Note**
>
> We use the safe navigation operator when accessing the `errors` property because when a form control does not have any errors, its value is `null`, which may break our components.

The Angular framework provides a set of built-in validators that we can use in our forms. A validator is a `function` that returns either a `ValidationErrors` object or `null` when the control does not have any errors. A validator can also return a value synchronously or asynchronously, according to the scenario. Later, in the *Building a custom validator* section, we will learn how to create a custom synchronous validator. For the time being, let's focus on form building and introduce another artifact that we can use to add form controls dynamically during runtime.

Modifying forms dynamically

So far, we have used the `FormGroup` and `FormControl` classes extensively throughout this chapter. However, we have not seen what `FormArray` is all about.

Suppose that we would like to enable the form of `HeroComponent` so that it allows us to add some powers to our hero. After all, superheroes are all about having special powers, aren't they? A hero can have more than one superpower, so let's modify the `heroDetails` form accordingly:

1. Add a `powers` property to the `heroDetails` form group and set its value to an instance of the `FormArray class`. The `constructor` of the `FormArray class` accepts a list of `FormControl` instances as a parameter. For now, the list is empty since the hero does not have any powers initially:

```
heroDetails = new FormGroup({
  name: new FormControl(''),
  realName: new FormControl(''),
  biometricData: new FormGroup({
    age: new FormControl(''),
    eyes: new FormControl(''),
    hair: new FormControl('')
  }),
  powers: new FormArray([])
});
```

2. Define a getter property that returns the `powers` form array and cast it as a `FormArray` type. Typecasting here is very important since we want to manipulate the `powers` property using standard array methods such as `push`:

```
get powers(): FormArray {
  return this.heroDetails.controls.powers as FormArray;
}
```

3. Create a method in the component that adds a new `FormControl` instance to the `powers` form array:

```
addPower() {
  this.powers.push(new FormControl(''));
}
```

4. Open the `hero.component.html` file and add a `button` element right after the `biometricData` form element. Bind the `click` event of the `button` element to the newly created `addPower` method:

```
<button (click)="addPower()">Add power</button>
```

5. The `addPower` method populates the `controls` property of the `powers` form array. We can use the `ngFor` directive to iterate over the `controls` property and create an `input` element for each one:

```
<div *ngFor="let power of powers.controls; let i=index">
  <label>
    Power:
    <input type="text" [formControlName]="i">
  </label>
</div>
```

6. We use the `index` keyword of the `ngFor` directive to give a dynamically created name to each form control.

The real power of the `FormArray class` is that it can be used not only with `FormControl` instances but also with more complicated structures and other form groups.

With `FormArray`, we have completed our knowledge range about the most basic building blocks of an Angular form. In the next section, we'll learn how to build an Angular form without using them explicitly.

Creating elegant reactive forms

So far, we have been using the `FormGroup`, `FormControl`, and `FormArray` classes to create our forms, as follows:

```
loginForm = new FormGroup({
  username: new FormControl('', Validators.required),
  password: new FormControl('', [
    Validators.required,
    Validators.minLength(6)
  ])
});
```

The previous way, however, constitutes a lot of noise, especially in forms that contain many controls. Alternatively, we can use an Angular service called `FormBuilder` to take away a lot of that noise. We can import `FormBuilder` from the `@angular/forms` npm package, inject it into the `constructor` of the component, and rewrite `loginForm` as follows:

```
constructor(private builder: FormBuilder) { }
private buildForm() {
  this.loginForm = this.builder.group({
    username: ['', Validators.required],
    password: ['', [
      Validators.required,
      Validators.minLength(6)
    ]]
  });
}
```

We use the `group` method of the `FormBuilder` service to group form controls together. `FormControl` is now an array that contains two items: the first is the default value of the control, while the second is the list of validators. The `FormBuilder` service also contains the following methods:

- `control`: Initializes a `FormControl` object
- `array`: Initializes a `FormArray` object

Using the `FormBuilder` service looks a lot easier to read, and we don't have to deal with the `FormGroup`, `FormControl`, and `FormArray` data types explicitly, although that is what is being created under the hood.

We have already seen some of the built-in validators provided by the Angular framework. However, forms are so extensible in Angular that this allows us to create custom validators tailored to our needs. In the next section, we'll learn how to create such a validator from scratch.

Building a custom validator

Sometimes, default validators won't cover all the scenarios that we might encounter in our application. Luckily, it is quite easy to write a custom validator and use it in our Angular reactive forms. In our case, we are building a validator to check whether the name of a hero already exists.

We have already learned that a validator is a `function` that needs to return a `ValidationErrors` object with the error specified or a `null` value. Let's define such a `function`:

reserved-name.directive.ts

```
import { ValidatorFn, AbstractControl } from '@angular/forms';

const heroes = [
  { id: 1, name: 'Boothstomper' },
  { id: 2, name: 'Drogfisher' },
  { id: 3, name: 'Bloodyllips' },
  { id: 4, name: 'Mr Bu Moverse' },
  { id: 5, name: 'Piranhaelli' }
];

export function reservedNameValidator():
ValidatorFn {
  return (control: AbstractControl): {[key: string]: any} |
  null => {
    const reserved = heroes.find(hero => hero.name === control.
    value);
    return reserved ? {<reservedName': true} : null;
  };
}
```

The validator is a `function` that returns another `function`, called the configured validator `function`. It accepts the form control object to which it will be applied as a parameter. If the value of the control matches the name of a hero from the `heroes` list, it returns a validation error object. Otherwise, it returns `null`.

The key of the validation error object specifies a descriptive name for the validator error. This is a name that we can later check in the `errors` object of the control to find out if it has any errors. The value of the validation error object can be any arbitrary value that we can pass in the error message.

To use our new validator, all we must do is import it into our component `class` and add it to the `name` `FormControl` instance:

```
heroDetails = new FormGroup({
  name: new FormControl('',
  reservedNameValidator()),
  realName: new FormControl(''),
  biometricData: new FormGroup({
    age: new FormControl(''),
    eyes: new FormControl(''),
    hair: new FormControl('')
  }),
  powers: new FormArray([])
});
```

We can then display an error message in the template of the component, if that specific error occurs:

```
<div>
  <input type="text" placeholder="Name"
formControlName="name">
  <span class="help-block" *ngIf="heroDetails.
  controls.name.hasError('reservedName')">Hero name is
  already taken</span>
</div>
```

Here, we use the `hasError` method of the `FormControl` `class`, passing the name of the error to check if it has occurred.

Angular forms are not only about checking statuses but also about setting values. In the next section, we'll learn how to set values in a form.

Manipulating form data

The `FormGroup` `class` contains two methods that we can use to change the values of a form programmatically:

- `setValue`: Replaces values in all the controls of the form
- `patchValue`: Updates values in specific controls of the form

The `setValue` method accepts an object as a parameter that contains key-value pairs *for all the controls* of the form. Let's add a button to our `heroDetails` form that creates a new hero in order to illustrate the usage of `setValue`:

1. Open the `hero.component.html` file and add a `button` element named `Add hero` before the button that adds powers.
2. Bind the `click` event of the `Add hero` button to a component method named `addHero`:

```
<button (click)="addHero()">Add hero</button>
```

3. Open the `hero.component.ts` file and add the `addHero` method, which uses the `setValue` method to fill in the form with details of a new hero:

```
addHero() {
  this.heroDetails.setValue({
    name: 'Maleward',
    realName: 'Agavens Jenmar',
    biometricData: {
      age: 30,
      eyes: '#006400',
      hair: '#8b4513'
    },
    powers: []
  });
}
```

   Each key of the object that's passed in the `setValue` method must match the name of each control in the form. If we omit one, Angular will throw an error.

Run the application using `ng serve` and click on the **Add hero** button. You should see the following output on the screen:

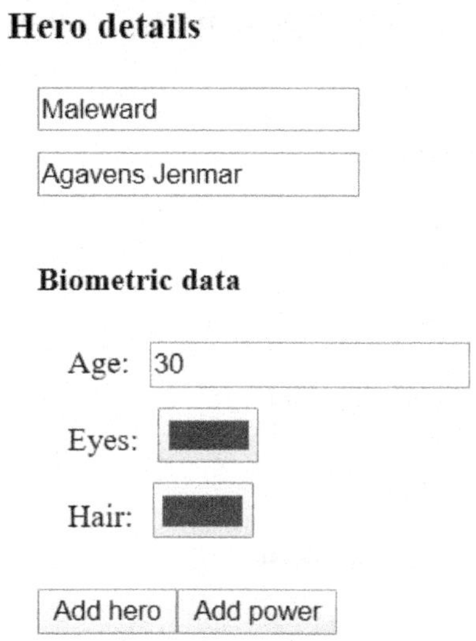

Hero details

Maleward

Agavens Jenmar

Biometric data

Age: 30

Eyes:

Hair:

Add hero | Add power

Figure 8.4 – Edit hero form

If, on the contrary, we want to fill in *some* of the details of a hero, we can use the `patchValue` method:

1. Create a new `button` element named `Add biometric` and bind its `click` event to a new method named `addBio`:

```
<button (click)="addBio()">Add biometric</button>
```

2. Create the `addBio` method, which uses the `patchValue` method to set values in some of the biometric data of the hero:

```
addBio() {
  this.heroDetails.patchValue({
    biometricData: {
      age: 35,
      hair: '#ff0000'
    },
  })
}
```

Rerun the application and click on the **Add biometric** button. You should now see the following output:

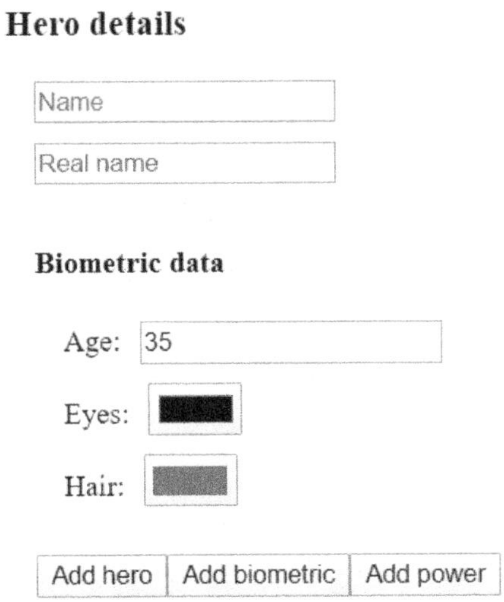

Hero details

Name

Real name

Biometric data

Age: 35

Eyes:

Hair:

Add hero | Add biometric | Add power

Figure 8.5 – Setting hero biometric data

The `setValue` and `patchValue` methods of the `FormGroup class` help us when it comes to setting data in a form. Another interesting aspect of reactive forms is that we can also be notified when these values change.

Watching state changes and being reactive

So far, we have learned how to create forms programmatically and how to specify all our fields and their validations in the code. A reactive form can listen to changes in the controls of the form when they happen and react accordingly. A suitable reaction could be to disable/enable a control, provide a visual hint, or something else according to your needs. You get the idea.

How can we make this happen? Well, a `FormControl` instance contains two observable properties: `statusChanges` and `valueChanges`. The first one notifies us when the status of the control changes, such as going from `invalid` to `valid`. On the other hand, the second one notifies us when the value of the control changes. Let's explore this one in more detail, using an example.

The `password` field in the `ReactiveLoginComponent` form contains a validator to check the minimum length of the value entered by the user. From an end user point of view, it would be better to display a hint about this validation as soon as the user has started entering values in the field:

1. First, add a `span` element to the template of the component. This will contain an appropriate hint message:

```
<div>
  <input type="password" name="password"
  placeholder="Password" formControlName="password"
  required>
  <span class="help-block" *ngIf="password.touched &&
  password.errors?.required">The password is required</
  span>
  <span class="help-block" *ngIf="password.touched &&
  password.errors?.minlength">The password is too short</
  span>
  <span *ngIf="showPasswordHint">Password should be
  minimum six characters long</span>
</div>
```

   The hint will be displayed according to the `showPasswordHint` property of the component.

2. Create the `showPasswordHint` `boolean` property in the component.

3. Subscribe to the `valueChanges` property of the `password` form control inside the `ngOnInit` method. It checks if the password that's been entered is smaller than six characters long and sets `showPasswordHint` appropriately. The `valueChanges` subscription provides values for each keystroke in the input control:

```
ngOnInit() {
  this.password.valueChanges.subscribe((value:
  string) => {
    this.showPasswordHint = value.length < 6;
  });
}
```

> **Important Note**
>
> `valueChanges` and `statusChanges` are standard observable streams. Do not forget to unsubscribe from them, as we learned in *Chapter 6, Enrich Components with Asynchronous Data Services.*

Of course, there is more that we can do with the `valueChanges` and `statusChanges` observables. For example, we could check if the username is taken by sending it to a backend server, but this code shows off the reactive nature. Hopefully, this has conveyed how you can take advantage of the reactive nature of forms and respond accordingly.

Summary

In this chapter, we have learned that Angular provides two different flavors for creating forms – template-driven and reactive forms – and that neither approach can be said to be better than the other. We have merely focused on reactive forms because of their many advantages and learned how to build them. We have also covered the different types of validations that exist, and we now know how to create our custom validations. We also learned how to fill in our forms with values and get notified when they change.

In the next chapter, we will learn how to skin our application so that it looks more beautiful with the help of Angular Material. Angular Material comes with a lot of components and styling ready for you to use in your projects. So, let's give your Angular project the love it deserves.

9 Introduction to Angular Material

When you develop a web application, you need to decide how to create your UI. It should use proper contrasting colors, have a consistent look and feel, be responsive, and work well on different devices, as well as browsers. In short, there are many things to consider when it comes to the UI and UX. It is no wonder that most developers consider the UI/UX to be a daunting task, and therefore turn to UI frameworks that do a lot of the heavy lifting. Some frameworks are used more than others, namely the following:

- **Bootstrap**
- **Foundation**
- **Pure**
- **Tailwind CSS**

There is, however, a new kid on the block—Angular Material—that is based on Google's Material Design techniques. In this chapter, we will explain what Material Design is and how Angular Material implements its principles, and we will have a look at some of its core components.

In this chapter, we will do the following:

- Learn what Material Design is and a little bit of its history.
- Delve deeper into Angular Material and its parts.
- Review some of the core components of Angular Material.
- Learn about the Angular **Component Dev Kit (CDK)**, which is the basis of Angular Material components.
- Integrate **Angular Flex Layout**, a UI layout implementation that uses Flexbox, by Angular.

Technical requirements

The code files for this chapter can be found at `https://github.com/PacktPublishing/Learning-Angular--Third-Edition/tree/master/ch09`.

Introducing Material Design

Material Design is a design language that was developed by Google in 2014. Google states that its new design language is based on paper and ink. The creators of Material Design tried to explain the goal they were trying to reach in the following way:

> *"We challenged ourselves to create a visual language for our users that synthesizes the classic principles of good design with the innovation and possibility of technology and science."*

They further explained their goals as follows:

- Develop a single underlying system that allows for a unified experience across platforms and device sizes.
- Mobile precepts are fundamental, but touch, voice, mouse, and keyboard are all first-class input methods.

The purpose of a design language is to have the user deal with how the UI and user interaction should look and feel across devices. Material Design is based on three main principles:

- **Material is the metaphor**: It is inspired by the physical world with different textures and mediums, such as paper and ink.

- **Bold, graphic, intentional**: It is guided by different methods of print design, such as typography, grids, and color, to create an immersive experience for the user.
- **Motion provides meaning**: Elements are displayed on the screen by creating animations and interactions that reorganize the environment.

All in all, it can be said that there is much theory behind the design language, and there is proper documentation on the topic should you wish to delve further. You can find more information at the official documentation site, `https://material.io/`.

Now, all of this is probably very interesting if you are a designer. But we are web developers—why should we bother looking at this at all? Well, every time Google sets out to build something, it becomes big, and while not everything stays big forever, there is sufficient muscle behind it to indicate that Material Design will be around for quite a while. Google has paved the way for it by using it extensively in their products, such as Firebase, Gmail, and Google Analytics.

But of course, a design language by itself isn't that interesting, at least not for a developer, which brings us to the following section, where we will learn about known implementations based on Material Design principles.

Known implementations

The design is there to make sense of the code and give the user a pleasant experience, both visually and from a usability standpoint. Currently, there are three major implementations of Material Design:

- **Materialize**: Almost 40K stars on GitHub tells you that this is very well used. It used to work as a standalone library, but there are also bindings to other frameworks, such as AngularJS and React. It offers navigation elements, components, and much more. You can read more at `https://materializecss.com/`.
- **AngularJS Material**: This is Google's implementation for AngularJS. It is quite capable and comes with themes, navigation elements, components, and, of course, directives. You can read more at `https://material.angularjs.org/`.
- **Angular Material**: It is maintained internally by the Angular team, and it is Google's implementation for the Angular framework. We will focus on this one throughout the rest of this chapter. You can read more at `https://material.angular.io/`.

Angular Material is made for the Angular framework alone. An advantage of using it is that the Angular team itself maintains it, so we can be sure that it is fully aligned and up to date with the latest versions of the framework. In the following section, we will learn how to install Angular Material 10 in an Angular app.

Introducing Angular Material

The Angular Material library was developed to implement Material Design for the Angular framework. It promotes itself with the following features:

- **Sprint from zero to app**: The intention is to make it very easy for you as an app developer to hit the ground running. The amount of effort in setting it up should be minimal.
- **Fast and consistent**: Performance has been a significant focus point, and it is guaranteed to work well on all major browsers.
- **Versatile**: There are a multitude of themes that should be easy to customize, and there is also great support for localization and internationalization.
- **Optimized for Angular**: The fact that the Angular team itself has built it means that the support for Angular is a big priority.

The library is split into the following parts:

- **Components**: There are a ton of UI components in place to help you be successful, such as different kinds of input, buttons, layout, navigation, modals, and different ways to show tabular data.
- **Themes**: The library comes with a set of preinstalled themes, but there is also a theming guide if you want to create your own at `https://material.angular.io/guide/theming/`.
- **Icons**: Material Design comes with over 900 icons, so you are likely to find exactly the icon you need. You can browse through the full collection at `https://material.io/resources/icons/`.

We have already covered all basic theory about Angular Material, so let's put it in to practice in the following section by integrating Angular Material 10 with an Angular 10 app.

Creating your first Angular Material app

The Angular Material 10 library is an npm package. To install it, we need to manually execute the `npm install` command and import several Angular modules into an Angular 10 app. Luckily, the Angular team has automated these interactions by creating the necessary schematics to install it using the Angular CLI. We can use the `ng add` Angular CLI command to install Angular Material 10 in an existing Angular 10 app:

```
ng add @angular/material
```

The Angular CLI will ask us whether we want to use a prebuilt theme for our Angular app or a custom one. Accept the default value **Indigo/Pink** and press *Enter*:

```
? Choose a prebuilt theme name, or "custom" for a custom theme: (Use arrow keys)
> Indigo/Pink          [ Preview: https://material.angular.io?theme=indigo-pink ]
  Deep Purple/Amber    [ Preview: https://material.angular.io?theme=deeppurple-amber ]
  Pink/Blue Grey       [ Preview: https://material.angular.io?theme=pink-bluegrey ]
  Purple/Green         [ Preview: https://material.angular.io?theme=purple-green ]
  Custom
```

Figure 9.1 – Theme selection

After selecting a theme, the Angular CLI will ask if we want to set up global typography styles in our app. Typography refers to how the text is arranged in our application. Angular Material typography is based on Material Design guidelines and uses the **Roboto** Google font for styling.

We want to keep our application as simple as possible, so type `N` (No) and press *Enter*:

```
? Set up global Angular Material typography styles? (y/N)
```

Figure 9.2 – Set up typography

The next question is about animations. We want our application to display a beautiful animation when we click on a button or open up a modal dialog. It isn't strictly necessary for it to work, but we want some cool animations, right? Type `Y` (Yes) and press *Enter*:

```
? Set up browser animations for Angular Material? (Y/n)
```

Figure 9.3 – Set up animations

> **Important Note**
>
> If the question contains y or n in uppercase, then this is the default choice and you can select it by pressing enter

The Angular CLI will start installing Angular Material into our app. It will scaffold and import all necessary artifacts so that we can start working with Angular Material straight away. After the installation is finished, we can begin adding controls from the Angular Material library into our app.

Adding Angular Material controls

To start using a UI control from the Angular Material library, such as a button or a checkbox, we need to import its corresponding module. Let's see how this is done by adding a button control in our `AppComponent`. Go through the following steps:

1. Import `MatButtonModule` into `AppModule`. We do not import it directly from `@angular/material` because every module has a dedicated namespace. The button control can be found in the `@angular/material/button` namespace:

```
import { BrowserModule } from '@angular/platform-
browser';
import { NgModule } from '@angular/core';

import { AppComponent } from './app.component';
import { BrowserAnimationsModule } from '@angular/
platform-browser/animations';
import { MatButtonModule } from '@angular/material/
button';

@NgModule({
  declarations: [
    AppComponent
  ],
  imports: [
    BrowserModule,
    BrowserAnimationsModule,
    MatButtonModule
  ],
  providers: [],
  bootstrap: [AppComponent]
})
export class AppModule { }
```

2. Open the `app.component.html` file and remove all content. Add a `button` element and set the `mat-button` directive to it. The `mat-button` directive, in essence, modifies the `button` element so that it resembles and behaves as a Material Design button:

```
<button mat-button>I am an Angular Components button</
button>
```

That's it! You now have an Angular 10 app that is decorated with Material Design. But there is more—much more. For instance, we can apply several colors to the button that we created according to the selected theme, which is the topic of the following section.

Theming Angular Material components

As we saw in the previous section, the Angular Material comes with four built-in themes:

- **Indigo/Pink**
- **Deep Purple/Amber**
- **Pink/Blue-Gray**
- **Purple/Green**

When we add Angular Material to an Angular CLI 10 project, the Indigo/Pink theme is the default one. We can always change the selected theme by modifying the included CSS file in the `angular.json` configuration file:

```
"styles": [
  "./node_modules/@angular/material/prebuilt-themes/indigo-
  pink.css",
  "src/styles.css"
]
```

Each theme consists of a set of color palettes, the most common ones being the following:

- Primary
- Accent
- Warn

So, if we want to apply the primary palette to a button, we would write the code as follows:

```
<button mat-
button color="primary">I am an Angular Components button</
button>
```

Theming in Angular Material is so extensive that we can use existing CSS variables to create custom themes, a topic that is out of the scope of this book.

To continue our magical journey to the land of styling with Angular Material, let's talk about some of the essential core components in the next section.

Adding core UI controls

Angular Material consists of many components of different types. Some of the most basic ones are as follows:

- **Buttons**: These are what they sound like: buttons that you can push. But there are several different types that you can use, such as icon buttons, raised buttons, and more.
- **Form controls**: These are any type of control that we use to collect data from a form, such as autocomplete, checkbox, input, radio button, and drop-down list.
- **Navigation**: Controls that are used to perform navigation, such as a menu, a sidenav, or a toolbar.
- **Layout**: Controls that define how data is arranged on a page, such as a list, a card, or tabs.
- **Popups/modals**: Overlay windows that block any user interaction until they are dismissed in any way.
- **Tables**: Controls that are used to display data in a tabular way. What kind of table you need depends on whether your data is massive and needs pagination or needs to be sorted, or both.

Buttons

We have already learned how to create a simple button with Angular Material. There are, however, a lot more button types, namely the following:

- `mat-raised-button`: A button that is displayed with a shadow to indicate its raised state. A variation of this button is `mat-flat-button`, which is the same button but without a shadow.
- `mat-stroked-button`: A button with a border.
- `mat-icon-button`: A button that displays an icon only, without text.
- `mat-fab`: A rounded button with an icon. A variation of this type is `mat-mini-fab`, which displays a smaller button.
- `mat-button-toggle`: A button with on/off capabilities that indicates whether it has been pressed or not.

In the following snippet, you can see how to use each button type:

buttons.component.html

```
<button mat-raised-button>Raised button</button>
<button mat-flat-button>Flat button</button>
<button mat-stroked-button>Stroked button</button>
<button mat-icon-button>
  <mat-icon>favorite</mat-icon>
</button>
<button mat-fab>
  <mat-icon>delete</mat-icon>
</button>
<mat-button-toggle-group>
  <mat-button-toggle value="left">
    <mat-icon>format_align_left</mat-icon>
  </mat-button-toggle>
  <mat-button-toggle value="center">
    <mat-icon>format_align_center</mat-icon>
  </mat-button-toggle>
  <mat-button-toggle value="right">
    <mat-icon>format_align_right</mat-icon>
  </mat-button-toggle>
</mat-button-toggle-group>
```

There are some things to note in setting up buttons:

- To use a `mat-icon-button`, we need to import `MatIconModule` from the `@angular/material/icon` namespace and add a `mat-icon` element inside the button. The content of a `mat-icon` element is a text that indicates which icon to display. Each icon in the Material Design icon website consists of an image and a piece of descriptive text. To use a specific image, we just need to insert the appropriate text inside the `mat-icon` element.
- A `mat-icon` element is also the basis for the `mat-fab` and `mat-mini-fab` buttons, but it can also be used with other button types. Use your imagination to create awesome buttons.

- To use a `mat-button-toggle` button, we need to import `MatButtonToggleModule` from the `@angular/material/button-toggle` namespace. A `mat-button-toggle` button is rarely used standalone; instead, it is combined with other buttons of the same type in a `mat-button-toggle-group` element.

The resulting output is shown in the following image:

Figure 9.4 – Different types of buttons

Buttons are a fundamental element of the Angular Material library. In the following section, we will learn some of the Angular Material controls that are suitable for forms.

Form controls

As we learned in *Chapter 8, Orchestrating Validation Experiences in Forms*, form controls are about collecting input data in different ways and taking further action, such as sending data to a backend API over HTTP.

There are quite a few controls in the Angular Material library of varying types, namely the following:

- **Autocomplete**: Enables the user to start typing in an input field and be presented with a list of suggestions while typing. It helps to narrow down the possible values that the input can take.
- **Checkbox**: A classic checkbox that represents a state either checked or unchecked.
- **Date picker**: Allows the user to select a date in a calendar.
- **Input**: A classic input control enhanced with meaningful animation while typing.
- **Radio button**: A classic radio button enhanced with animations and transitions while editing to create a better user experience.
- **Select**: A drop-down control that prompts the user to select one or more items from a list.

- **Slider**: Enables the user to increase or decrease a value by pulling a slider button to either the right or the left.
- **Slide toggle**: A switch that the user can slide to set it either on or off.

In the following sections, we will take a look at some of the previous form controls in more detail.

Input

The input field is a classic input control that we can set different validation rules on. We can quite easily add the ability to display errors in the input field nicely and reactively. To accomplish this, we need to go through the following steps:

1. Create a `FormControl` instance and add a validation rule so that the control is required to have a value:

```
name = new FormControl('', Validators.required);
```

> **Important Note**
>
> A `FormControl` instance can be used as a standalone control without necessarily needing to be inside a `FormGroup` instance.

2. Create an `input` native HTML element inside a `mat-form-field` element and associate it with the previously created form control. To use a `mat-form-field` element, we need to import `MatFormFieldModule` from the `@angular/material/form-field` namespace:

```
<mat-form-field>
  <input type="text" [formControl]="name"
  placeholder="Name">
</mat-form-field>
```

> **Important Note**
>
> We use `formControl` property binding to associate the `input` element with the `FormControl` instance because `name` is now a variable and not a key, as in the case of `FormBuilder`.

3. Add the `matInput` directive to the `input` field to indicate that it is an Angular Material input control. To use the `matInput` directive properly, we need to import the `MatInputModule` from the `@angular/material/input` namespace.
4. Add a `mat-error` element just below the `input` field to display error messages in `mat-form-field` elements. The `mat-error` element should be displayed only when the validation rule is violated:

```
<mat-form-field>
  <input matInput type="text" [formControl]="name"
  placeholder="Name">
  <mat-error *ngIf="!name.valid">Name is required</
  mat-error>
</mat-form-field>
```

In the following section, we will learn how we can combine such an input with an autocomplete control to suggest values to the user.

Autocomplete

The idea with autocomplete is to help the user narrow down the possible values that an input field can have. In a regular input field, you would just type something and hope a validation tells you whether what you have entered is correct. With autocomplete, you are presented with a list of inputs that you are most likely to want as you type, and at any point, you can decide to stop typing and select an item from the list. It is a time saver, as you don't have to type the entire item's name, and it also enhances accuracy because typing is often error-prone.

To learn how autocomplete works, let's provide a list of possible values in the input control that we created in the previous section. We can create an autocomplete control with Angular Material by adding a `mat-autocomplete` element right after our `mat-form-field` element:

```
<mat-autocomplete #heroesAuto="matAutocomplete">
  <mat-option *ngFor="let hero of heroes" [value]="hero.
  name">{{hero.name}}</mat-option>
</mat-autocomplete>
```

To use it, we first need to import `MatAutocompleteModule` from the `@angular/material/autocomplete` namespace. The `mat-autocomplete` element contains a set of `mat-option` elements that represent the list of suggested values. We use the `ngFor` directive to iterate over a list of heroes that we have created in the `heroes.ts` file and display them as options:

heroes.ts

```
import { Hero } from './hero.model';

export const heroes: Hero[] = [
  { id: 1, name: 'Boothstomper' },
  { id: 2, name: 'Drogfisher' },
  { id: 3, name: 'Bloodyllips' },
  { id: 4, name: 'Mr Bu Moverse' },
  { id: 5, name: 'Piranhaelli' }
];
```

We define a `heroesAuto` template reference variable and set it to `matAutocomplete` so that we can reference it later in the `input` field. This way, when the input control is focused, it triggers the autocomplete control to display the suggested hero names:

```
<input matInput type="text" [formControl]="name"
placeholder="Name" [matAutocomplete]="heroesAuto">
```

If we run our application with `ng serve` and focus on the input control, a drop-down list will appear that contains the suggested values from the autocomplete control:

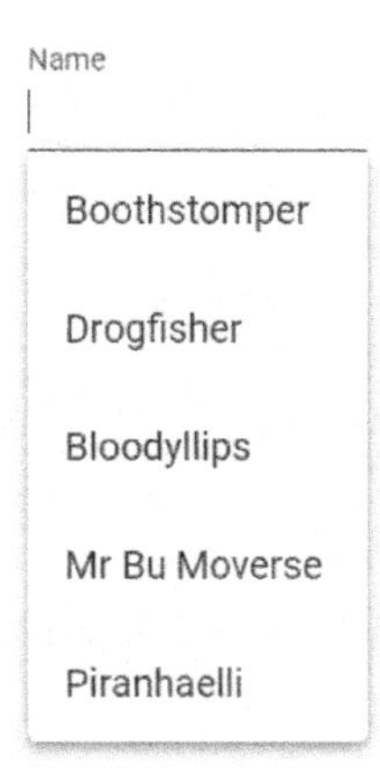

Figure 9.5 – Autocomplete control

We are halfway there. Currently, the autocomplete control displays all suggested values. Ideally, we would like to filter them as we type. Specifically, we would like to display heroes whose name starts with the text that we type in the input control.

As we learned in *Chapter 8, Orchestrating Validation Experiences in Forms*, a form control contains a `valueChanges` observable property. We can subscribe to that property and get notified when the user types in the input control. As soon as the observable emits a new value, we can filter the `heroes` array according to that value:

```
filteredHeroes$: Observable<Hero[]>;

ngOnInit() {
  this.filteredHeroes$ = this.name.valueChanges.pipe(
    map(name => this.heroes.filter(hero => hero.name.
    startsWith(name)))
  );
}
```

Now we just need to change our template so that the `mat-option` element iterates over the `filteredHeroes$` observable using the `async` pipe:

```
<mat-autocomplete #heroesAuto="matAutocomplete">
  <mat-option *ngFor="let hero of filteredHeroes$ | async"
  [value]="hero.name">{{hero.name}}</mat-option>
</mat-autocomplete>
```

If we rerun the application and start typing the character `B` in the input control, we can see that it displays all heroes whose name starts with `B` as suggested values:

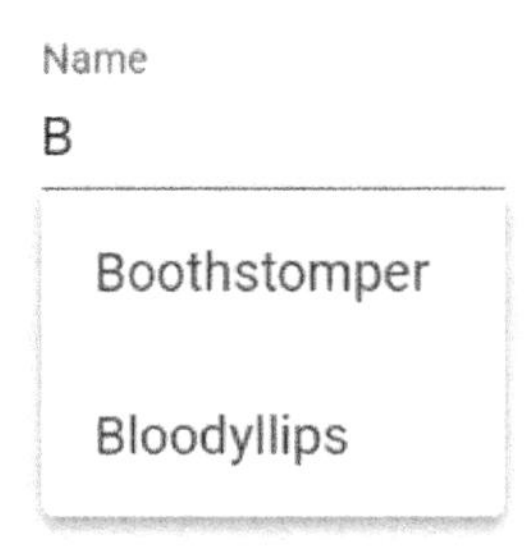

Figure 9.6 – Autocomplete filtering

We could also have implemented a more advanced filtering mechanism, such as a case-insensitive search through all the names or a live search. Imagine that, instead of filtering a local array, we sent a request to a backend API and got live results. The possibilities are endless. The only limit is your imagination in crafting good user experiences with an autocomplete control.

In the following section, we explore how to use a checkbox control from the Angular Material library.

Checkbox

The checkbox is a tristate control, and can have checked, unchecked, or undetermined values. To use it, we first need to import `MatCheckboxModule` from the `@angular/material/checkbox` namespace and then add a `mat-checkbox` element to our template:

```
<mat-checkbox [checked]="isChecked">Check me</mat-checkbox>
```

In the previous snippet, we added a property binding to the `checked` property of the checkbox control to indicate whether it is checked using the `isChecked` component property.

We will finally complete our walkthrough using the form controls of the Angular Material 10 library by having a look at the date-picker control, in the following section.

Date picker

We can do a lot more with a date-picker control than just select a date from a pop-up calendar. We can disable date ranges, format the date, show it on a yearly and monthly basis, and so on. In this chapter, we will only learn how to get up and running with it.

To use a date-picker control, we first need to import the following modules:

- `MatDatepickerModule` from the `@angular/material/datepicker` namespace.
- `MatNativeDateModule` from the `@angular/material/core` namespace. `MatNativeDateModule` provides parsing and formatting utilities for dates, and it is based on the native `Date` object implementation.

A date-picker control in Angular Material 10 must be used in conjunction with an input control, like the autocomplete control that we saw earlier:

```
<mat-form-field>
  <input matInput type="text" placeholder="Select a date">
</mat-form-field>
```

The idea is that the input control triggers the date-picker control to be displayed. To create a date-picker control, we need to add a `mat-datepicker-toggle` and a `mat-datepicker` element inside the `mat-form-field` element:

```
<mat-datepicker-toggle matSuffix [for]="picker"></mat-
datepicker-toggle>
<mat-datepicker #picker></mat-datepicker>
```

The `mat-datepicker-toggle` is a button element with a calendar icon on it. It is positioned at the end of the input control, as defined by the `matSuffix` directive, and displays the calendar pop-up when clicked by the user. The `mat-datepicker` element defines a `picker` template reference variable that we can use to associate it both with the `input` field and the `mat-datepicker-toggle` element:

```
<input matInput type="text" placeholder="Select a date"
[matDatepicker]="picker">
```

The date picker is a form control that is used extensively in enterprise Angular applications. We encourage you to explore its capabilities further at `https://material.angular.io/components/datepicker/overview`.

In the following section, we will learn about navigation techniques in Angular Material 10.

Navigation

There are different ways of navigating in an Angular 10 app, such as clicking on a link or a menu item. Angular Material 10 offers the following components for this type of interaction:

- **Menu**: A pop-up list where you can choose from a predefined set of options.
- **Sidenav**: A component that acts as a menu docked to the left or the right of the page. It can be presented as an overlay over the application while dimming the application content.
- **Toolbar**: A standard toolbar that is a way for the user to reach commonly used actions.

In the following section, we will demonstrate how to use the menu. We encourage you to keep exploring by learning to use the sidenav and the toolbar component on the official Angular Material documentation website. However, you will get a basic knowledge of both them in *Chapter 13, Develop a Real-World Angular App*.

Menu

A menu control in Angular Material is composed of the following artifacts:

- `mat-menu`: The main menu element
- `mat-menu-item`: Represents the individual items of the menu element
- `matMenuTriggerFor`: Triggers the menu element

> **Important Note**
>
> A `mat-menu-item` is a directive that we usually attach in `button` elements, but you could also use other elements, such as an anchor, as well. The `matMenuTriggerFor` binding is also usually used in `button` elements.

To create a menu control, go through the following steps:

1. First, we need to import `MatMenuModule` from the `@angular/material/menu` namespace.
2. Create an Angular Material `button` control that will be used to trigger the menu control to appear:

```
<button mat-icon-button>
  <mat-icon>more_vert</mat-icon>
</button>
```

3. Create a `mat-menu` element and add some `mat-menu-item` elements to it:

```
<mat-menu>
  <button mat-menu-item>Option A</button>
  <button mat-menu-item>Option B</button>
</mat-menu>
```

4. Add a template reference variable to the `mat-menu` element and use it in conjunction with the `matMenuTriggerFor` property binding on the `button` element to associate them with each other:

```
<button mat-icon-button [matMenuTriggerFor]="menu">
  <mat-icon>more_vert</mat-icon>
</button>
<mat-menu #menu>
  <button mat-menu-item>Option A</button>
  <button mat-menu-item>Option B</button>
</mat-menu>
```

If we run the application using `ng serve` and click on the button with three dots, a menu with two options will appear:

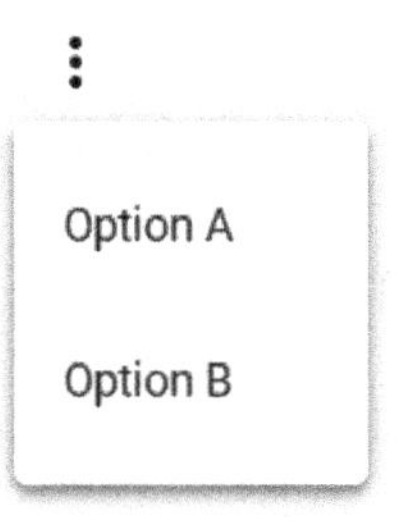

Figure 9.7 – Menu control

Not all menus are so simple, of course. Sooner or later, you will encounter a scenario where you need a menu to be nested. Angular Material 10 can easily support this approach. In a nutshell, we can define a `mat-menu` element for each menu that we need and then connect them. Finally, we need to define what action triggers which menu. Sound hard? It's not. Let's add a submenu in the menu that we have already created:

1. Create a new menu control and define a different template reference variable to it:

```
<mat-menu #submenu>
  <button mat-menu-item>Option B1</button>
  <button mat-menu-item>Option B2</button>
</mat-menu>
```

2. Add a `matMenuTriggerFor` property binding to the `Option B` item of the first menu control and set it to the template reference variable of the submenu control that you have just created:

```
<mat-menu #menu>
  <button mat-menu-item>Option A</button>
  <button mat-menu-item [matMenuTriggerFor]="submenu"
  >Option B</button>
</mat-menu>
```

If we rerun the application and hover over the **Option B** item, we will notice that the submenu appears:

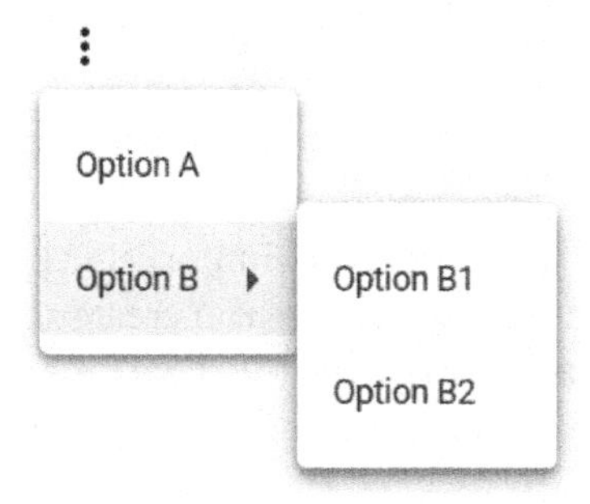

Figure 9.8 – Nested menu control

There are more things that you can do with a menu than just rendering a few menu items and setting them up to be triggered by a button. Now that you know the basics of how to create a nested hierarchy of menus, you can explore further possibilities.

Layout

When we refer to the layout, we are talking about how we place content in our templates. Angular Material 10 gives us different components for this purpose, namely the following:

- **List**: Visualizes the content as a list of items. It can be enriched with links and icons, and can even be multiline.
- **Grid list**: This helps us arrange the content in blocks. We only need to define the number of columns and the component will fill out the visual space.
- **Card**: Wraps content and adds a box shadow. We can define a header for it as well.
- **Tabs**: Divides up the content into different tabs.
- **Stepper**: Divides up the content into wizard-like steps.

- **Expansion panel**: Works in a similar way to an accordion. It enables us to place the content in a list-like way with a title for each item. Items can only be expanded one at a time.

In the following sections, we will cover the list and grid-list components.

List

The list control is built up by a `mat-list` element that contains a set of `mat-list-item` elements:

```
<mat-list>
  <mat-list-item *ngFor="let hero of heroes">
    {{hero.name}}
  </mat-list-item>
</mat-list>
```

To use a `mat-list` element, we first need to import `MatListModule` from the `@angular/material/list` namespace. We can create simple lists, such as the previous snippet, or more advanced lists by enriching them with a multiselect functionality:

```
<mat-selection-list>
  <mat-list-option *ngFor="let hero of heroes">
    {{hero.name}}
  </mat-list-option>
</mat-selection-list>
```

In the previous snippet, we are using the `mat-selection-list` flavor of the `mat-list` element that contains `mat-list-option` elements. A `mat-list-option` element is a list item with a label and a checkbox that we can check to select the item:

Boothstomper

Drogfisher

Bloodyllips

Mr Bu Moverse

Piranhaelli

Figure 9.9 – Selection list

The list control of Angular Material 10 has a rich set of capabilities, and the combinations that we can use are endless.

Grid list

A grid list is similar to a list control, but the content is arranged in a list of rows and columns while ensuring that it fills out the page viewport. It is an excellent fit if you want maximum freedom to decide how to display content. To use it, we must first import `MatGridListModule` from the `@angular/material/grid-list` namespace. The component consists of a `mat-grid-list` element and several `mat-grid-tile` elements:

```
<mat-grid-list cols="3" rowHeight="100px" gutterSize="50">
  <mat-grid-tile *ngFor="let hero of heroes">
    {{hero.name}}
  </mat-grid-tile>
</mat-grid-list>
```

> **Important Note**
>
> The viewport of a page is defined as the area of the page that is visible to the user. It varies according to the device that we use for browsing the content. For example, the viewport in mobile devices is smaller than a desktop one.

We can set the number of columns and the height of each row by using the `cols` and `rowHeight` properties, respectively. We can also define the space between rows by setting the `gutterSize` property that is measured in pixels.

In the previous snippet, we are using the `ngFor` directive to iterate over a list of heroes and display one tile for each hero. The output after running the application should be the following:

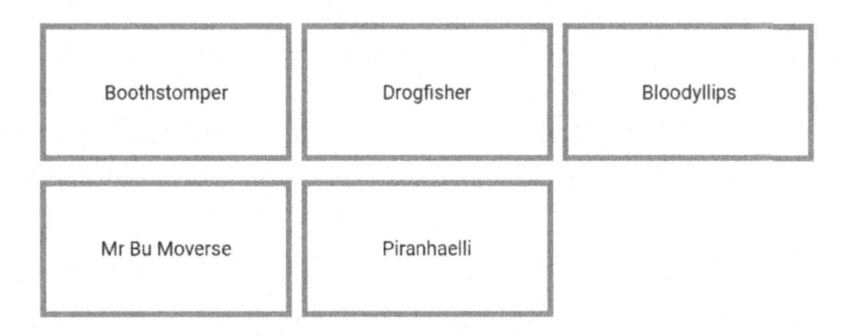

Figure 9.10 – Grid list

The `mat-grid-tile` element also contains the `colspan` property, which decides how much column space it should take and the `rowspan`, which indicates how many rows it should take. We encourage you to explore the preceding properties along with the remaining card and tab components to learn more.

Popups and modals

There are different ways that we can capture the user's attention in a web application. One of them is to show a pop-up dialog over the content of the page and prompt the user to act accordingly. Another way is to display information about a part of the page when the user hovers over that particular part with the mouse.

Angular Material 10 offers three different components for handling such cases:

- **Dialog**: A modal pop-up dialog that is displaying itself on top of the page content.
- **Tooltip**: A piece of text that is displayed when we hover over a specific area.
- **Snackbar**: An information message that is displayed at the bottom of a page and is visible for a short amount of time. Its purpose is to notify the user of the result of an action, such as saving a form.

In this chapter, we will focus on the dialog component, which is widely used in Angular apps. In the following section, we learn how to create a simple dialog.

Creating a simple dialog

The dialog component is quite powerful and can easily be customized and configured. It is an ordinary Angular component and uses custom directives that force it to behave like a dialog. To create an Angular Material dialog, go through the following steps:

1. First, we need to import `MatDialogModule` from the `@angular/material/dialog` namespace.
2. Create an Angular component that will be the host for our dialog. The template of the component contains various directives and elements that `MatDialogModule` exports and we can use. The `mat-dialog-title` directive defines the title of the dialog, and the `mat-dialog-content` is the actual content of the dialog. The `mat-dialog-actions` element defines the actions that can be performed by the dialog, and it usually wraps `button` elements:

```
<h1 mat-dialog-title>Confirmation needed!</h1>
<mat-dialog-content>Do you like Angular?</mat-dialog-
content>
```

```
<mat-dialog-actions>
  <button mat-button [mat-dialog-close]="true">
  Absolutely!</button>
  <button mat-button mat-dialog-close>Not sure</button>
</mat-dialog-actions>
```

3. We use the `mat-dialog-close` directive on a `button` element to indicate that the dialog will be closed when that button is clicked. In our case, we use the `mat-dialog-close` directive twice. In the first case, we use it as a property binding and set it to a value that is finally passed back to the caller of the dialog. In the second case, we close the dialog right away.
4. A dialog must be triggered to be displayed on a page. Add a `button` element to the template of `AppComponent` that will call a `showDialog` method:

```
<button mat-button (click)="showDialog()">Open dialog</
button>
```

5. Open the `app.component.ts` file and create the `showDialog` method that uses the `MatDialog` service to display the dialog component. The `MatDialog` service accepts the type of component that represents our dialog as a parameter:

```
import { Component } from '@angular/core';
import { MatDialog } from '@angular/material/dialog';
import { DialogComponent } from './dialog/dialog.
component';

@Component({
  selector: 'app-root',
  templateUrl: './app.component.html',
  styleUrls: ['./app.component.css']
})
export class AppComponent {

  constructor(private dialog: MatDialog) {}

  showDialog() {
    this.dialog.open(DialogComponent);
  }
}
```

Run the application using `ng serve` and click on the **Open dialog** button. The following dialog will appear on the screen:

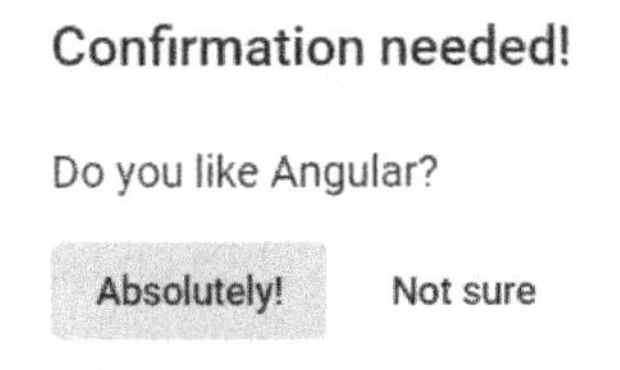

Figure 9.11 – Confirmation dialog

You may notice that the **Absolutely!** button is focused by default. In the following section, we will learn how to configure our dialog and change that.

Configuring a dialog

We can configure a dialog by passing configuration options using the second parameter of the `open` method:

```
showDialog() {
  this.dialog.open(DialogComponent, {autoFocus: false});
}
```

The `autoFocus` property is part of the `MatDialogConfig` object that contains various options that we can use to configure a dialog, such as setting its `width` or `height`. We can also use this object to pass data to our dialog component.

In a real-world scenario, you will probably need to create a reusable component for displaying a dialog in an Angular project. Even better, the component may end up in an Angular library as a package. Therefore, you should configure the dialog component to accept data dynamically, such as the title of the dialog:

1. Inject the `MAT_DIALOG_DATA` token in the `constructor` of `DialogComponent`. The `MAT_DIALOG_DATA` is not an Angular service, and that's the reason why we cannot inject it normally as we do with services. It is an injection token, and we use the `@Inject` decorator to inject it, as we learned in *Chapter 5, Structure an Angular App*. The `data` variable will contain any data that we pass to the dialog when we call its `open` method:

```
import { Component, Inject } from '@angular/core';
import { MAT_DIALOG_DATA } from '@angular/material/
dialog';

```

```
@Component({
  selector: 'app-dialog',
  templateUrl: './dialog.component.html',
  styleUrls: ['./dialog.component.css']
})
export class DialogComponent {

  constructor(@Inject(MAT_DIALOG_DATA) public data:
  any) { }

}
```

2. Use interpolation to bind the `data` property into the header element of the template:

```
<h1 mat-dialog-title>{{data}}</h1>
```

3. Open the `app.component.ts` file and set the `data` property in the configuration object of the dialog:

```
showDialog() {
  this.dialog.open(DialogComponent, {
    autoFocus: false,
    data: 'My dialog'
  });
}
```

> **Important Note**
>
> The `MAT_DIALOG_DATA` property is set to type `any` so that we can pass any arbitrary structure of data to the dialog. In a real-world scenario, you will possibly use more advanced data structures, such as objects.

We have already seen that the dialog is closed automatically when we click on each of the defined buttons. The first button also sends a value back to the caller of the dialog. How could we read this value? In the following section, we will learn how to do that.

Getting data back from a dialog

The open method of the `MatDialog` service returns an `afterClosed` observable property that we can subscribe to, which will enable us to be notified when the dialog closes. The `afterClosed` observable emits any value that is sent back from the dialog:

```
showDialog() {
  this.dialog.open(DialogComponent, {
    autoFocus: false,
    data: 'My dialog'
  }).afterClosed().subscribe(result => {
    if (result) { window.alert(result); }
  });
}
```

Note that we check whether there is a value returned from the dialog because the second button does not return a value at all, and so we will probably want to take action *only* if the dialog returns valid data.

Instead of using the `mat-dialog-close` directive to close a dialog declaratively, we could use the `MatDialogRef` service. The `MatDialogModule` exports the `MatDialogRef` service that contains a `close` method that we can use:

dialog.component.ts

```
import { Component, Inject } from '@angular/core';
import { MAT_DIALOG_DATA, MatDialogRef } from '@angular/
material/dialog';

@Component({
  selector: 'app-dialog',
  templateUrl: './dialog.component.html',
  styleUrls: ['./dialog.component.css']
})
export class DialogComponent {

  constructor(@Inject(MAT_DIALOG_DATA) public data:
  any, private dialogRef: MatDialogRef<DialogComponent>) { }

  closeDialog(data?: boolean) {
```

```
        this.dialogRef.close(data);
    }

}
```

The `close` method accepts a single parameter that defines data that we want to send back to the caller.

> **Important Note**
> When we inject the `MatDialogRef` service in the `constructor`, we also set its type to `DialogComponent`, which is the same as the dialog component itself.

We should also modify the `button` elements accordingly for the previous snippet to work properly:

```
<mat-dialog-actions>
  <button mat-button (click)="closeDialog(true)">Absolutely!</
  button>
  <button mat-button (click)="closeDialog()">Not sure</button>
</mat-dialog-actions>
```

Both ways of closing a dialog are valid, and we could also use them simultaneously in our components.

Dialogs are a dominant feature of Angular Material 10, and it seems inevitable that you will need to use them in your Angular project, especially if you are using Angular Material.

Data table

There are different ways in which we can visualize data in an Angular component. An efficient way of getting a quick overview is by displaying it in a tabular format with rows and columns. We might, however, need to sort data by column to find the information we are looking for. Also, the amount of data might be so large that it needs to be shown in parts by page. Angular Material 10 addresses these issues by offering the following components:

- **Table**: Lays out data in rows and columns with headers
- **Sort table**: Allows you to sort data in a table
- **Paginator**: Allows you to slice up data in pages that we can navigate

In the following sections, we learn more about each component in detail.

Table

The table component allows us to display our data in columns and rows. To create a table, we first need to import `MatTableModule` from the `@angular/material/table` namespace.

An Angular Material table is a standard HTML `table` element that contains specific Angular directives to conform to the Material Design guidelines. To create the table initially, we use the `mat-table` directive:

```
<table mat-table [dataSource]="heroes"></table>
```

The `dataSource` property of the `mat-table` directive defines the data that we want to display on the table. It can be any sort of data that can be enumerated, such as an observable stream or an array. In our case, we bind it to the `heroes` array that we declared in our component `class`, along with the `columnNames` property that indicates the column names of the table:

```
import { Component } from '@angular/core';
import { heroes } from '../heroes';

@Component({
  selector: 'app-table',
  templateUrl: './table.component.html',
  styleUrls: ['./table.component.css']
})
export class TableComponent {

  heroes = heroes;
  columnNames = ['id', 'name'];
}
```

The names of columns match the properties of a hero object and are used twice in the `table` element—once to define the header row of the table that displays the names of the columns and the second time to define the actual rows that contain data:

```
<tr mat-header-row *matHeaderRowDef="columnNames"></tr>
<tr mat-row *matRowDef="let row; columns: columnNames;"></tr>
```

Finally, we use an `ng-container` element for each column to display the header and data cells:

```
<ng-container matColumnDef="id">
  <th mat-header-cell *matHeaderCellDef> ID </th>
  <td mat-cell *matCellDef="let hero"> {{hero.id}} </td>
</ng-container>
<ng-container matColumnDef="name">
  <th mat-header-cell *matHeaderCellDef> Name </th>
  <td mat-cell *matCellDef="let hero"> {{hero.name}} </td>
</ng-container>
```

> **Important Note**
>
> The `ng-container` element is a unique-purpose element that is used to group elements with similar functionality. It does not interfere with the styling of the child elements, nor is it rendered on the screen.

The `ng-container` element uses the `matColumnDef` directive to set the name of the specific column, as defined in the `columnNames` component property.

> **Important Note**
>
> The value of `matColumnDef` must match with a value from the `columnNames` component property; otherwise, the application will throw an error that it cannot find the name of the defined column.

It contains a `th` element with a `mat-header-cell` directive that indicates the header of the cell and a `td` element with a `mat-cell` directive for the data of the cell. The `td` element uses the `matCellDef` directive to create a local template variable for the data of the current row that we can bind to later.

If we run the application, the output should be the following:

ID	Name
1	Boothstomper
2	Drogfisher
3	Bloodyllips
4	Mr Bu Moverse
5	Piranhaelli

Figure 9.12 – Table control

You did great! You managed to create a good-looking table in no time using Angular Material.

Sorting

At this point, we have created a nice-looking table, but it lacks a pretty standard functionality—namely, sorting. We would typically expect that if we click the header, it will sort data into ascending and descending order, respectively, and that it will be able to recognize common data types, such as text and numbers, and sort them properly. The good news is that Angular Material can help us to achieve this behavior. We just need to use the suitable Angular Material directives for the job:

1. Import `MatSortModule` from the `@angular/material/sort` namespace and add it to the `imports` property of `AppModule`.
2. `MatSortModule` exports a variety of directives that we can use to sort a table. Add the `matSort` and `matSortDisableClear` directives to the `table` element and add the `mat-sort-header` directive to each header cell that you want to sort:

```
<table mat-table [dataSource]="heroes" matSort
matSortDisableClear="true">
  <ng-container matColumnDef="id">
    <th mat-header-cell *matHeaderCellDef> ID </th>
    <td mat-cell *matCellDef="let hero"> {{hero.id}}
    </td>
  </ng-container>
  <ng-container matColumnDef="name">
    <th mat-header-cell *matHeaderCellDef
    mat-sort-header> Name </th>
```

```
        <td mat-cell *matCellDef="let hero"> {{hero.name}}
        </td>
      </ng-container>
      <tr mat-header-row *matHeaderRowDef="columnNames"></tr>
      <tr mat-row *matRowDef="let row; columns:
      columnNames;"></tr>
    </table>
```

We set the value of the `matSortDisableClear` directive to `true` because sorting by default contains three states: ascending, descending, and the original ordering. The last one clears the ordering, and that is why we disable it.

3. Use the `@ViewChild` decorator to get a reference to the `matSort` directive that we defined earlier:

```
@ViewChild(MatSort, {static: true}) sort: MatSort;
```

We set the `static` property to `true` because we already know that the `matSort` directive is available at component initialization, as we learned in *Chapter 6, Enrich Components with Asynchronous Data Services*.

4. To use sorting, wrap the data in a `MatTableDataSource` instance and set the `sort` property of that instance to the `MatSort` property that we defined previously:

```
heroes = new MatTableDataSource(heroes);

ngOnInit() {
  this.heroes.sort = this.sort;
}
```

Sorting a table is a feature that you will possibly need when writing Angular applications. The configuration of sorting looks simple as soon as you have a simple table model.

Pagination

So far, our table is starting to look quite good. As well as displaying data, it can even be sorted. We are aware, though, that in most cases, the data for a table is usually quite long, which means that the user either has to scroll up and down or browse the data page by page. We can solve the latter problem with the help of the pagination element. To use it, we need to do the following:

1. Import `MatPaginatorModule` from the `@angular/material/paginator` namespace and add it to the `imports` property of `AppModule`.

2. Add a `mat-paginator` element immediately after the `table` element. Set the `pageSize` property to display two rows each time. Also set the `pageSizeOptions` property so that the user can change the page size:

```
<mat-paginator [pageSize]="2"
[pageSizeOptions]="[2,4,6]"></mat-paginator>
```

3. Use the `@ViewChild` decorator to get a reference to the `mat-paginator` element that we created:

```
@ViewChild(MatPaginator, {static: true}) paginator:
MatPaginator;
```

4. Set the `paginator` property of the `heroes` data source to the `MatPaginator` property that we defined previously:

```
ngOnInit() {
  this.heroes.sort = this.sort;
  this.heroes.paginator = this.paginator;
}
```

If we rerun the application, we will notice that the table now displays two heroes each time; however, we can navigate through all of the pages using the paginator control that is shown at the bottom of the table:

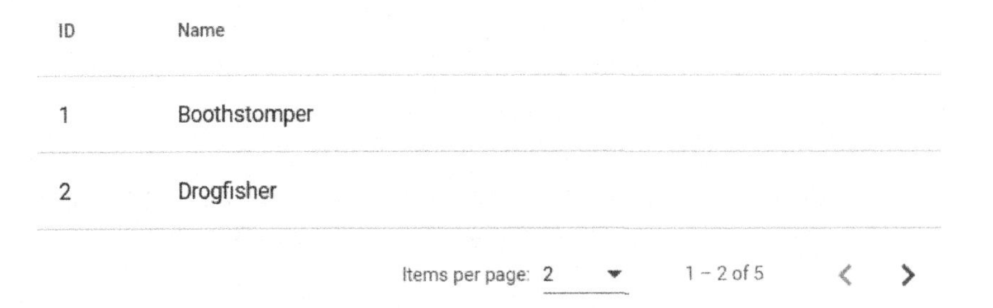

Figure 9.13 – Table with pagination

The paginator component also displays the total length of our data, even if we did not set it explicitly. Well, we did when we set the `paginator` property of the data source to the paginator element. It is smart enough to understand how to handle the data by itself.

In this section, we learned about some of the core components of the Angular Material library and how we can leverage them to create compelling and engaging user interfaces. We covered UI controls that span a broad range of uses, such as navigation, layout, popups, and form controls.

In the next section, we will learn about the backbone of the Angular Material library, the Angular CDK, and how we can use it to create custom controls that adhere to Material Design guidelines.

Introducing the Angular CDK

The Angular CDK is the core of the Angular Material library. It is a collection of tools that implement similar interaction patterns; however, they are not tied to any presentation style, such as Material Design. The behavior of Angular Material components has been designed using the Angular CDK. The Angular CDK is so abstract that you can use it to create custom components. You should seriously consider it if you are a UI library author.

The capabilities of the Angular CDK are enormous and certainly cannot fit in a single chapter. For the sake of demonstration, we are going to describe two elements of the library:

- **Clipboard**: Provides a copy–paste functionality with the system clipboard
- **Drag and Drop**: Provides drag-and-drop features in elements

Angular CDK elements are imported from the `@angular/cdk` npm package. Each element must be imported from its module, which resides in a different namespace, similar to the Angular Material components.

Clipboard

We can easily create a *copy-to-clipboard* button using the `cdkCopyToClipboard` directive. All we have to do is import `ClipboardModule` from the `@angular/cdk/clipboard` namespace and attach the directive to a `button` element:

copy-text.component.html

```
<mat-form-field>
  <textarea matInput [(ngModel)]="content" placeholder="Enter
  some text and click the Copy button"></textarea>
</mat-form-field>
<button mat-flat-button [cdkCopyToClipboard]="content">
  <mat-icon>content_copy</mat-icon>
  Copy
</button>
```

We set the value of the directive to the `content` component property:

copy-text.component.ts

```
import { Component } from '@angular/core';

@Component({
  selector: 'app-copy-text',
  templateUrl: './copy-text.component.html',
  styleUrls: ['./copy-text.component.css']
})
export class CopyTextComponent {
  content: string;
}
```

This is the actual content that is going to be copied to the clipboard once we click the `Copy` button.

Drag and drop

A powerful application of the drag-and-drop functionality is when using lists in an Angular app, which we do in most cases! To use it, we must first import `DragDropModule` from the `@angular/cdk/drag-drop` namespace. The drag-and-drop component of Angular CDK is spread across various directives that we can apply to a `mat-list` element:

```
<mat-list cdkDropList>
  <mat-list-item *ngFor="let hero of heroes" cdkDrag>
    {{hero.name}}
  </mat-list-item>
</mat-list>
```

The `cdkDropList` directive indicates that the `mat-list` element is a container for items that can be dragged. The `cdkDrag` directive indicates that the `mat-list-item` element can be dragged. We have also applied a bit of styling to quickly identify the items as draggable:

```
mat-list-item {
  cursor: move;
  border: 1px lightgray solid;
}
```

If we run the application using `ng serve`, we will notice that even if we can drag an item from the list, the application will not respect the movement of the item when we drop it. The drag-and-drop component does not have reordering baked in, but we must implement it on our own. We can use the `cdkDropListDropped` event binding to achieve that:

```
<mat-list cdkDropList (cdkDropListDropped)="reorder($event)">
  <mat-list-item *ngFor="let hero of heroes" cdkDrag>
    {{hero.name}}
  </mat-list-item>
</mat-list>
```

When we drag a `mat-list-item` element and drop it, the `reorder` component method will be called:

list.component.ts

```
import { Component } from '@angular/core';
import { heroes } from '../heroes';
import { CdkDragDrop, moveItemInArray } from '@angular/cdk/
drag-drop';
import { Hero } from '../hero.model';

@Component({
  selector: 'app-list',
  templateUrl: './list.component.html',
  styleUrls: ['./list.component.css']
})
export class ListComponent {

  heroes = heroes;

  reorder(event: CdkDragDrop<Hero[]>) {
    moveItemInArray(this.heroes, event.previousIndex,
    event.currentIndex);
  }

}
```

It accepts a `CdkDragDrop` event of the `Hero[]` type. Although Angular CDK cannot reorder items by itself, it gives us the necessary artifacts to perform reordering efficiently. We use the built-in `moveItemInArray` method from the `@angular/cdk/drag-drop` namespace that performs reordering out of the box. It accepts three parameters: the array that we want to sort, the index of the current item that we drag it from, and the new index that we are going to drop it in.

The Angular CDK sits on the core of Angular Material and contains a ton of other elements that we use at our disposal. In the following section, we learn about how to lay out applications that contain Angular Material components using a pattern called **flexbox**.

Designing layouts using flexbox

Flexbox is a popular CSS pattern that is concerned with the layout of items in a container. It helps us to align and distribute elements inside a container efficiently and responsively. The container can dynamically adapt to the size of its elements accordingly in the best way. It can expand to fill the available space or collapse to prevent overflow.

The flexbox API contains various CSS properties that we can use to define the layout of our application. Some of the most important ones are as follows:

- `display`: Sets its value to `flex` to indicate that we want to use flexbox.
- `flex-direction`: Defines how items are placed inside the container.
- `flex-grow`: Indicates that an item can grow if necessary.
- `flex-shrink`: Opposite to `flex-grow`; indicates that an item can shrink if necessary.
- `flex-wrap`: Indicates that items will not try to fit in just one line, but instead will wrap to accommodate all space.
- `justify-content`: Indicates how items are aligned in the main axis.

> **Important Note**
> The flexbox layout is currently supported in all desktop and mobile browsers, as we can see at `https://caniuse.com/#feat=flexbox`.

The Angular team has created the **Angular Flex Layout** library that provides a more sophisticated layout API based on flexbox that we can use in our Angular apps. It is written in pure TypeScript, and we need to make sure that we have Angular CDK installed before using it.

The Angular Flex Layout library is an npm package that can be installed using the following command:

```
npm install @angular/flex-layout
```

The library contains `FlexLayoutModule`, an Angular module that we can add to the `imports` property of `AppModule`. It exports various Angular directives that we can use in our components:

flex.component.html

```
<div fxLayout="row" fxLayoutAlign="center center">
  <span *ngFor="let hero of heroes" fxFlexOffset="5%">
    {{hero.name}}
  </span>
</div>
```

The previous snippet aligns `span` elements in a single row and places them in the center of both axes. Each `span` element has a margin of `5%` of the width of the containing element. The output should be the following:

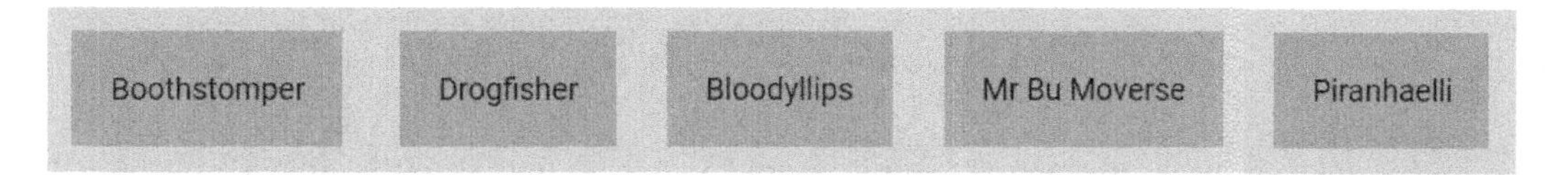

Figure 9.14 – Flexbox layout

The Angular Flex Layout library contains many more properties that we can use to make our application responsive. You can find them at `https://github.com/angular/flex-layout/wiki/Declarative-API-Overview`.

Summary

We set about trying to explain what Material Design is, a design language with paper and ink in mind. After that, we looked at the most well-known implementations of Material Design.

Next, we put most of our focus on Angular Material, the Material Design implementation meant for Angular, and how it consists of different components. We looked at a hands-on explanation of how to install it, set it up, and even how to use some of its core components and themes.

We also learned about the core of Angular Material, which is the Angular CDK, and demonstrated some of its style-aware components.

Time was also spent covering other aspects of styling, such as how to design the layout of our app using flexbox and the Angular Flex Layout library.

Hopefully, you will have read this chapter and found that you now have a grasp of Material Design in general and Angular Material in particular, and can determine whether it is a good match for your next Angular app. In the next chapter, we will complete our journey of styling an Angular app by learning how to apply beautiful animations to our components.

10

Giving Motion to Components with Animations

Nowadays, animations are one of the cornerstones of modern user experience design. Far from just representing visual eye candy to beautify the UI, they have become an essential part of the visual narrative. Animations pave the way to convey messages in a non-intrusive way, becoming a powerful tool for informing the user about the underlying processes and events that happen while they interact with an application, thus enhancing the application's user experience. Animations are language-agnostic, not necessarily bound to a single device or environment (web, desktop, or mobile). In other words, animations are here to stay, and Angular has a strong commitment to this aspect of modern visual development.

With all modern browsers embracing the newest features of CSS for animation handling, Angular offers support for implementing imperative animation scripting through an incredibly simple but powerful API. In this chapter, we will cover several approaches to implementing animation effects. We will start by leveraging plain vanilla CSS for applying class-based animations. Furthermore, we will implement script routines where Angular takes full responsibility for handling DOM transitions.

In this chapter, we cover the following topics:

- Creating animations with plain vanilla CSS
- Leveraging class-named animations using a class binding to better handle transitions
- Looking at Angular's built-in CSS hooks for defining styles for each transition state
- Introducing animation triggers and declaratively attaching those animations to elements in our templates
- Animating components with the AnimationBuilder API
- Designing directives that handle animations

Technical requirements

You can find the code files present in this chapter on GitHub at `https://github.com/PacktPublishing/Learning-Angular--Third-Edition/tree/master/ch10`.

Creating animations with plain vanilla CSS

The inception of CSS-based animation is a critical milestone in modern web design. Before that, we used to rely on JavaScript to accommodate animations in our web applications. We were manipulating DOM elements through complex and cumbersome scripts based on intervals, timeouts, and loops. Unfortunately, this was neither maintainable nor scalable.

Then, modern browsers embraced the functionalities brought by the recent CSS transformation: transitions, keyframes, and animation properties. It soon became a game-changer in the context of web interaction design. While support for these techniques in old browsers is far from optimal, the rest of them provide full support for these CSS APIs.

We assume that you have a broad understanding of how CSS animation works in the context of building keyframe-driven or transition-based animations. Providing coverage of these techniques is obviously beyond the scope of this book. CSS-based animations are usually implemented by either of the following approaches or even a combination of both:

- Transition properties that act as observers of either all or just a subset of the CSS properties applied to DOM elements. Whenever any of these properties are changed, the DOM element will not apply the new value right away but will experience a steady transition into its new state.

- Named keyframe animations that define different steps for animating one or several CSS properties under a unique name. Each keyframe corresponds to an animation property of a given selector. We can set additional parameters of the animation, such as the delay, the duration, or the number of iterations in which the animation can be applied.

As we can see in the previous cases, the use of a CSS selector populated with animation settings is the starting point for all things related to animation. To better illustrate this, let's build a fancy pulse animation to emulate a heartbeat-style effect in an Angular Material button:

1. We use a keyframe animation that is based on a simple interpolation. We'll take an object, scale it up by 15%, and scale it back down again to its initial state.
2. We'll then wrap it in a CSS class named `pulse`, which executes the animation in an infinite loop where each iteration takes 1 second to complete.
3. We define the animation routine in the CSS file of `AppComponent`:

app.component.css

```
@keyframes pulse {
  0% {
    transform: scale3d(1, 1, 1);
  }
  50% {
    transform: scale3d(1.5, 1.5, 1.5);
  }
  100% {
    transform: scale3d(1, 1, 1);
  }
}

.pulse {
  animation: pulse 1s infinite;
}
```

4. Any DOM element annotated with the `pulse` class name will visually beat like a heart. The visual effect is a good hint that the element is undertaking some kind of action.

To make it even better, we can apply such an effect only when a condition is met. We use a class binding to toggle the `pulse` class only when the `isBeating` component property is truthy. The value of the `isBeating` property is toggled by clicking on the `button` element itself. The following code in the template of `AppComponent` puts it simply:

```
<button mat-icon-
button [class]="{pulse: isBeating}" color="accent"
(click)="isBeating = !isBeating">
  <mat-icon>favorite</mat-icon>
</button>
```

And that's it! Run the application using `ng serve` and check the visual effect live after clicking on the heart button. Click on it and resume it again to see the effect applied when the value of the `isBeating` property changes.

Pure CSS animations are great to use in a web application, but when it comes to the Angular context, there is a better alternative. The Angular framework saves us much boilerplate code by providing a robust animation API to use, as we'll learn in the following section.

Introducing Angular animations

The Angular framework provides an API for handling animations through the `@angular/animations` npm package. In an Angular CLI project, we do not need to install it separately, as it is automatically available when creating a new Angular app. It provides all the necessary artifacts for performing animations through `BrowserAnimationsModule`. We need to import this module into `AppModule` to start using animations in an Angular app:

```
import { BrowserModule } from '@angular/platform-browser';
import { NgModule } from '@angular/core';

import { AppComponent } from './app.component';
import { BrowserAnimationsModule } from '@angular/platform-
browser/animations';

@NgModule({
  declarations: [
    AppComponent
  ],
```

```
  imports: [
    BrowserModule,
    BrowserAnimationsModule
  ],
  providers: [],
  bootstrap: [AppComponent]
})
export class AppModule { }
```

> **Important Note**
>
> We already met `BrowserAnimationsModule` in *Chapter 9, Introduction to Angular Material,* when we added Angular Material in our Angular app. The Angular CLI asked us for the first time whether we wanted to set up browser animations.

The idea with Angular animations is that we can show a specific animation when a particular property of the component changes. `BrowserAnimationsModule` exports a set of artifacts that we can use to define an animation trigger:

- `trigger`: Defines the property in the component that the animation targets. It accepts a name as the first argument and an array of states and transitions as the second.
- `state`: Defines the value of the component property and what CSS properties it should have. We need to define one of these for each value that the property can take.
- `transition`: Defines how the animation should perform when we go from one property value to another.
- `animate`: Performs the defined animation when we move from one state value to the next.

In the following section, we'll use several of the preceding artifacts to create our first Angular animation.

Creating our first animation

Let's now see what an Angular animation looks like, and then explain the parts:

```
animations: [
  trigger('sizeAnimation', [
    state('small', style({
```

```
        transform:'scale(1)',
        backgroundColor: 'green'
      })),
      state('large', style({
        transform: 'scale(1.4)',
        backgroundColor: 'red'
      })),
      transition('small => large', animate('100ms ease-in')),
      transition('large => small', animate('100ms ease-out'))
    ])
  ]
```

When we want to define an animation in an Angular component, we use the `animations` property of the `@Component` decorator. It contains an array of `trigger` definitions where each one has a name and an array of items that can be either a `state` definition or a `transition`. A `state` indicates that when the value defined by the name has changed, a `style` is applied.

> **Important Note**
>
> Style properties are camel-cased and not kebab-cased. For example, the background color is defined as `backgroundColor` and not `background-color`, as it is in CSS.

The animation that we defined in the previous example has the following behavior:

- If an animation with the name `sizeAnimation` is triggered and the value is set to `small`, then apply the `transform: 'scale(1)'` and `backgroundColor: 'green'` CSS rules.
- If an animation with the name `sizeAnimation` is triggered and the value is set to `large`, then apply the `transform: 'scale(1.4)'` and `backgroundColor: 'red'` CSS rules.

The two remaining items in the animation are two calls to the `transition` method, which defines how to apply the animation smoothly. It indicates that when a state changes from one value to another, an animation should execute using the `animate` method. The previous example is interpreted in the following way:

- When the value of the state changes from `small` to `large`, the animation is applied for `100ms` using the `ease-in` effect.

- When the value of the state changes the other way round, from `large` to `small`, the animation is applied for `100ms` using the `ease-out` effect.

Now that we have defined the different parts that compose an animation, let's see how we can connect it to our components.

Setting up the animation with our component

Following these steps will help you better understand how the animation of the previous section works:

1. We have created a new Angular component, and we have added the `animations` property inside the `@Component` decorator:

```
import { Component } from '@angular/core';
import { trigger, state, style, transition, animate }
from '@angular/animations';

@Component({
  selector: 'app-size',
  templateUrl: './size.component.html',
  styleUrls: ['./size.component.css'],
  animations: [
    trigger('sizeAnimation', [
      state('small', style({
        transform: 'scale(1)',
        backgroundColor: 'green'
      })),
      state('large', style({
        transform: 'scale(1.4)',
        backgroundColor: 'red'
      })),
      transition('small => large', animate('100ms
      ease-in')),
      transition('large => small', animate('100ms
      ease-out'))
    ])
  ]
})
```

```
export class SizeComponent {
  state: string;
}
```

2. We apply the animation in a paragraph element in the template of the component using the `[@animationName]` notation:

```
<div>
  <button mat-icon-button (click)="state = 'large'">
    <mat-icon>zoom_in</mat-icon>
  </button>
  <button mat-icon-button (click)="state = 'small'">
    <mat-icon>zoom_out</mat-icon>
  </button>
  <p class="animate" [@sizeAnimation]="state">Hello
  Angular 10</p>
</div>
```

That is, `sizeAnimation` is applied in the paragraph element according to the value of the `state` component property. Two buttons control the value of the `state` property. One sets it to `large` and the other to `small`.

Using animations based on a component is pretty simple if we know how to handle the animations API of the Angular framework. However, two special-case animations operate independently of a component property:

- The wildcard state
- The void state

We'll explain both states in the following sections.

The wildcard state

An animation can have more than the two states that we defined in our trigger previously. In some cases, it makes more sense to apply transitions regardless of what state we are currently coming from. For those cases, we can use the wildcard state. Using it is relatively easy. We only need to go to our `transition` definition and replace a state value with `*`, like so:

```
transition('* => larger')
```

That means that regardless of what state we were in before, a transition will happen when the `state` property has the value `larger`.

The void state

The `void` state is different from the wildcard state. We can think of it as an element that didn't exist before, and it has the `void` value. Upon exiting, we assume that it has value. The definition of a `transition` with the `void` state looks like this:

```
transition('void => *')
```

Let's make this more realistic by creating an Angular component that uses the `void` state:

invisible.component.html

```
<button mat-button color="primary" (click)="appear()">Show me</
button>
<button mat-
button color="accent" (click)="disappear()">Good bye!</button>
<p [@flyInOut]="state" *ngIf="showMe">You asked for me?</p>
```

We have added one `button` element that calls the `appear` component method to show the element and another one that calls the `disappear` method, which hides the element. The `appear` method sets the `state` component property to `in` and the `showMe` component property to `true`. The `disappear` method reverts the value of the `showMe` property to `false`:

```
export class InvisibleComponent {
  state: string;
  showMe: boolean;

  appear() {
    this.state = 'in';
    this.showMe = true;
  }

  disappear() {
    this.showMe = false;
  }

}
```

Actually, the `appear` method triggers the `in state` and the `'void => *' transition` of the animation. The `disappear` method activates the `'* => void' transition`:

```
trigger('flyInOut', [
  state('in', style({transform: 'translateX(0)'})),
  transition('void => *', [
    style({transform: 'translateX(-100%)'}),
    animate(500)
  ]),
  transition('* => void', [
    animate(500, style({transform: 'translateX(200%)'}))
  ])
])
```

In a nutshell, if an element goes from the state not existing to existing, that is `void => *`, then it animates from `-100%` to x position `0`. When going from existing to non-existing, then it moves out of the page by moving it to x position `200%`. That is, the primary purpose of the `void` state is to be used when prior elements don't exist.

There are occasions where we want to know when a particular animation is kicked off as well as knowing when it finishes. We can use animation callbacks for this purpose, as we'll learn in the following section.

Animation callbacks

Sometimes we want to get notified about the life cycle of animation in our components. The animation API provides two properties that we can use to listen for the start and the end of an animation:

```
<p class="animate" [@sizeAnimation]="state"
(@sizeAnimation.start)="started($event)"
(@sizeAnimation.done)="finished($event)">
  Hello Angular 10
</p>
```

The `start` property of the specific animation name denotes that animation has already started. The `done` property of the animation indicates that the animation has finished. Both properties can be accessed from the `@animationName` object. In our case, this is the `@sizeAnimation` because the name of the animation is `sizeAnimation`. Also, both properties expose a `$event` object of the `AnimationEvent` type that we can use in our component:

```
export class SizeComponent {
  state: string;

  started(evt: AnimationEvent) {
    console.log('Animation started');
  }

  finished(evt: AnimationEvent) {
    console.log('Animation finished');
  }
}
```

While we are working with animations in our components, we may reach a point where we want to create an animation programmatically. In the following section, we will learn how to create such animations using the `AnimationBuilder` service.

Animating components programmatically

So far, we have covered how to perform animations either with pure CSS or using the `animation` property of the `@Component` decorator. There is another more programmatic approach that uses the `AnimationBuilder` service. There are some artifacts involved in making this approach work, namely:

- `AnimationBuilder`: This is the Angular service that we need to inject into our components.
- `AnimationFactory`: This is the result of calling the `build` method of the `AnimationBuilder` instance and contains the animation definition.
- `AnimationPlayer`: This is an object created from the `AnimationFactory` instance and requires an element on which to apply the animation.

Let's cover these bullets in more detail so we can understand how `AnimationBuilder` works. First things first, we need to inject the `AnimationBuilder` service into the `constructor` of our component. We are also injecting the `ElementRef` instance to get a reference to the native element of the component:

```
import { Component, OnInit, ElementRef } from '@angular/core';
import { AnimationBuilder } from '@angular/animations';

@Component({
  selector: 'app-text-resize',
  templateUrl: './text-resize.component.html',
  styleUrls: ['./text-resize.component.css']
})
export class TextResizeComponent implements OnInit {

  constructor(private builder: AnimationBuilder, private el:
  ElementRef) { }

  ngOnInit() {
  }

}
```

At this point, we are ready to start building our style transformations and animations:

```
ngOnInit() {
  const factory = this.builder.build([
    style({ width : '0px' }),
    animate(1000, style({ width: '200px' }))
  ]);
}
```

We use the `build` method of the `AnimationBuilder` instance that accepts an array of animation metadata as a parameter. We define a transformation that sets the `width` of the target element to `0` pixels initially, and an animation that sets its width to `200px` after `1` second.

Finally, we set the result of the `build` method to the `factory` variable, which is of the `AnimationFactory` type. We later use this variable to create an `AnimationPlayer` object:

```
const factory = this.builder.build([
  style({ width : '0px' }),
  animate(1000, style({ width: '200px' }))
]);
const textEl = this.el.nativeElement.querySelector('.text');
const player = factory.create(textEl);
```

In the previous snippet, we use the `nativeElement` of the component to locate the element where we want to apply the animation. We also create an instance of an animation player by calling the `create` method of the `AnimationFactory` instance, passing the target element as a parameter.

> **Important Note**
>
> We assume that the template of the component contains an HTML element with a `text` class.

We then call the `play` method on our animation player instance so that the animation can start immediately:

```
const textEl = this.el.nativeElement.querySelector('.text');
const player = factory.create(textEl);
player.play();
```

`AnimationBuilder` is a powerful way to create reusable animations that you can easily apply to an element of your choice. An alternate approach is to create an animation directive, as we will see in the following section.

Creating a reusable animation directive

So far, we have seen how we can create an `AnimationBuilder` and use it to create and apply animations programmatically. One way of making it reusable is to wrap it inside a directive. We have already learned how to create a custom directive in *Chapter 4, Enhance Components with Pipes and Directives*. In our case, we need an attribute directive that will be applied to an element, and this element is the one that will be animated. For the sake of simplicity, we are going to use the same animation as in the previous section:

1. Use the Angular CLI to create a directive with the name `highlight`.
2. Inject `AnimationBuilder` and `ElementRef` into the `constructor` of the directive.
3. Implement the `OnInit interface` of the directive.
4. Use the `build` method of `AnimationBuilder` to describe the flow of the animation.
5. Create an `AnimationPlayer` object using the `create` method of `AnimationFactory`.
6. Use the `play` method of the `AnimationPlayer` object to start the animation.

The resulting directive should look like the following:

highlight.directive.ts

```
import { Directive, ElementRef, OnInit } from '@angular/core';
import { AnimationBuilder, style, animate } from '@angular/
animations';

@Directive({
  selector: '[appHighlight]'
})
export class HighlightDirective implements OnInit {

  constructor(private builder: AnimationBuilder, private el:
  ElementRef) { }

  ngOnInit() {
    const animation = this.builder.build([
      style({ width: '0' }),
```

```
            animate(1000, style({ width : '200px' }))
        ]);
        const player = animation.create( this.el.nativeElement );
        player.play();
    }

}
```

We are all set. Now we can just apply our directive to any element that needs to be animated.

Summary

We have only scratched the surface of dealing with animations. To read up on everything you can do, we suggest looking at the official documentation at `https://angular.io/guide/animations`.

In this chapter, we started looking at how to define vanilla CSS animations. Then, we explained animation triggers and how you can declaratively attach a defined animation to an element. Then, we looked at how to define animations and attach them to an element programmatically. The very last thing we did was to bundle our programmatic animations in a directive. There is a lot more to learn about animations, but now you should have a basic understanding of what APIs exist and when to use them. Go out there and make your app full of life, but remember, less is more.

Web applications must be testable to make sure that they are functioning correctly and according to the application requirements. In the next chapter, we will learn how to apply different testing techniques in the context of Angular web apps.

11
Unit test an Angular App

In the previous chapters, we have gone through many aspects of how to build an enterprise Angular 10 application from scratch. But how can we ensure that an application can be maintained in the future without much hassle? A comprehensive automated testing layer can become our lifeline once our application begins to scale up and we have to mitigate the impact of bugs.

Testing (and, more specifically, unit testing) is meant to be carried out by the developer as the project is being developed; however, we will cover all the intricacies of testing an Angular application briefly in this chapter, now that our knowledge for the framework is at a mature stage.

In this chapter, we will learn how to use testing tools to perform proper unit testing of our Angular application artifacts. In more detail, we will do the following:

- Look at the importance of testing and, more specifically, unit testing.
- Learn how to test components, with or without dependencies, and how to override them.
- Learn how to test pipes and routes.
- Implement tests for services, mocking dependencies, and stubs.

- Intercept XHR requests and provide mocked responses for refined control.
- Discover how to test directives.
- Learn how to test reactive forms and use page objects to group controls under test together.

Technical requirements

- **GitHub link**: `https://github.com/PacktPublishing/Learning-Angular--Third-Edition/tree/master/ch11`.
- **Jasmine**: `https://jasmine.github.io/`
- **Karma**: `https://karma-runner.github.io/`

Why do we need tests?

What is a unit test? If you're already familiar with unit testing and test-driven development, you can safely skip to the next section. If not, let's just say that unit tests are part of an engineering philosophy that takes a stand for efficient and agile development processes. They add a layer of automated testing to the application code before it is developed. The core concept is that a piece of code is accompanied by its test, and both of them are built by the developer who works on that code. First, we design the test against the feature we want to deliver, checking the accuracy of its output and behavior. Since the feature is still not implemented, the test is going to fail, and so the developer's job is to build the feature in such a way that it passes the test.

Unit testing is quite controversial. While test-driven development is beneficial for ensuring code quality and maintenance over time, not everybody undertakes unit testing in the daily development workflow. Why is that? Well, building tests while we develop our code can feel like a burden sometimes. Especially when the test results become larger than the piece of functionality it aims to test.

However, the arguments in favor of testing outnumber the arguments against it:

- Building tests contributes to better code design. Our code must conform to the test requirements and not the other way around. If we try to test an existing piece of code and we find ourselves blocked at some point, the chances are that the code is not well designed and requires some rethinking. On the other hand, building testable features can help with early detection of side effects.

- Refactoring tested code is the lifeline against introducing bugs in later stages. Development is meant to evolve with time, and with every refactor, the risk of introducing a bug is high. Unit tests are an excellent way to ensure that we catch bugs at an early stage, either when introducing new features or updating existing ones.
- Building tests is an excellent way to document our code. It becomes a priceless resource when someone not acquainted with the code base takes over the development endeavor.

These are only a few arguments, but you can find countless resources on the web about the benefits of testing your code. If you do not feel convinced yet, give it a try; otherwise, let's continue with our journey and look at the overall form of a test.

The anatomy of a unit test

There are many different ways to test a piece of code. In this chapter, we will look at the anatomy of a test—the different parts that it's made of. To test any code, we need two things: a framework for writing the test and a runner to run it on. The test framework should provide utility functions for building test suites, containing one or several test specs each. As a result, unit testing involves the following concepts:

- **Test suite**: A suite that creates a logical grouping for a bunch of tests. A suite, for example, can contain all the tests for a specific feature.
- **Test spec**: The actual unit test.

We are going to use **Jasmine**, a popular test framework, which is also used by default in Angular CLI projects. Here is how a unit test looks in Jasmine:

```
describe('Calculator', () => {
  it('should add two numbers', () => {
    expect(1+1).toBe(2);
  });
});
```

The `describe` method is used to define a test suite and accepts a name and an arrow `function` as parameters. The arrow `function` is the body of the test suite and contains several unit tests. The `it` method is used to define a single unit test. It accepts a name and an arrow `function` as parameters.

Each test spec checks out a specific functionality of the feature described in the suite name and declares one or several expectations in its body. Each expectation takes a value, called the expected value, which is compared against an actual value using a matcher `function`. The `function` checks whether the expected and actual values match accordingly, which is called an **assertion**. The test framework passes or fails the spec depending on the result of such assertions. In the previous example, `1+1` will return the actual value that is supposed to match the expected value, `2`, which is declared in the `toBe` matcher `function`.

> **Important Note**
>
> The Jasmine framework contains various matcher functions according to the user specific needs, as we will see later in the chapter.

Suppose that the previous code contains another mathematical operation that needs to be tested. It would make sense to group both operations under one suite:

```
describe('Calculator', () => {
  it('should add two numbers', () => {
    expect(1+1).toBe(2);
  });

  it('should subtract two numbers', () => {
    expect(1-1).toBe(0);
  });
});
```

So far, we have learned about test suites and how to use them to group tests according to their functionality. Furthermore, we have learned about invoking the code we want to test and affirming that it does what we think it does. There are, however, more concepts involved in unit tests that are worth knowing about, namely the setup and tear-down functionalities.

A setup functionality is something that prepares your code before you start running the tests. It's a way to keep your code cleaner so that you can focus on just invoking the code and checking the assertions. A tear-down functionality is the opposite of a setup functionality and is responsible for tearing down what we initially set up, which is involved in activities such as cleaning up resources. Let's see what this looks like in practice with a code example:

```
describe('Calculator', () => {
  let total: number;

  beforeEach(() => total = 1);

  it('should add two numbers', () => {
    total = total + 1;
    expect(total).toBe(2);
  });

  it('should subtract two numbers', () => {
    total = total - 1;
    expect(total).toBe(0);
  });

  afterEach(() => total = 0);
});
```

The `beforeEach` method is used for the setup functionality, and it runs before every unit test. In this example, we set the value of the `total` variable to `1` before each test. The `afterEach` method is used to run tear-down logic. After each test, we reset the value of the `total` variable to `0`.

It is therefore evident that the test only has to care about invoking application code and asserting the outcome, which makes tests cleaner; however, in a real-world application, tests tend to have much setup going on. Most importantly, the `beforeEach` method tends to make it easier to add new tests, which is great. What you want at the end of the day is well-tested code; the easier it is to write and maintain such code, the better for your software.

Now that we have covered the basics of a unit test, let's see how we can put them in action in the context of the Angular framework.

Introducing unit tests in Angular

In the previous section, we familiarized ourselves with unit testing and its general concepts, such as test suites, test specs, and assertions. It is now time to venture into unit testing with Angular, armed with that knowledge. Before we start writing tests for Angular, though, let's have a look at the tooling that the Angular framework and the Angular CLI provide us to make unit testing a pleasant experience:

- **Jasmine**: We have already learned that this is the testing framework.
- **Karma**: The test runner for running our unit tests.
- **Angular testing utilities**: A set of helper methods that assist us in setting up our unit tests and writing our assertions in the context of the Angular framework.

Configuring Karma as the test runner

In terms of configuration, when using the Angular CLI, we don't have to do anything to make it work. As soon as we create a new Angular CLI project, unit testing works out of the box. As we venture deeper into unit testing in Angular, we need to be aware of a few concepts that leverage our ability to test different artifacts, such as components and directives. The Angular CLI uses Karma as the test runner. As we learned in *Chapter 5, Structure an Angular App*, the `karma.conf.js` file is responsible for configuring the Karma test runner. In this file we can specify the following:

- Various plugins that enhance the Karma test runner.
- The location of the tests that we need to run. There is a `files` property that specifies where to find the application code and the unit tests; however, for the Angular CLI, this property can be found in the `tsconfig.spec.json` file.
- Setup of a selected coverage tool that measures to what degree our tests cover the application code.
- Reporters that report every executed test in a console window, a browser, or by some other means.
- Different browsers to run our tests.

Using the Angular CLI, you most likely won't need to change or edit this file yourself, but it is good to know of its existence and its capabilities.

Angular testing utilities

Angular testing utilities help us to create a testing environment that makes writing tests for our Angular artifacts easy. It consists of the `TestBed` `class` and various helper methods that can be found under the `@angular/core/testing` namespace. We will learn what these are and how they can help us to test various artifacts as this chapter progresses. For now, let's have a look at the most commonly used concepts so that you are familiar with them when we look at them in more detail later on:

- The `TestBed` `class` is the most crucial concept. It essentially creates a testing module that behaves like an ordinary Angular module. In reality, when we test an Angular artifact, we detach it from the Angular module that it resides in and we attach it to this testing module. The `TestBed` `class` contains the `configureTestingModule` method that we use to set up the test module as needed.
- The `ComponentFixture` is a wrapper `class` around an Angular component instance. It allows us to interact with the component and its corresponding element.
- The `DebugElement` is also a wrapper around the DOM element of the component. It is an abstraction that operates cross platform so that our tests are platform independent.

Now that we have got to know our testing environment and the frameworks and libraries that are used, we can start writing our first unit tests in Angular. We will embark on this great journey from the most fundamental building block in Angular, the component.

Testing components

You may have noticed that every time we used the Angular CLI to scaffold a new Angular app or generate an Angular artifact, it would also create some test files for us.

Test files in the Angular CLI contain the word `spec` in their filename so that it is easier for the Karma runner to find and run them. Mainly, the filename of a test is the same as the Angular artifact that is testing followed by the suffix `.spec.ts`. For example, the test file for the main component of an Angular app, `app.component.ts`, would be `app.component.spec.ts` and would reside in the same path as the component file.

> **Important Note**
>
> We should think about an Angular artifact and its corresponding test as one thing. When we change the logic of the artifact, we need to modify the unit test as well. Placing unit test files together with their Angular artifacts makes it easier for us to remember and edit both of them. It also helps us when we need to do some refactoring to our code, such as moving artifacts (not forgetting to move the unit test as well).

The Angular CLI automatically creates a test for the main component, `AppComponent`, when we scaffold a new Angular app:

1. At the beginning of the file, there is a `beforeEach` statement that is used for setup purposes:

```
beforeEach(async(() => {
  TestBed.configureTestingModule({
    declarations: [
      AppComponent
    ],
  }).compileComponents();
}));
```

   It uses the `configureTestingModule` method of the `TestBed class` and passes an object as a parameter. The properties of this object are the same as those of the `@NgModule` decorator, and so we can take our knowledge of how to configure an Angular module and apply that to set up a testing module, as it is the same thing. We can specify a `declarations` array that contains `AppComponent`. As far as testing is concerned, `AppComponent` now belongs to the declarables of the testing module. Finally, we call the `compileComponents` method, and the setup is completed.

> **Important Note**
>
> The `compileComponents` method, as per its name, compiles components that are configured in the testing module. During the compilation process, it also inlines external CSS files as well as templates. We are not going to use this method for the rest of this chapter because Angular CLI does it for us anyway under the hood; however, do not forget that Angular testing utilities can be used with build tools other than the Angular CLI.

2. The first unit test verifies whether we can create a new instance of `AppComponent` using the `createComponent` method:

```
it('should create the app', () => {
  const fixture = TestBed.createComponent(AppComponent);
  const app = fixture.componentInstance;
  expect(app).toBeTruthy();
});
```

The result of the `createComponent` method is a `ComponentFixture` instance of the `AppComponent` type that can give us the instance of the component using the `componentInstance` property. We also use the `toBeTruthy` matcher `function` to check whether the resulting instance is valid.

3. As soon as we have access to the component instance, we can typically query its `public` properties and methods:

```
it(`should have as title 'my-app'`, () => {
  const fixture = TestBed.createComponent(AppComponent);
  const app = fixture.componentInstance;
  expect(app.title).toEqual('my-app');
});
```

In the previous test, we check whether the `title` property of the component is equal to the `my-app` value using another matcher `function`, the `toEqual`.

4. As we learned, a component consists of a TypeScript `class` and a template file. So testing it only from the class perspective, as in the previous test, is not sufficient. We should also test whether the `class` interacts correctly with the DOM:

```
it('should render title', () => {
  const fixture = TestBed.createComponent(AppComponent);
  fixture.detectChanges();
  const compiled = fixture.nativeElement;
  expect(compiled.querySelector('.content span').
  textContent).toContain('my-app app is running!');
});
```

> **Important Note**
> Many developers tend to favor class testing over DOM testing, and they rely on **end-to-end (E2E)** testing, which is slower and has poor performance. E2E tests often validate the integration of an application with a backend API and are easy to break. Thus, it is recommended that you perform DOM unit testing in your Angular apps.

We are creating the component in a similar way to what we did before, and we call the `detectChanges` method of the `ComponentFixture`. The `detectChanges` method triggers the Angular change-detection mechanism, forcing the data bindings to be updated. It executes the `ngOnInit` life cycle event of the component the first time it is called and the `ngOnChanges` in any subsequent calls, so we can then query the DOM element of the component using the `nativeElement` property. In this example, we check the `textContent` of the HTML element that corresponds to the `title` property.

To run our tests, we use the `test` command of the Angular CLI:

```
ng test
```

The previous command starts the Karma runner, fetches all unit test files, and executes them. Depending on the runner configuration, a browser will open and display the results of each test. The Angular CLI uses the Google Chrome browser by default. The output will look like this:

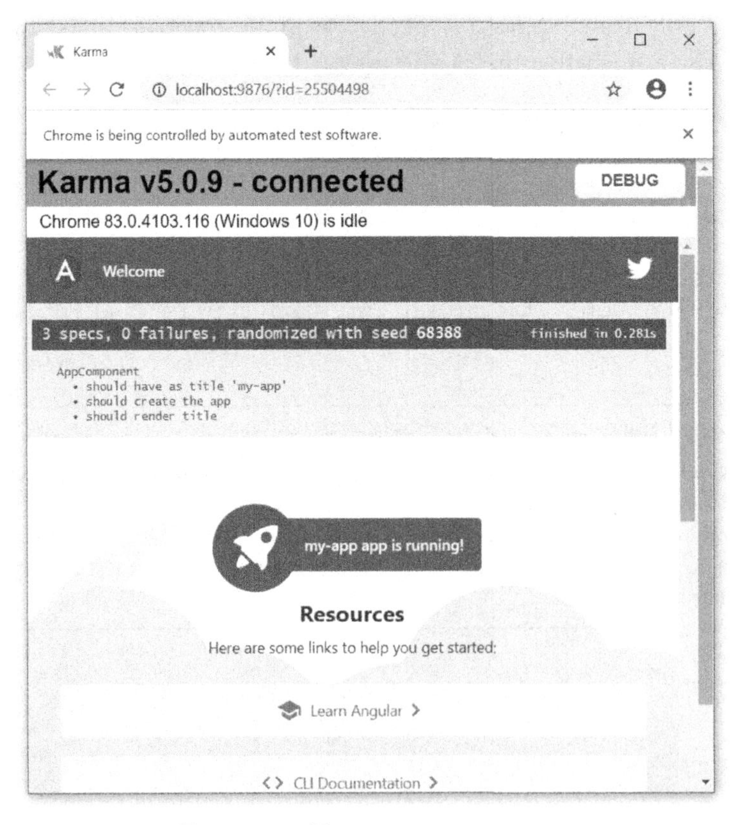

Figure 11.1 – Karma test runner output

In the previous figure, we can see the result of each test at the top of the page. We can also see how Karma visually groups each test by suite. In our case, the only test suite is the **AppComponent**.

> **Important Note**
>
> The page also renders the last component that we tested. In our case, this happens to be the `AppComponent`, since we only have one in a new Angular app. As we progress throughout the chapter, the rendered component may change because Karma runs unit tests in a random order.

Now let's make one of our tests fail. Open the `app.component.ts` file, change the value of the `title` property to `my-new-app`, and save the file. Karma will re-execute our tests and display the results on the page:

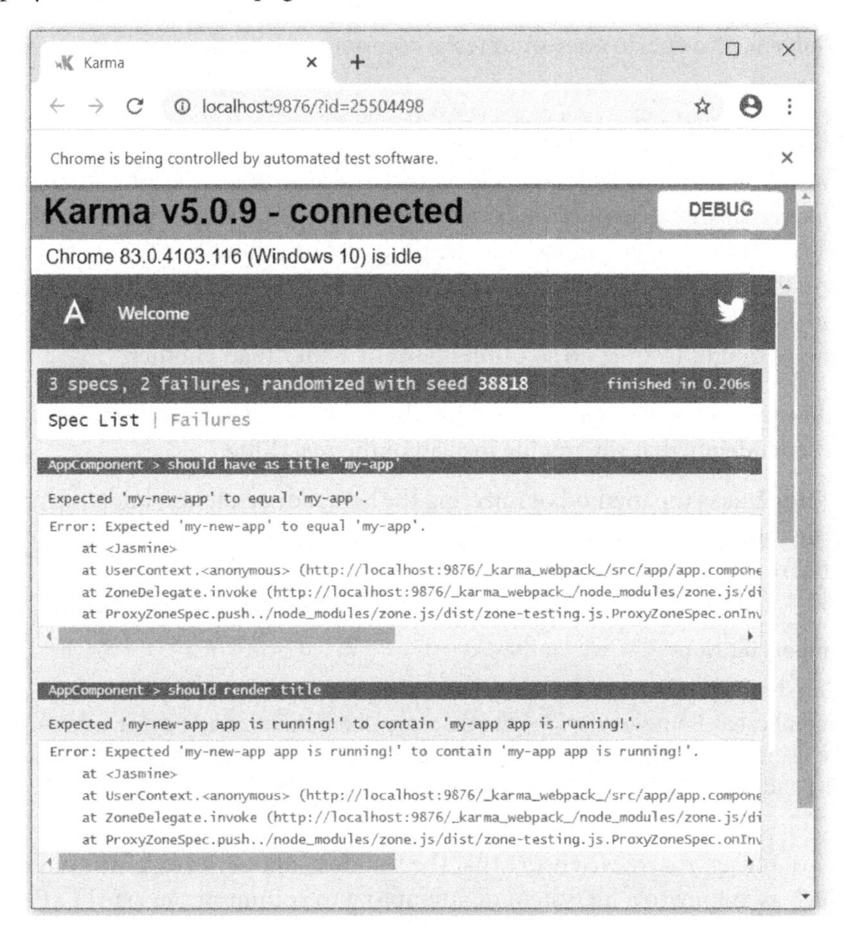

Figure 11.2 – Test failure

> **Important Note**
>
> Karma runs in watch mode, so we do not need to execute the Angular CLI test command every time we make a change.

In some cases, it is not very convenient to read the output of tests in the browser. Alternatively, we can inspect the console window that we used to run the `ng test` command, which contains a trimmed version of the test results:

```
Chrome 83.0.4103.116 (Windows 10): Executed 3 of 3 SUCCESS (0.286 secs / 0.204 secs)
TOTAL: 3 SUCCESS
TOTAL: 3 SUCCESS
```

Figure 11.3 – Console test output

We've gained quite a lot of insight just by looking at the test of `AppComponent` that Angular CLI created automatically for us. In the following section, we will have a look at a more advanced scenario on how to test a component with dependencies.

Testing with dependencies

In a real-world scenario, usually, components are not as simple as `AppComponent`. They will almost certainly be dependent on one or more services. We have different ways of dealing with testing in such a situation. One thing is clear, though: if we are testing the component, then we should not test the service as well. So when we set up such a test, the dependency should not be the real thing. There are different ways of dealing with that when it comes to unit testing; no solution is strictly better than another:

- **Stubbing**: This is the method of telling the dependency injector to inject a stub of the dependency that we provide instead of the real thing.
- **Spying**: This is the method of injecting the actual dependency, but attaching a spy to the method that we call in our component. We can then either return mock data or let the method call through.

> **Important Note**
>
> You should prefer to use stubbing over spying when a dependency is complicated. Some services inject other services in their `constructor`, so using the real dependency in a test requires you to compensate for other dependencies, too.

Regardless of the approach, we ensure that the test does not perform any unintended actions, such as talking to a filesystem or attempting to communicate via HTTP; that is, we are testing the component in complete isolation.

Replacing the dependency with a stub

Replacing a dependency with a stub means that we completely replace the dependency with a fake one. We can create a fake dependency in one of two ways:

- Create a constant variable that contains properties and methods of the real dependency.
- Create a mock definition of the actual `class` of the dependency.

Both approaches are not so different. In this section, we will look at the first one. Feel free to explore the second one at your own pace. Consider the following component:

stub.component.ts

```
import { Component, OnInit } from '@angular/core';
import { StubService } from '../stub.service'

@Component({
  selector: 'app-stub',
  template: `<span>{{msg}}<span>`
})
export class StubComponent implements OnInit {

  msg: string;

  constructor(private stub: StubService) { }

  ngOnInit() {
    this.msg = !this.stub.isBusy
      ? this.stub.name + ' is available'
      : this.stub.name + ' is on a mission';
  }

}
```

It injects `StubService` that contains just two `public` properties. Providing a stub for this service would be pretty straightforward, as shown in the following example:

```
const serviceStub: Partial<StubService> = {
  name: 'Boothstomper'
};
```

We have declared the service as `Partial` because we want to only set the `name` property initially. We can now use the object-literal syntax to inject the stub service in our testing module:

```
TestBed.configureTestingModule({
  declarations: [StubComponent],
  providers: [
    { provide: StubService, useValue: serviceStub }
  ]
});
```

The `msg` property of the component relies on the value of the `isBusy` `boolean` property of the service. Therefore, we need to get a reference to the service in the test suite and provide alternate values for this property in each test. We can get the injected instance of `StubService` using the `inject` method of the `TestBed` `class`:

```
beforeEach(() => {
  TestBed.configureTestingModule({
    declarations: [StubComponent],
    providers: [
      { provide: StubService, useValue: serviceStub }
    ]
  });
  fixture = TestBed.createComponent(StubComponent);
  component = fixture.componentInstance;

  msgDisplay = fixture.nativeElement.querySelector('span');
  service = TestBed.inject(StubService);
});
```

Important Note

We pass the real `StubService` as a parameter to the `inject` method and *not* the stubbed version that we created. Modifying the value of the stub will not have any effect on the injected service since our component uses an instance of the real service. The `inject` method asks the root injector of the application for the requested service. If the service was provided from the component injector, we would need to get it from the component injector using `fixture.debugElement.injector.get(StubService)`.

We can now write our tests to check whether the `msg` property of the component behaves correctly during data binding:

```
describe('status', () => {
  it(<should be on a mission>, () => {
    service.isBusy = true;
    fixture.detectChanges();
    expect(msgDisplay.textContent).
    toContain('is on a mission');
  });

  it('should be available', () => {
    service.isBusy = false;
    fixture.detectChanges();
    expect(msgDisplay.textContent).toContain('is available');
  });
});
```

Stubbing a dependency is not always viable, especially when the root injector does not provide it. A service can be provided in the component injector level. Providing a stub using the process we saw earlier doesn't have any effect. So how do we tackle such a scenario? We are using the `overrideComponent` method of the `TestBed class`:

```
TestBed.configureTestingModule({
  declarations: [StubComponent],
}).overrideComponent(StubComponent, {
  set: {
    providers: [
      { provide: StubService, useValue: serviceStub }
```

```
      ]
    }
  });
```

The `overrideComponent` method accepts two parameters: the type of component that provides the service and an override metadata object. The metadata object contains a property `set` that is used to provide services to the component.

Stubbing a dependency is very simple, but it is not always possible, as we will see in the following section.

Spying on the dependency method

The previously mentioned approach, using a stub, is not the only way to isolate ourselves in a unit test. We don't have to replace the entire dependency—only the parts that our component is using. Replacing certain parts means that we point out specific methods on the dependency and assign a spy to them. A spy can answer what you want it to answer, but you can also see how many times it was called and with what arguments. So a spy gives you a lot more information about what is going on.

There are two ways to set up a spy in a dependency:

- Inject the actual dependency and spy on its methods.
- Use the `createSpyObj` method of Jasmine to create a fake instance of the dependency. We can then spy on the methods on this dependency as we would with the real one.

Let's see how to set up the first case. Consider the following component that uses the `Title` service of the Angular framework:

spy.component.ts

```
import { Component, OnInit } from '@angular/core';
import { Title } from '@angular/platform-browser';

@Component({
  selector: 'app-spy',
  template: '{{caption}}'
})
export class SpyComponent implements OnInit {

```

```
  caption: string;

  constructor(private title: Title) { }

  ngOnInit() {
    this.title.setTitle('My Angular app');
    this.caption = this.title.getTitle();
  }

}
```

> **Important Note**
>
> The `Title` service is used to interact with the title of the HTML document of an Angular app and can be imported from the `@angular/platform-browser` npm package.

We do not have any control over the `Title` service since it is built into the framework. It may have dependencies that we are not aware of. The easiest and safest way to use it in our tests is by spying on its methods. We inject it normally in the `providers` property of the testing module and then use it in our test like this:

```
it('should set the title', () => {
  const title = TestBed.inject(Title);
  const spy = spyOn(title, 'setTitle');
  fixture.detectChanges();
  expect(spy.calls.mostRecent().args[0]).
  toBe('My Angular app');
});
```

We use the `spyOn` method of Jasmine that accepts two parameters: the object to spy on and the specific method. Note that we use it before calling the `detectChanges` method since we want to attach the spy before triggering the `ngOnInit` lifecycle hook. The `expect` statement then validates the arguments passed in the `setTitle` method. There are cases where a service method might be called many times throughout the lifecycle of a component, so it is safer to check the most recent call, as we do in this case with the `spy.calls.mostRecent` method.

Our component also uses another method of the `Title` service—the `getTitle` method—to get the title of the document. We can leverage the second case, which we defined before, to spy on the method and return mock data:

1. First of all, we need to define the `Title` service as a spy object:

```
let titleSpy: jasmine.SpyObj<Title>;
```

2. We use the `createSpyObj` method to initialize the spy object, passing two parameters: the name of the service and an array of the method names that the component currently uses:

```
titleSpy = jasmine.
createSpyObj('Title', ['getTitle', 'setTitle']);
```

3. We attach a spy to the `getTitle` method and return a custom title using the `returnValue` method of Jasmine:

```
titleSpy.getTitle.and.returnValue('My title');
```

As soon as we add it to the `providers` array of the testing module, we can use it in our tests. The resulting test suite should look like the following:

```
let titleSpy: jasmine.SpyObj<Title>;

beforeEach(() => {
  titleSpy = jasmine.
createSpyObj('Title', ['getTitle', 'setTitle']);
  titleSpy.getTitle.and.returnValue('My title');

  TestBed.configureTestingModule({
    declarations: [SpyComponent],
    providers: [
      { provide: Title, useValue: titleSpy }
    ]
  });
  fixture = TestBed.createComponent(SpyComponent);
  component = fixture.componentInstance;
});

it('should get the title', () => {
```

```
    fixture.detectChanges();
    expect(fixture.nativeElement.textContent).
  toContain('My title');
  });
```

Very few services are well behaved and straightforward, such as the `Title` service, in the sense that they are synchronous. Most of the time, they are asynchronous and can return either observables or promises. In the following section, we will learn in detail how to test such scenarios.

Testing asynchronous services

Angular testing utilities provide two artifacts to tackle asynchronous testing scenarios:

- `async`: An asynchronous approach to unit test async services. It is combined with the `whenStable` method of `ComponentFixture`.
- `fakeAsync`: A synchronous approach to unit test async services. It is used in combination with the `tick` function.

Both approaches provide roughly the same functionality; they only differ in the way that we use them.

> **Important Note**
> A notable limitation of the `fakeAsync` is that it cannot be used when the body of the test makes an `XMLHttpRequest` call, which is a rare case.

Let's see how we can use each one by looking at an example. Consider the following component that displays a list of items:

async.component.ts

```
import { Component, OnInit } from '@angular/core';
import { Observable } from 'rxjs';
import { AsyncService } from '../async.service';

@Component({
  selector: 'app-async',
  template: `
    <p *ngFor="let hero of data$ | async">
      {{hero}}
```

```
    </p>
  `
})
export class AsyncComponent implements OnInit {

  data$: Observable<string[]>;

  constructor(private asyncService: AsyncService) { }

  ngOnInit() {
    this.data$ = this.asyncService.getData();
  }

}
```

It injects the `AsyncService` and calls its `getData` method inside the `ngOnInit` method. As we can see, the `getData` method of the `AsyncService` returns an observable of strings. It also introduces a slight delay so that the scenario looks asynchronous:

```
getData(): Observable<string[]> {
  return of(heroes).pipe(delay(500));
}
```

The unit test queries the native element of the component and checks whether the `ngFor` directive loops through the `data$` observable correctly:

```
it('should get data with async', async(() => {
  fixture.detectChanges();

  fixture.whenStable().then(() => {
    fixture.detectChanges();
    expect(fixture.nativeElement.querySelectorAll(‹p›).length).
    toBe(5);
  });
}));
```

We wrap the body of the test inside the `async` method, and initially, we call the `detectChanges` method to trigger the `ngOnInit` lifecycle hook. Furthermore, we call the `whenStable` method that returns a promise, which is resolved immediately when the `data$` observable is complete. When the promise is resolved, we call `detectChanges` once more to trigger data binding and query the DOM accordingly.

> **Important Note**
>
> The `whenStable` method is also used when we want to test a component that contains a template-driven form. The asynchronous nature of this method makes us prefer using reactive forms in our Angular apps.

If you are sure that you are going to run your tests in a modern evergreen browser or some other environment that supports the new `async/await` syntax, then you can easily refactor the unit test as follows:

```
it('should get data with async/await', async () => {
  fixture.detectChanges();

  await fixture.whenStable();
  fixture.detectChanges();
  expect(fixture.nativeElement.querySelectorAll(‹p›).length).
  toBe(5);
});
```

In this approach, we have unwrapped the test body from the `async` *method* and replaced it with the `async` *keyword*. We added the `await` keyword in front of the `whenStable` method call and now it looks more readable and synchronous.

An alternative synchronous approach would be to use the `fakeAsync` method and write the same unit test as follows:

```
it('should get data with fakeAsync', fakeAsync(() => {
  fixture.detectChanges();

  tick(500);
  fixture.detectChanges();
  expect(fixture.nativeElement.querySelectorAll(‹p›).length).
  toBe(5);
}));
```

In the previous snippet, we have wrapped the test body in a `fakeAsync` method and replaced `whenStable` with `tick`. The `tick` method advances the time by *500 ms*, which is the virtual delay that we introduced in the `getData` method of `AsyncService`.

Testing components with asynchronous services can sometimes become a nightmare. Still, each of the described approaches can significantly help us in this task; however, components are not only about services but also input and output bindings. In the following section, we will learn how to test the public API of a component.

Testing with inputs and outputs

So far, we have learned how to test components with simple properties and tackle dependencies, and synchronous and asynchronous services. But there is more to a component than that. As we learned in *Chapter 3, Component Interaction and Inter-Communication*, a component has a public API that consists of inputs and outputs that should be tested as well.

Since we want to test the public API of a component, it makes sense to test how it interacts when hosted from another component. Testing such a component should be done in two ways:

- We should verify that our input binding is correctly set.
- We should verify that our output binding triggers correctly and that what it emits is received.

Suppose that we have the following simple component with an input and output binding:

bindings.component.ts

```
import { Component, Input, Output, EventEmitter } from '@
angular/core';

@Component({
  selector: 'app-bindings',
  template: `
    <p>{{title}}</p>
    <button (click)="liked.emit()">Like!</button>
  `
})
export class BindingsComponent {
```

```
  @Input() title: string;
  @Output() liked = new EventEmitter();
}
```

Before we start writing our tests, we should create a test host component that is going to use the component under test:

```
@Component({
  template: '<app-bindings [title]="testTitle"
  (liked)="isFavorite = true"></app-bindings>'
})
export class TestHostComponent {
  testTitle = 'My title';
  isFavorite: boolean;
}
```

Note that in the setup phase, we declare both components in the testing module, but the `ComponentFixture` is of the `TestHostComponent` type:

```
let component: TestHostComponent;
let fixture: ComponentFixture<TestHostComponent>;

beforeEach(() => {
  TestBed.configureTestingModule({
    declarations: [
      BindingsComponent,
      TestHostComponent
    ]
  });
  fixture = TestBed.createComponent(TestHostComponent);
  component = fixture.componentInstance;
  fixture.detectChanges();
});
```

We follow this approach because we want to test `BindingsComponent` when it is used with a host component, not by itself. Our unit tests will validate the behavior of `BindingsComponent` when interacting with `TestHostComponent`.

The first test checks whether the input binding to the `title` property has been applied correctly:

```
it('should display the title', () => {
  const titleDisplay: HTMLElement = fixture.nativeElement.
  querySelector(<p>);
  expect(titleDisplay.textContent).toBe(component.testTitle);
});
```

The second one validates whether the `isFavorite` property is wired up correctly with the `liked` output event:

```
it('should emit the liked event', () => {
  const button: HTMLButtonElement = fixture.nativeElement.
  querySelector('button');
  button.click();
  expect(component.isFavorite).toBeTrue();
});
```

In the previous test, we query the DOM for the `button` element using the `nativeElement` property of `ComponentFixture` and then click on it for the output event to emit. Alternatively, we could have used the `debugElement` property to find the `button` element and use its `triggerEventHandler` method to click on it:

```
it('should emit the liked event using debugElement', () => {
  const button: DebugElement = fixture.debugElement.query(By.
  css('button'));
  button.triggerEventHandler('click', null);
  expect(component.isFavorite).toBeTrue();
});
```

We are using the `query` method that accepts a predicate `function` as a parameter. The predicate uses the `css` method of the `By class` to locate an element by its CSS selector.

> **Important Note**
>
> As we learned in the *Introducing unit tests in Angular* section, the `debugElement` is framework agnostic. If you are sure that your tests are only going to run in a browser, you should go with the `nativeElement` property.

The `triggerEventHandler` method accepts two parameters. The first is the name of the event to trigger; in our case, it is the `click` event. The second one is additional optional data that we can pass to the event, such as which mouse button was clicked.

We could have avoided a lot of code if we had tested our `BindingsComponent` as standalone, and it would still have been valid. But we would have missed the opportunity to test it as a real-world scenario. The public API of a component is intended to be used by other components, so we should test it in this way.

We have gone through many ways on how to test a component with a dependency. Now it is time to learn how to test the dependency by itself.

Testing services

As we learned in *Chapter 5, Structure an Angular App*, a service can inject other services to use them as well. Testing a standalone service is pretty straightforward: we get an instance from the injector and then start to query its `public` properties and methods.

> **Important Note**
>
> We are only interested in testing the public API of a service, which is the interface that components and other artifacts interact with. Private symbols do not have any value in being tested, except if they have any public side effects. For example, a `public` method can call a `private` one that may set a `public` property as a side effect.

There are three different types of test that we can perform in a service:

- Testing a synchronous operation, such as a method that returns a simple array
- Testing an asynchronous operation, such as a method that returns an observable
- Testing services with dependencies, such as a method that makes HTTP requests

Let's go through each of them in more detail in the following sections.

Testing a synchronous method

Before starting to write our tests, we need to set up our testing module:

```
let service: AsyncService;

beforeEach(() => {
```

```
    TestBed.configureTestingModule({});
    service = TestBed.inject(AsyncService);
  });
```

The `AsyncService` is not dependent on anything, and it is also provided with the root injector of the Angular app, so we pass an empty object to the `configureTestingModule` method. We can then get an instance of the service under test using the `inject` method of the `TestBed class`.

> **Important Note**
>
> When a service is provided from an injector other than the root, we should add it to the `providers` property of the testing module, as we did with the components.

The first test is pretty straightforward as it calls the `setData` method and inspects its result:

```
it('should set data', () => {
  const result = service.setData('Fake hero');
  expect(result.length).toBe(6);
});
```

Writing a test for synchronous methods is relatively easy most of the time; however, things are different when we want to test an asynchronous method.

Testing an asynchronous method

The second test is a bit tricky because it involves an observable. We need to subscribe to the `getData` method and inspect the value as soon as the observable is complete:

```
it('should get data', (done: DoneFn) => {
  service.getData().subscribe(heroes => {
    expect(heroes.length).toBe(5);
    done();
  });
});
```

Karma does not know when an observable is going to complete, so we provide the `done` method to signal that the observable has completed, and the framework can now assert the `expect` statement.

Testing services with dependencies

Testing services with dependencies is similar to testing components with dependencies. Every different way that we saw in the *Testing components* section can be applied in exactly the same way; however, we follow a different approach when testing a service that injects `HttpClient`. Consider the following service that makes HTTP requests to an imaginary backend API:

data.service.ts

```
import { Injectable } from '@angular/core';
import { HttpClient } from '@angular/common/http';
import { Observable } from 'rxjs';

@Injectable({
  providedIn: 'root'
})
export class DataService {

  constructor(private http: HttpClient) { }

  getHeroes(): Observable<string[]> {
    return this.http.get<string[]>('api/heroes');
  }

  addHero(name: string) {
    return this.http.post<string>('api/heroes', {hero: name});
  }

}
```

Angular testing utilities provide two artifacts for mocking HTTP requests in unit tests: the `HttpClientTestingModule` that replaces `HttpClientModule` and the `HttpTestingController` that mocks the `HttpClient` service. We can import both of them from the `@angular/common/http/testing` namespace:

```
TestBed.configureTestingModule({
  imports: [HttpClientTestingModule]
});
httpTestingController = TestBed.inject(HttpTestingController);
```

Our tests do not make a real HTTP request. They only need to validate that it will be made with the correct options and that we will receive a proper answer. The following is the first test that validates the `getHeroes` method:

```
it('should get heroes', () => {
  const heroes = [‹Boothstomper', 'Drogfisher'];
  service.getHeroes().subscribe(heroes => expect(heroes.
  length).toBe(2));
  const req = httpTestingController.expectOne('api/heroes');
  expect(req.request.method).toEqual('GET');
  req.flush(heroes);
});
```

We initiate a fake request using the `expectOne` method of the `HttpTestingController` that takes a URL as an argument. The `expectOne` method not only creates a mock request object that we can inspect, but also asserts that only one request is made to the specific URL. After we have created our request, we can validate that its method is `GET` and return a response using the `flush` method. The response from the `flush` method is used when we call the `getHeroes` method that we want to test and subscribe to it.

We follow a similar approach when testing a **POST** method, except that we need to make sure that the body of the request contains proper data:

```
it('should add a hero', () => {
  service.addHero('Bloodyllips').subscribe();
  const req = httpTestingController.expectOne('api/heroes');
  expect(req.request.method).toEqual('POST');
  expect(req.request.body).toEqual({hero: 'Bloodyllips'})
  req.flush('');
});
```

In this case, we do not care about a response, so we pass an empty string to the `flush` method.

In the following section, we continue our journey through the testing world by learning how to test a pipe.

Testing pipes

As we learned in *Chapter 4, Enhance Components with Pipes and Directives*, a pipe is a TypeScript `class` that implements the `PipeTransform interface`. It exposes a `transform` method that is usually synchronous, which means that it is straightforward to test. Let's create a simple pipe that converts a comma-separated `string` into a list:

list.pipe.ts

```
import { Pipe, PipeTransform } from '@angular/core';

@Pipe({
  name: 'list'
})
export class ListPipe implements PipeTransform {

  transform(value: string): string[] {
    return value.split(',');
  }

}
```

Writing a test for it is really simple. The only thing that we need to do is to instantiate an object of `ListPipe` and verify the outcome of the `transform` method with some mock data:

```
it('should return an array', () => {
  const pipe = new ListPipe();
  expect(pipe.transform('A,B,C')).toEqual(['A', 'B', 'C']);
});
```

It is worth noting that Angular testing utilities are not involved when testing a pipe. We just create an instance of the pipe `class`, and we can start calling methods. Pretty simple!

In the following section, we take a look at a more advanced testing scenario—that of routing.

Testing routing

Just like components, routes play an essential role in the way our applications deliver an efficient user experience. As such, route testing becomes paramount in ensuring a flawless performance. There are different things that we can do with routing, and we need to test for different scenarios:

- Ensure that the navigation targets the right route URL.
- Ensure that the correct parameters are made available so you can fetch the correct data for the component or filter the dataset that the component needs.
- Ensure that a particular route ends up loading the intended component.

Let's learn more about how to test all of the scenarios in the following sections.

Testing the navigation URL

The most common feature of an Angular app with routing is a component that contains some anchor elements with `routerLink` directives on them. As we learned in *Chapter 7, Navigate through Components with Routing*, a `routerLink` directive can also contain parameters such as the following:

```
<a routerLink="home">Home</a>
<a [routerLink]="['heroes', 1]">Hero</a>
```

One way to test this is to check whether `routerLink` directives have been set up correctly. But we do not want to set up routing during testing because this involves configuring a lot of moving parts. So we will need to create a directive stub for this:

router-link-directive-stub.ts

```
import { Directive, Input } from "@angular/core";

@Directive({
  selector: '[routerLink]'
})
export class RouterLinkDirectiveStub {
  @Input('routerLink') linkParams: any;
}
```

The `selector` must match that of the actual `routerLink` directive for the stubbing to work correctly. Note that we pass the `routerLink` value to the `@Input` decorator. Why is that? Well, the value that we pass to an `@Input` decorator represents an *alias* of the input binding. Instead of using the `linkParams` property to pass an input parameter in the directive, we use the `routerLink` binding to emulate the original behavior of the `routerLink` directive.

> **Important Note**
>
> The use of aliases in `@Input` decorators is not recommended for components because having two names for the same property becomes confusing.

As a result, the `linkParams` property passes the URL of the `routerLink` directive to the stub `class`.

> **Important Note**
>
> The `routerLink` directive is probably used in many places throughout an application, so we would likely want to reuse it. Consider placing reusable stubs and other helper methods in a `testing` folder inside the `src` folder of your Angular project.

Before we can start using the stub of the `routerLink` directive, we need to add it to the `declarations` property of the testing module. After that, we can write our unit test:

```
it('should set up routerLink directives', () => {
  const linkDe = fixture.debugElement.queryAll(By.
  directive(RouterLinkDirectiveStub));
  const links = linkDe.map(de => de.injector.
  get(RouterLinkDirectiveStub));
  expect(links.length).toBe(2);
  expect(links[0].linkParams).toEqual('home');
  expect(links[1].linkParams).toEqual(['heroes', 1]);
});
```

We are using another predicate `function` of the `By` `class`—the `directive` method—that can locate an Angular component or directive by its type. Since we have more than one `routerLink` directive, we use the `queryAll` method of the `debugElement` property to find them. As soon as we get the directive instance from the injector of the debug elements, we can check whether they exist and what their parameters are.

Testing route parameters

An Angular app has some components that perform routing and others that are routed to, possibly with a parameter. In the latter case, the components have the mission of digging out the value of the parameter and act accordingly such as calling a service. Consider the following component:

```
export class MenuComponent implements OnInit {

  heroId: number;

  constructor(private route: ActivatedRoute) { }

  ngOnInit() {
    this.route.paramMap.subscribe(params =>
    this.heroId = +params.get('id'));
  }

}
```

It subscribes to the `paramMap` observable of the `ActivatedRoute` service and gets the value of a parameter named `id`. Currently, we want to test whether the component gets the parameter correctly, and we do not care what it does afterward with its value, so we need to stub the `ActivatedRoute` service. It might sound a bit daunting, but it isn't.

We have already learned about the `Subject class` in *Chapter 6, Enrich Components with Asynchronous Data Services*. We could use a flavor of this `class` to build the behavior of the `paramMap` observable. With that knowledge, let's start to create our `ActivatedRouteStub`:

activated-route-stub.ts

```
import { convertToParamMap, ParamMap, Params } from '@angular/
router';
import { ReplaySubject } from 'rxjs';

export class ActivatedRouteStub {

  private subject = new ReplaySubject<ParamMap>();

```

```
  constructor(initialParams?: Params) {
    this.setParamMap(initialParams);
  }

  readonly paramMap = this.subject.asObservable();

  setParamMap(params?: Params) {
    this.subject.next(convertToParamMap(params));
  }
}
```

We define a `paramMap` observable that takes values from a `ReplaySubject` instance. We use the `asObservable` method to convert values from the `ReplaySubject` type into an observable.

> **Important Note**
>
> The `ReplaySubject` is similar to the `Subject`, except that it *replays* old values to new subscribers.

Route parameters can be set either through the `constructor` or the `setParamMap` method. We use the built-in `convertToParamMap` method to convert them into a `ParamMap` because the `ReplaySubject` variable is of the `ParamMap` type.

Now we can easily emulate the process of passing route parameters to a component in our test:

1. First of all, we create an instance of the `ActivatedRouteStub class` in the `beforeEach` statement of the setup phase and pass a value for the `id` parameter:

   ```
   const activatedRoute = new ActivatedRouteStub();
   activatedRoute.setParamMap({id: 1});
   ```

2. Then, we add the `activatedRoute` variable to the `providers` property of the testing module:

   ```
   TestBed.configureTestingModule({
     declarations: [
       MenuComponent,
       RouterLinkDirectiveStub
     ],
   ```

```
    providers: [
      { provide: ActivatedRoute, useValue: activatedRoute }
    ]
  });
```

3. Finally, in our unit test, we check whether the component property has been set from the route parameters correctly:

```
  it('should get the id parameter', () => {
    expect(component.heroId).toBe(1);
  });
```

> **Important Note**
>
> You can extend the `ActivatedRouteStub class` to support passing parameters through the `snapshot` property of the `ActivatedRoute`. We encourage you to do so!

Testing routes

So far, we have relied on stubbing to test routing in an Angular app; however, there is a way to test the behavior of real routing by incorporating `RouterTestingModule`. It is a very qualified stub version of the routing, so in that sense, there is not much difference in principle from creating our own, as we saw earlier.

The real benefit of `RouterTestingModule` is that it allows us to define only the routes that we need for our tests:

```
TestBed.configureTestingModule({
  imports: [
    RouterTestingModule.withRoutes([{
      path: 'heroes/:id',
      component: MenuComponent
    }])
  ],
  declarations: [MenuComponent]
});
```

We can then write our tests generally as we did with all the other methods, and they should work. Using this approach, we can also validate that a specific route activates the correct component. If your Angular app contains advanced routing techniques, then this should be the way to go.

Another critical aspect of route testing is the `router-outlet` directive. As we have already learned in *Chapter 7, Navigate through Components with Routing*, it is the placeholder for rendering routed components. The usual way is to provide a component stub with the appropriate `selector` and an empty `template`:

router-outlet-component-stub.ts

```
import { Component } from '@angular/core';

@Component({
  selector: 'router-outlet',
  template: ''
})
export class RouterOutletComponentStub { }
```

Instead of creating another stub, we could use the `NO_ERRORS_SCHEMA` schema from the `@angular/core` npm package and add it to the `schemas` property of the testing module:

```
TestBed.configureTestingModule({
  declarations: [
    MenuComponent,
    RouterLinkDirectiveStub
  ],
  providers: [
    { provide: ActivatedRoute, useValue: activatedRoute }
  ],
  schemas: [NO_ERRORS_SCHEMA]
});
```

With the previous snippet, the Angular compiler silently ignores any components in the template that it does not recognize.

> **Important Note**
>
> The `NO_ERRORS_SCHEMA` approach can be used for other components, but it should not be overused. Be aware that the Angular compiler will not tell you whether there are any other errors in your component, thereby preventing you from finding bugs, so use it with precaution. You should prefer stubbing most of the time.

Angular directives are an Angular artifact that we may not create very often, since the built-in collection that the framework provides is more than enough; however, if we create custom directives, we should test them as well. We will learn how to accomplish this task in the following section.

Testing directives

Directives are usually quite straightforward in their overall shape, being pretty much components with no view attached. The fact that directives usually work with components gives us a very good idea of how to proceed when testing them.

A directive can be simple in the sense that it has no external dependencies. Consider the following directive that we created in *Chapter 4, Enhance Components with Pipes and Directives*:

copyright.directive.ts

```
import { Directive, ElementRef, Renderer2 } from '@angular/
core';

@Directive({
  selector: '[appCopyright]'
})
export class CopyrightDirective {

  constructor(el: ElementRef, renderer: Renderer2) {
    renderer.addClass(el.nativeElement, 'copyright');
    renderer.setProperty(
      el.nativeElement,
      'textContent',
```

```
        `Copyright ©${new Date().getFullYear()} All Rights
        Reserved.`
      );
    }

}
```

A directive is always used in conjunction with a component, so it makes sense to unit test it while using it on a component. Let's create a test host component and add it to the `declarations` property of the testing module along with the directive under test:

```
@Component({
  template: '<span appCopyright></span>'
})
class TestHostComponent { }
```

We can now write our tests that check whether the `span` element that the directive is attached to satisfies the following criteria:

- It sets the `copyright` class.
- It displays the current year in its `textContent` property:

```
import { Component } from '@angular/core';
import { TestBed } from '@angular/core/testing';

import { CopyrightDirective } from './copyright.
directive';

@Component({
  template: '<span appCopyright></span>'
})
class TestHostComponent { }

describe('CopyrightDirective', () => {
  let container: HTMLElement;

  beforeEach(() => {
```

```
    const fixture = TestBed.configureTestingModule({
      declarations: [
        CopyrightDirective,
        TestHostComponent
      ]
    })
    .createComponent(TestHostComponent);

    container = fixture.nativeElement.
    querySelector('span');
  });

  it('should have copyright class', () => {
    expect(container.classList).toContain('copyright');
  });

  it('should display copyright details', () => {
    expect(container.textContent).toContain(new Date().
    getFullYear().toString());
  });
});
```

This is how simple it can be to test a directive. The key takeaways are that you need an element to place the directive on and that you implicitly test the directive using the element.

We will end our testing journey by looking at reactive forms.

Testing reactive forms

As we saw in *Chapter 8, Orchestrating Validation Experiences in Forms*, forms are an integral part of an Angular app. It is rare for an Angular app not to at least have a simple form , such as a search form. We have already learned that reactive forms are better than template-driven forms in many ways, and are easier to test, so in this section, we are going to focus only on testing reactive forms.

Consider the following component that behaves like a search form:

search.component.ts

```
import { Component } from '@angular/core';
import { FormControl, FormGroup, Validators } from '@angular/
forms';

@Component({
  selector: 'app-search',
  template: `
    <form [formGroup]="searchForm" (ngSubmit)="search()">
      <input type="text" placeholder="Username"
      formControlName="searchText">
      <button type="submit"
      [disabled]="searchForm.invalid">Search</button>
    </form>
  `
})
export class SearchComponent {

  get searchText(): FormControl {
    return this.searchForm.controls.searchText as FormControl;
  }
  searchForm = new FormGroup({
    searchText: new FormControl('', Validators.required)
  });

  search() {
    if(this.searchForm.valid) {
      console.log('You searched for: ' + this.searchText.value)
    }
  }
}
```

From this, we can identify three test cases:

- The `searchText` property can be set correctly.
- The `Search` button is disabled when the form is invalid.
- The `console.log` method is called when the form is valid.

For testing a reactive form, we first need to import `ReactiveFormsModule` into the testing module, as we would at runtime:

```
TestBed.configureTestingModule({
  imports: [ReactiveFormsModule],
  declarations: [SearchComponent]
});
```

For the first test, we need to test whether the value propagates to the `searchText` form control when we type something into the input control:

```
it('should set the searchText', () => {
  const input: HTMLInputElement = fixture.nativeElement.
  querySelector('input');
  input.value = 'Angular';
  input.dispatchEvent(newEvent('input'));
  expect(component.searchText.value).toBe('Angular');
});
```

We use the `querySelector` method of the `nativeElement` property to find the `input` element and set its value to `Angular`. But this alone will not be sufficient for the value to propagate to the form control. The Angular framework will not know whether the value of the `input` element has changed until we trigger a specific native DOM event to that element. The event that does the trick is the `input` event, which indicates that the value of an `input` element has changed. We are using the `dispatchEvent` method of the `input` element to trigger the event. It accepts a single method as a parameter that points to the `newEvent` method, a helper that creates a custom native event.

Now that we are sure that the `searchText` form control is wired up correctly, we can use it to write the remaining tests:

```
it('should disable search button', () => {
  component.searchText.setValue('');
  expect(button.disabled).toBeTrue();
```

```
});

it('should log to the console', () => {
  const spy = spyOn(console, 'log');
  component.searchText.setValue('Angular');
  fixture.detectChanges();
  button.click();
  expect(spy.calls.first().args[0]).
  toBe('You searched for: Angular');
});
```

Note that in the second test, we set the value of the `searchText` form control, and then we call the `detectChanges` method for the `button` to be enabled. Clicking on the button triggers the `submit` event of the form, and we can finally assert the expectation of our test.

In cases where a form has many controls, it is not convenient to query them inside our tests. Alternatively, we can create a `Page` object that takes care of querying HTML elements and spying on services:

```
class Page {
  get searchText() { return this.
  query<HTMLInputElement>('input'); }
  get submitButton() { return this.
  query<HTMLButtonElement>('button'); }

  private query<T>(selector: string): T {
    return fixture.nativeElement.querySelector(selector);
  }
}
```

We can then create an instance of the `Page` object in the `beforeEach` statement and get access to its properties and methods in our tests.

As we have seen, the nature of reactive forms makes them very easy to test since the form model is the single source of truth.

Summary

We are at the end of our testing journey, and it's been a long but exciting one. In this chapter, we saw the importance of introducing unit testing in our Angular applications, the basic shape of a unit test, and the process of setting up Jasmine for our tests.

We also learned how to write robust tests for our components, directives, pipes, routes, and services. We also discussed how to test reactive forms.

With this unit testing chapter, we have almost completed the puzzle of building a complete Angular application. Only the last piece remains, a piece that is so important because web applications are, ultimately, destined for the web. Therefore, in the next chapter, we will learn how to build our awesome application and share it with the rest of the world!

Section 4: Deployment and Practice

This section explains how to use the Angular CLI 10 to deploy an Angular 10 application to a hosting provider, and how to use the knowledge acquired to build a real-world Angular 10 application.

This part comprises the following chapters:

12 Bringing an Angular App to Production

A web application should typically run on the web and be accessible by anyone and from anywhere. As such, it needs two essential ingredients: a web server that is going to host the application and a production build of the application to deploy to that server. In this chapter, we are going to focus on the second part of the recipe. But what do we mean by production build?

In a nutshell, a production build of a web application is an optimized version of the application code that is smaller, faster, and more performant. Primarily, it is a process that takes all the code files of the application, applies optimization techniques, and converts them to a single bundle file.

In the previous chapters, we have gone through many parts that are involved when building an Angular 10 application. We need just one last piece to connect the dots and make our application available for anyone to use, which is to build it and deploy it to a web server.

In this chapter, we will do the following:

- Learn how to create a production build of an Angular 10 app
- Get to know how to limit the size of the build using budgets
- Learn how to apply optimization techniques to the build
- Investigate available built-in hosting providers and learn how to deploy to one of them

Technical requirements

The source code for this chapter can be found in the GitHub repository at `https://github.com/PacktPublishing/Learning-Angular--Third-Edition/tree/master/ch12`.

Building an Angular app

To build an Angular 10 app, we use the following command of the Angular CLI:

```
ng build
```

The build process boots up the Angular compiler that primarily collects all TypeScript files of our application code and converts them into JavaScript. An Angular application contains various TypeScript files that are not generally used during runtime, such as unit tests or tooling helpers. How does the compiler know which files to collect for the build process? Well, it reads the `files` property of the `tsconfig.app.json` file that indicates the main entry point of an Angular 10 app:

```
"files": [
  "src/main.ts",
  "src/polyfills.ts"
]
```

From there, it can go through all components, services, and other Angular artifacts that are needed by our application, as we have already learned in *Chapter 1, Building Your First Angular App*. The Angular compiler outputs the resulting JavaScript files into a folder named according to the name of the Angular CLI project, which is created inside the `dist` folder:

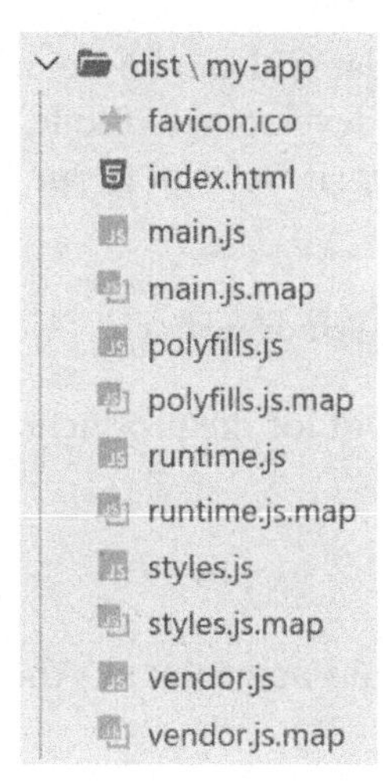

Figure 12.1 – Output folder in development mode

The output folder contains several files, including the following:

- `favicon.ico`: the icon of the Angular app
- `index.html`: the main HTML file of the Angular app
- `main.js`: contains the source code of the application that we wrote
- `polyfills.js`: contains feature polyfills for older browsers
- `runtime.js`: contains Angular CLI related code that is needed to run all other files
- `styles.js`: contains the global application CSS styles
- `vendor.js`: contains the Angular framework and any third-party libraries that we are using in the Angular app

The folder also contains several files with the `.map` extension. They are called **source map** files, and they are primarily used for debugging purposes. The `index.html` file is the same HTML file that exists in the `src` folder except that the Angular CLI has modified it so that it includes the rest of the JavaScript build files:

```
<body>
  <app-root></app-root>
<script src="runtime.js" defer></script><script src="polyfills.
js" defer></script><script src="styles.
js" defer></script><script src="vendor.js" defer></
script><script src="main.js" defer></script></body>
```

The `build` command of the Angular CLI can be run in two modes: development and production. By default, it is run in development mode. As we have already learned in *Chapter 5, Structure an Angular App*, if we want to run it in production mode, we should run the following command:

```
ng build --configuration=production
```

Alternatively, we could use a shortcut for the production configuration using the `--prod` switch:

```
ng build --prod
```

The output of the `dist` folder should now look like the following:

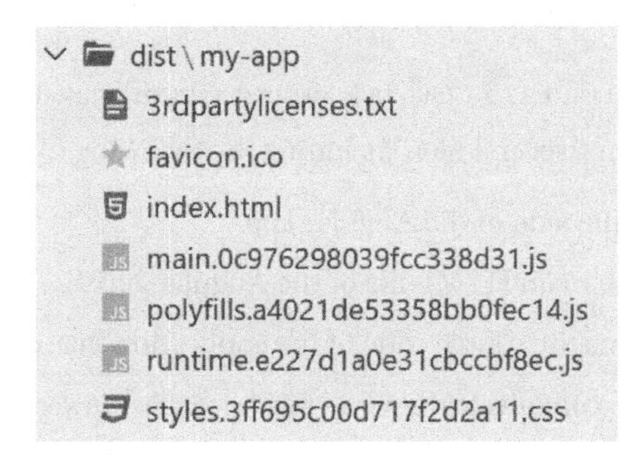

Figure 12.2 – Output folder in production mode

The Angular CLI performs various optimization techniques on the application code so that the final output is suitable for hosting in a web server and a production environment. The output folder does not contain source map files because we don't want to enable debugging in a production environment. It also adds a *hash* number to each file so that the cache of a browser will quickly invalidate them upon deploying a newer version of the application.

An Angular 10 app may use files that are not imported as ES6 modules, but instead, they need to be attached in the global `window` object, such as a third-party **jQuery** plugin. In this case, we need to tell the Angular CLI about their existence so that it can include them in the final bundle. The `angular.json` configuration file contains an `options` object in the `build` configuration that we can use to define such files. It is separated into three categories, `assets`, `styles`, and `scripts` according to the type of file that we want to include:

```
"options": {
  "outputPath": "dist/my-app",
  "index": "src/index.html",
```

```
    "main": "src/main.ts",
    "polyfills": "src/polyfills.ts",
    "tsConfig": "tsconfig.app.json",
    "aot": true,
    "assets": [
      "src/favicon.ico",
      "src/assets"
    ],
    "styles": [
      "src/styles.css"
    ],
    "scripts": []
  }
```

> **Important Note**
>
> The `assets` folder is already included, but it is empty, and that is the reason that it did not make it into the final output folder. The `styles.css` file is also included by default from the Angular CLI. It corresponds to the `styles.js` generated file in the output folder.

As we add more and more features in an Angular application, the final bundle is going to grow bigger at some point. In the following section, we'll learn how to mitigate such an effect using budges.

Limiting the application bundle size

As developers, we always want to build impressive applications that contain cool features for the end user. As such, we end up adding more and more features to our Angular app – sometimes according to the specifications and at other times to provide additional value to users. However, adding new functionality in an Angular app will cause it to grow in size, which may not be acceptable at some point. To overcome this problem, we can use Angular CLI budgets for our production build.

Budgets are thresholds that we can define in the `angular.json` configuration file and make sure that the size of our application does not exceed those thresholds. To set budgets, we can use the `budgets` property of the `production` configuration in the `build` environment:

```
"budgets": [
  {
    "type": "initial",
    "maximumWarning": "2mb",
    "maximumError": "5mb"
  },
  {
    "type": "anyComponentStyle",
    "maximumWarning": "6kb",
    "maximumError": "10kb"
  }
]
```

The Angular CLI does a pretty good job by defining some default budgets for us when creating a new Angular CLI project.

We can define a budget for different types, such as the whole Angular app or some parts of it. The threshold of a budget can be defined in bytes, kilobytes, megabytes, or a percentage of it. The Angular CLI displays a warning or throws an error when the size is reached or exceeds the defined value of the threshold.

To better understand it, let's describe the previous default example:

- A warning is shown when the size of the Angular app exceeds 2 MB and an error when it goes over 5.
- A warning is shown when the size of any component style exceeds 6 KB and an error when it goes over 10.

To see all available options that you can define when configuring budgets in an Angular app, check out the guide on the official documentation website at `https://angular.io/guide/build#configuring-size-budgets`.

Budgets are great to use when we want to provide an alert mechanism in case our Angular app grows significantly. However, they are just a level of information and precaution. In the following section, we will learn how to minimize the size of our bundle.

Optimizing the application bundle

As we learned in the *Building an Angular 10 app* section, the Angular CLI performs optimization techniques when we build an Angular 10 app in production mode. The optimization process that is performed in the application code includes modern web techniques and tools, including the following:

- **Minification**: Converts multiline source files into a single line by removing whitespaces and comments. It is a process that enables browsers to parse them faster later on.
- **Uglification**: Renames properties and methods to a non-human-readable form so that they are difficult to understand and used for malicious purposes.
- **Bundling**: Concatenates all source files of the application into a single file, called the **bundle**.
- **Tree-shaking**: Removes unused files and Angular artifacts such as components and modules, resulting in a smaller bundle.

As we can see, the Angular CLI does a tremendous job for us as far as build optimization is concerned. However, if the size of the final bundle remains considerably large, we can use the lazy-load module technique that we have already seen in *Chapter 7, Navigate through Components with Routing*.

In a nutshell, we can use the Angular router to load Angular modules upon request, when we are sure that they are not going to be used often. Thus, we reduce the size of the initial bundle dramatically because the Angular CLI creates one small bundle for each lazy-loaded module when building the application. For example, if we build the Angular app in *Chapter 7, Navigate through Components with Routing*, the output folder will look like this:

Figure 12.3 – Output folder with a lazy-loaded module in development mode

We can see that the Angular CLI has created a file named `about-about-module.js`, which is the bundle of `AboutModule` that is lazy-loaded by the router. If we had defined `AboutModule` to be eagerly loaded, the bundle would not have been created, and the source code of the module would be included in the `main.js` bundle.

The name of a lazy-loaded bundle contains the name of the related module when we build an Angular app in development mode by default, such as `about-about-module.js`. Angular renames the bundle when we build the application in production mode by appending a random number in front of the bundle filename:

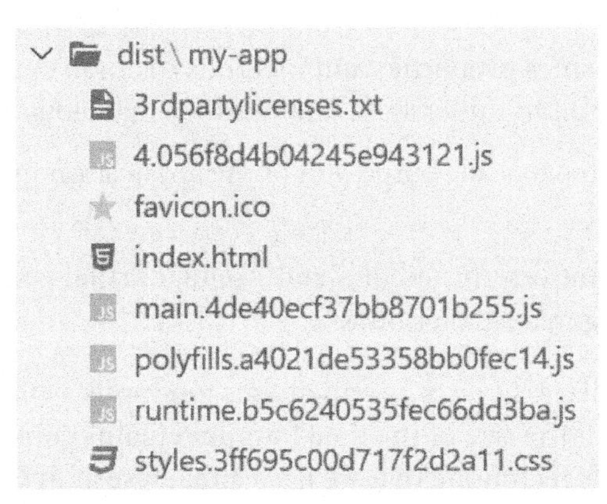

Figure 12.4 – Output folder with a lazy-loaded module in production mode

The `about-about-module.js` bundle in the previous screenshot has been replaced with `4.056f8d4b04245e943121.js`.

> **Important Note**
> A good practice when we design an Angular app is to think small at first and plan accordingly. Consider carefully which of the modules are not going to be used frequently and make them lazy-loaded. A good case for this is the menu links of a website. You can define one module for each link and load it lazily. As soon as you progress, if a module finally needs to be immediately available, make it eager-loaded. In this way, you will always start with the smallest bundle size available.

The lazy load technique also improves the launch time of an Angular app because a smaller bundle can be parsed faster from a browser.

The last resort technique when we have applied all previous optimizations, but the final bundle remains large, is using an external tool called **source-map-explorer**. It analyzes our application bundle and displays all Angular artifacts and libraries that we use in a visual representation. To start using it, do the following:

1. Install the `source-map-explorer` npm package:

```
npm install source-map-explorer --save-dev
```

2. Build your Angular app in production mode and enable source maps:

```
ng build --prod --source-map
```

3. Run the `source-map-explorer` binary against the main bundle file:

```
node_modules/.bin/source-map-explorer dist/my-app/
main.*.js
```

It will open up a visual representation of the application bundle in the default browser. We can then interact with it and inspect it so that we can understand why our bundle is still large enough. Some causes may be the following:

- A library is included twice in the bundle
- A library is included but not currently used

The last step after we build a production version of our Angular app is to deploy it to a web server, as we will learn in the following section.

Deploying an Angular app

If you already have a web server that you want to use for your shiny new Angular 10 app, simply copy the contents of the output folder to a path in your server. If you want to deploy it in another directory other than the root one, use the `--base-href` option of the `ng build` command:

```
ng build --prod --base-href=/myapp/
```

The previous command will build the Angular app in production mode and change the `href` value of the `base` tag in the `index.html` file to `/myapp/`.

If you do not want to deploy it to a custom server, you can use the Angular CLI infrastructure to deploy it in one of the built-in hosting providers that it supports out of the box, including the following:

- **Firebase hosting**: `https://firebase.google.com/docs/hosting`
- **Azure**: `https://azure.microsoft.com/en-us/`
- **Netlify**: `https://www.netlify.com/`
- **GitHub Pages**: `https://pages.github.com/`
- **Npm**: `https://npmjs.com/`

> **Important Note**
>
> Before using automatic deployment, you will probably need to create an account in the provider and configure it accordingly, a process that is out of the scope of this book.

However, the Angular CLI provides us the automation infrastructure so that we can deploy our Angular app directly from the comfort of our IDE. How? There are some third-party npm libraries, called **Angular builders**, that have implemented deployment capabilities for some of the providers mentioned previously. We can add them to an Angular CLI project and then use the Angular CLI to deploy directly to the respective provider. Let's see how easy it is to deploy a simple Angular 10 app to GitHub Pages:

1. Install the `angular-cli-ghpages` builder using the add command of the Angular CLI:

```
ng add angular-cli-ghpages
```

2. Run the `deploy` command of the Angular CLI to deploy a production version of your Angular app to GitHub Pages:

```
ng deploy
```

The Angular CLI builds the Angular 10 app in production mode and uploads it to the GitHub repository that is configured with the current Angular CLI project. That's it! Super easy and simple! The application is now available at `https://<username>.github.io/<repositoryname>`.

Summary

We finally took the last step toward the completion of our magical journey in the Angular framework. The deployment of an Angular app is the simplest and the most crucial part of the whole journey because it finally makes your awesome application available to the end user. Delivering experiences to the end user is what web applications are all about at the end of the day.

In this chapter, we learned how to build an Angular 10 app and make it ready for production. We also investigated different ways to optimize the final bundle and learned how to deploy an Angular 10 app into a custom server manually and automatically for other hosting providers.

In the next chapter, which is also the final chapter of the book, we are going to put a sample of what we have learned into practice and build a real-world Angular 10 app.

13 Develop a Real-World Angular App

We have come so far on our epic journey with the Angular framework. And what a journey! We began by setting up the environment and the tooling that enhanced our developer experience. We learned how to create components and group them in modules. We saw how to structure an Angular 10 application and how to use services to communicate via HTTP. We investigated how to apply routing in our Angular app and how to use forms to collect data from users. Finally, we saw how to build and test our Angular 10 app and deploy it to a web server.

Usually, at the end of a journey, we want to share our adventures—what we saw, what we did, and what we experienced—with other people. Don't we? Well, we are going to do something similar to share our experiences with the Angular framework. We are going to build a real-world Angular 10 app that showcases many of the exciting things that we learned during this journey.

In this chapter, we will do the following:

- Scaffold an Angular 10 app and break it down into features
- Design the layout of the application and build its core features
- Create a heroes feature to manage superheroes using CRUD techniques
- Create a missions feature to assign missions to heroes

Technical requirements

The source code for this chapter can be found in the GitHub repository at `https://github.com/PacktPublishing/Learning-Angular--Third-Edition/tree/master/ch13`.

Scaffolding the application structure

You may have noticed that the content of this book is all about heroes. After all, we are heroes in our everyday life – heroes of software development. So, the Angular 10 app that we want to create is not going to deviate from that.

We are going to create an **Angular Heroes Registry**. In a nutshell, the user of the application will be able to manage heroes and assign them to missions. The main features of the application are as follows:

- Displaying a list of heroes
- Adding a new hero
- Assigning a new mission to a hero
- Marking a mission as completed

For the design of the application, we'll use Angular Material together with Angular Flex Layout, which we learned about in *Chapter 9, Introduction to Angular Material*. We'll use the built-in *Deep Purple/Amber* Angular Material theme, and we'll also include Angular Material typography. Our application looks like the following:

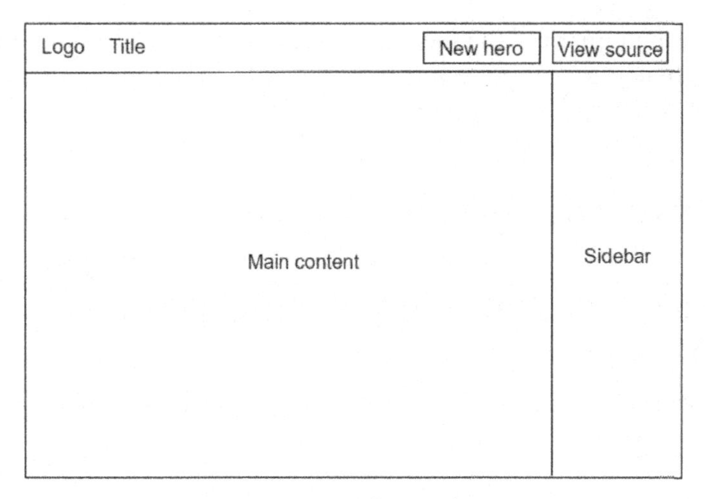

Figure 13.1 – Application layout

It consists of three main areas:

- A header that contains a title with a logo and two links – one to create a new hero and another that redirects to the source code repository of this chapter
- The main content, which displays either a list of heroes or a form to create a new hero
- A sidebar that contains information about a specific hero and any assigned missions

The application displays a list of heroes at startup by default. The sidebar is displayed when we select a hero from the list and contains the details of the selected hero. It also allows us to delete the hero or assign a new mission. Additionally, it displays a list of all the assigned missions of the selected hero, where we can select one to complete. We can always add a new hero by using the link in the header of the application.

> **Important Note**
>
> The purpose of the application is to put into practice the knowledge that we have gathered in all the previous chapters and not to be feature complete. So, expect some features that may make sense not to be covered in this chapter. However, feel free to clone the repository of the application that you will find in the *Technical requirements* section and use your Angular skills to add some more!
>
> This chapter provides a hands-on approach to what we have learned so far. Thus, we suggest that you read it along with the source code. The optimal way is to go through the source code and have the chapter as accompanying material to explain key parts of the code.

Now that we have summarized the specifications of our application and how it is going to work, let's start building it. First, we will start by building the core features that are going to be used application-wide.

Implementing core features

When we refer to core features in the application, we mean the following:

- Services that are going to be used globally in our application, such as a local cache or data access service
- Components that are going to be used only once, such as a header or footer component

In the following section, we will learn how to create a core service for handling local data.

Persisting data using local storage

In this application, we are going to use the Angular in-memory Web API that we have already seen in *Chapter 6, Enrich Components with Asynchronous Data Services.*

As we already know, it emulates the functionality of a backend API. Still, it keeps all data in memory, meaning that data will be gone when we refresh the browser, which is something that is not desirable. Thus, we are going to use the local storage of the browser as a means to persist it.

The local storage of the browser is an internal storage mechanism that can keep a limited amount of data. It is represented as key-value pairs and can be accessed using the `localStorage` JavaScript object. To use it in the Angular context, we create a wrapper Angular service:

storage.service.ts

```
import { Injectable } from '@angular/core';

@Injectable({
  providedIn: 'root'
})
export class StorageService {

  get(name: string): any[] | undefined {
```

```
    return JSON.parse(localStorage.getItem(name)) ?? undefined;
  }

  set(name: string, value: any[]) {
    localStorage.setItem(name, JSON.stringify(value));
  }

}
```

The `localStorage` object contains various methods for manipulating the local storage of the browser. We are only interested in the `get` and `set` methods, which read and write values, respectively. Each value of an entry in the local storage is of type `string`. So, if we want to store objects, we need to serialize them using the `stringify` method of the `JSON` object to set it and deserialize them using its corresponding `parse` method to get it.

> **Important Note**
>
> If we were using the `localStorage` object directly, we would limit the scope of our application only to a browser platform. It is a good practice to create wrappers for objects that are attached to the global `window` object. In this way, we can benefit from the Angular DI mechanism and inject a different service according to the platform that we are targeting.

The `get` method can return either a value from the local storage or `undefined` if it does not contain a specific key defined by `name`. In this way, we are making sure that the `parse` method of the `JSON` object will not throw an exception but instead fail gracefully.

`StorageService` is used internally from `DataService`, an Angular service that uses the Angular in-memory Web API library. We have already learned that such a service needs to implement the `createDb` method of `InMemoryDbService` to fill the in-memory database with some data:

```
createDb() {
  if (!this.storageService.get('heroes')) {
    this.storageService.set('heroes', []);
  }

  return {};
}
```

In our case, we do not want to keep data in memory, so we do not care about the return value of the `createDb` method. However, we do care about initializing our local storage so that we can interact with it later. So, initially, we add a new `heroes` entry in the local storage, if it does not exist already, that contains an empty array as a value.

We also need to provide interceptors for HTTP methods so that we can interact with `StorageService`. Each interceptor method accepts a `RequestInfo` object as a parameter that contains details about the HTTP request:

- `get`: Loads a collection from the local storage in memory and either returns the whole collection or an item of it, depending on whether there is an `id` property in the `RequestInfo` object or not. If there is an `id`, it uses the `findById` helper method to find the requested item in the collection:

```
const collection = this.storageService.get(reqInfo.
collectionName) as any[];
const result = reqInfo.id ? reqInfo.utils.
findById(collection, reqInfo.id) : collection;
```

- `post`: Uses the `getJsonBody` helper method to extract the new item from the request. It creates an `id` for the new item using the `guid` helper `function`, before appending it to the existing collection of the local storage:

```
const item = reqInfo.utils.getJsonBody(reqInfo.req);
item.id = guid();

const collection = this.storageService.get(reqInfo.
collectionName) as any[];

this.storageService.set(reqInfo.collectionName, [...
collection, item]);
```

- `put`: Loads a collection from the local storage in memory so that it can find the index of the item that needs to be updated. As soon as it finds the item, based on its `id` that's extracted from the `RequestInfo` object, it uses the `getJsonBody` helper method to replace it in the collection:

```
const collection = this.storageService.get(reqInfo.
collectionName) as any[];
const index = collection.findIndex(item => item.
id === reqInfo.id);
```

```
collection[index] = reqInfo.utils.getJsonBody(reqInfo.
req);

this.storageService.set(reqInfo.
collectionName, collection);
```

- `delete`: Loads the collection from the local storage in memory and creates a copy that does not include the `id` of the item that needs to be deleted. It then passes the filtered collection to the local storage so that it replaces the previous one:

```
const collection = this.storageService.get(reqInfo.
collectionName) as any[];
this.storageService.set(reqInfo.
collectionName, collection.filter(item => item.
id !== reqInfo.id));
```

All the previous methods return an HTTP response of status `OK` to emulate a successful response from a backend API:

```
return reqInfo.utils.createResponse$(() => {
  return { status: STATUS.OK }
});
```

The `get` method is the only one that also adds a `body` to the response that contains the requested data:

```
return reqInfo.utils.createResponse$(() => {
  return {
    body: result,
    status: STATUS.OK
  }
});
```

> **Important Note**
>
> The `DataService` has been designed so that it is model agnostic. That is, it can work with any collection that we want to pass. So, you can use your imagination to extend this service and integrate other collections that you may need.

As we have seen, core features contain not only services but also components. In the following section, we'll learn how to create a header component for our app.

Creating a header component

Our application contains a header that is loaded only once and remains rendered at all times. The header is an Angular component and exists in the `core` folder along with the services that we described in the previous section:

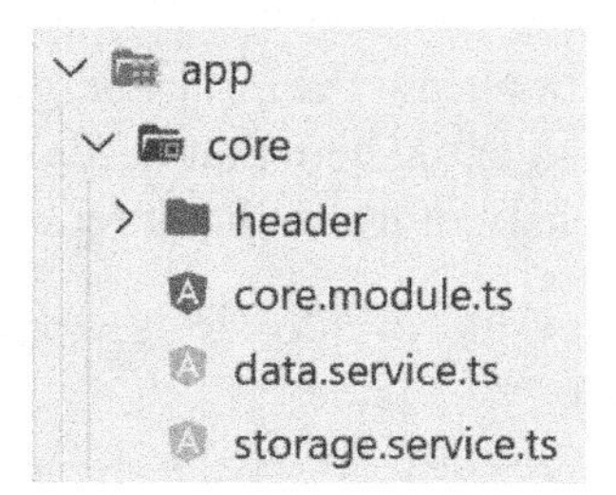

Figure 13.2 – Core folder structure

The organization of these Angular artifacts in the `core` folder does not have any special meaning as to the way that they are used in our Angular app but is instead a convention. We could have created them inside the app folder and they would work as they're supposed to. Having them in a dedicated folder is more clear, improves readability, and makes it easier to find them.

The `core` folder also contains its respective Angular module:

core.module.ts

```
import { HttpClientModule } from '@angular/common/http';
import { NgModule } from '@angular/core';
import { FlexLayoutModule } from '@angular/flex-layout';
import { RouterModule } from '@angular/router';
import { HttpClientInMemoryWebApiModule } from 'angular-in-memory-web-api';

import { AppMaterialModule } from '../app-material.module';
import { DataService } from './data.service';
import { HeaderComponent } from './header/header.component';

@NgModule({
  imports: [
    AppMaterialModule,
    FlexLayoutModule,
```

```
        HttpClientModule,
        HttpClientInMemoryWebApiModule.forRoot(DataService),
        RouterModule
    ],
    declarations: [HeaderComponent],
    exports: [HeaderComponent]
})
export class CoreModule { }
```

`CoreModule` imports several other Angular modules that our application requires. Among them, there is `AppMaterialModule`, a dedicated Angular module for Angular Material related modules. It imports and re-exports several Angular Material modules that our application may need. Whenever we want to use an Angular Material component in a module, we just need to import `AppMaterialModule` only.

We import `CoreModule` only once throughout the Angular app, into the main application module, `AppModule`. It exports `HeaderComponent` so that we can use it in the template of the main application component, `AppComponent`:

app.component.html

```
<div fxLayout="column" fxFill>
    <app-header></app-header>
    <div fxFlex class="content">
        <router-outlet></router-outlet>
    </div>
</div>
```

The main content of our application is denoted by the `div` element, which is styled with a `content` class. It contains a `router-outlet` element, which is the placeholder for loading the routed components of our app. The `app.component.html` file also defines a `column` flex layout that fills the remaining space.

The template of the header component is pretty simple:

header.component.html

```
<mat-toolbar color="primary">
    <a mat-icon-button href="https://www.angular.io/" target="_
    blank">
```

```
    <img src="assets/angular.png">
  </a>
  <h2 fxFlex>Angular Heroes Registry</h2>
  <a mat-button routerLink="new">
    <mat-icon>add</mat-icon>
    New hero
  </a>
  <a mat-button href="https://github.com/PacktPublishing/
Learning-Angular--Third-Edition/tree/master/ch13"
  target="_blank">
    <mat-icon>code</mat-icon>
    View source
  </a>
</mat-toolbar>
```

It uses a `mat-toolbar` component of the Angular Material to create a toolbar that contains the following:

- An Angular image logo that, when clicked, redirects to the official documentation website of the Angular framework
- A title named `Angular Heroes Registry`
- An anchor element that is styled as a `mat-button` component and contains a `routerLink` directive that navigates to the `new` route path
- An anchor element that is styled as a `mat-button` component and navigates to the GitHub repository of this chapter

This was the last time that we modified the main application module and component. From now on, we will work on feature modules. In the following section, we'll start building the heroes functionality of our application.

Adding heroes functionality

The primary goal of our application is to manage heroes. Thus, we need to create a feature module that groups similar functionality about heroes. The folder structure of the module should be as follows:

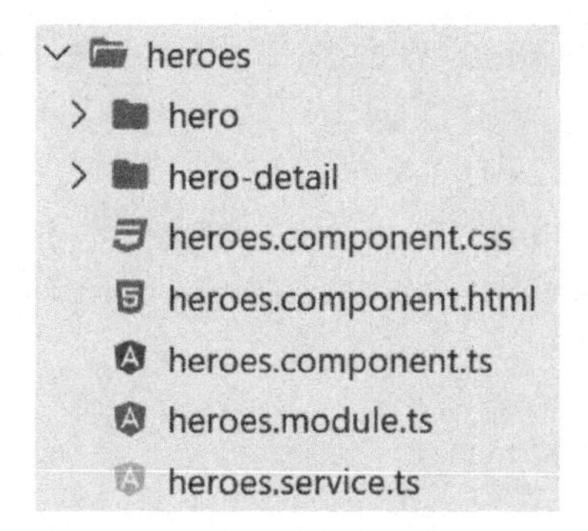

Figure 13.3 – The heroes folder structure

The `heroes` module contains the following Angular artifacts:

- `hero`: a component that is used to create a new hero
- `hero-detail`: a component that is used to display details of a specific hero
- `heroes.component.ts`: a component that hosts the list of heroes and the sidebar for displaying details of a specific hero
- `heroes.service.ts`: a service that uses the Angular HTTP client to provide CRUD operations for heroes data

> **Important Note**
>
> We have named the `heroes` host component the same as the module and placed it inside the same folder because it is the landing page of the `heroes` module. You can think of it as the main page of the feature. To create a component without a dedicated folder, we can use the `--flat` option when running the `generate` command of the Angular CLI.

The `hero` and `heroes` components are the routed components of our application. The first one is activated when the application navigates to the `new` route path. The second component is displayed when the application starts up. The routing configuration of the application is pretty simple, so we are going to use `AppRoutingModule` to define it:

app-routing.module.ts

```
import { NgModule } from '@angular/core';
import { RouterModule, Routes } from '@angular/router';

import { HeroComponent } from './heroes/hero/hero.component';
```

```
import { HeroesComponent } from './heroes/heroes.component';

const routes: Routes = [
  { path: '', component: HeroesComponent },
  { path: 'new', component: HeroComponent }
];

@NgModule({
  imports: [RouterModule.forRoot(routes)],
  exports: [RouterModule]
})
export class AppRoutingModule { }
```

We have defined two route configuration objects: one with a default empty path that loads `HeroesComponent` and another with the `new` route path that loads `HeroComponent`.

Now that we have got an insight into the `heroes` module, it is time to investigate all related artifacts in more detail. In the following section, we'll see how we can create a new hero.

Adding a new hero

We can add a new hero to our application by clicking on the **New hero** link of the header component. The application displays the following form for entering hero details:

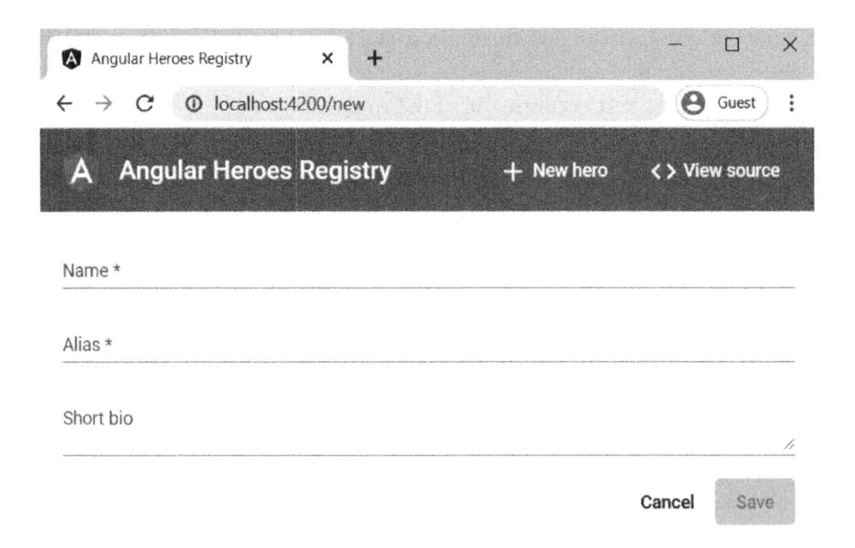

Figure 13.4 – Adding a new hero

The details of a hero are part of the `Hero` model that exists in the `core` folder of the application:

```
import { Mission } from '../core/mission';

export interface Hero {
  id: string;
  name: string;
  alias: string;
  shortBio: string;
  missions: Mission[];
}
```

> **Important Note**
>
> Each hero has a `missions` property of `Mission[]` type that is covered later in the *Integrating missions module* section.

The **Save** button is disabled until we type a value into the **Name** and **Alias** input fields that are required. We can fill in a short bio for our new hero optionally. The **Cancel** button redirects to the main landing page of the application without saving the hero.

The template of the `hero` component is as follows:

hero.component.html

```
<form class="form-
container" [formGroup]="heroForm" (ngSubmit)="save()">
  <mat-form-field>
    <mat-label>Name</mat-label>
    <input matInput formControlName="name" required>
  </mat-form-field>
  <mat-form-field>
    <mat-label>Alias</mat-label>
    <input matInput formControlName="alias" required>
  </mat-form-field>
  <mat-form-field>
    <mat-label>Short bio</mat-label>
    <textarea matInput formControlName="shortBio"></textarea>
  </mat-form-field>
```

```
  <div class="form-actions">
    <a mat-button [routerLink]="['/']">Cancel</a>
    <button mat-raised-button color="primary" type="submit"
    [disabled]="heroForm.invalid">Save</button>
  </div>
</form>
```

We have defined a `formGroup` for our form, and we have added an event binding on the `ngSubmit` form event that calls the `save` method of the component. Each field of the form contains a respective `formControlName` directive that binds it in the `HeroComponent` as follows:

```
ngOnInit() {
  this.heroForm = this.builder.group({
    name: ['', Validators.required],
    alias: ['', Validators.required],
    shortBio: ['']
  });
}
```

Required fields also contain the `required` attribute. We have already learned, that we can define whether an input control is required or not inside our component `class` and not in the template. It looks like we deviate from this rule. Why is that? We add the `required` attribute occasionally to offer advanced accessibility features in an Angular app, such as the asterisk character that is displayed in the label of the field.

The `disabled` property of the `Save` button is set according to the validity status of the form. The `Cancel` anchor element binds to the `routerLink` directive and passes the / path to navigate to the main page of our app.

The `save` method of the component calls the `createHero` method of `HeroService` to create a new hero, passing the `value` of the `heroForm` as a parameter. When the hero is created successfully, the application uses the `navigateByUrl` method of the `Router` service to navigate back to the main page of the application:

```
save() {
  this.heroService.createHero(this.heroForm.value).
  subscribe(() => this.router.navigateByUrl('/'));
}
```

> **Important Note**
>
> The `navigateByUrl` method differs from the classic `navigate` method in that it accepts an absolute representation of the URL to which we want to navigate.

After creating a new hero and redirecting to the main page, we should see the newly created hero on the list. In the following section, we'll take a look at the implementation of the component that is responsible for this behavior.

Displaying a list of heroes

The component that is responsible for displaying a list of heroes is `HeroesComponent`, and it is the main component of the `heroes` module:

```
<mat-drawer-container fxLayout="column" fxFill>
  <mat-drawer mode="over" position="end">
    <mat-tab-group>
      <mat-tab label="Details"></mat-tab>
      <mat-tab label="Missions"></mat-tab>
    </mat-tab-group>
  </mat-drawer>
  <mat-drawer-content>
    <mat-grid-list cols="4" rowHeight="250" gutterSize="10">
      <mat-grid-tile *ngFor="let hero of heroes">
        <h1>{{hero.name}}</h1>
        <mat-grid-tile-footer>
          <h3 mat-line>{{hero.alias}}</h3>
          <button mat-icon-button (click)="selectHero(hero)">
            <mat-icon>info</mat-icon>
          </button>
        </mat-grid-tile-footer>
      </mat-grid-tile>
    </mat-grid-list>
  </mat-drawer-content>
</mat-drawer-container>
```

It uses the `mat-drawer-container` component of Angular Material to create the main content area and the sidebar. The main content is indicated by the `mat-drawer-content` component and the sidebar by the `mat-drawer` component.

The sidebar is positioned at the far-right end of the page by setting the `position` property to `end`. The `mode` property indicates that the sidebar will open over the main content. The sidebar contains two tabs: one that displays the details of a specific hero and another that displays the missions assigned to that hero. We are going to discuss them later, in the following sections.

The main content contains a `mat-grid-list` component that displays a list of `mat-grid-tile` components equally spaced by *10px* from each other. Each row of the list contains four `mat-grid-tile` components where each one is *250px* tall.

It iterates over the `heroes` component property and creates one `mat-grid-tile` for each hero. Each `mat-grid-tile` displays the name of a hero and a `mat-grid-tile-footer` component. The `mat-grid-tile-footer` component displays the alias of a hero and a button to select that hero. The output should look like the following:

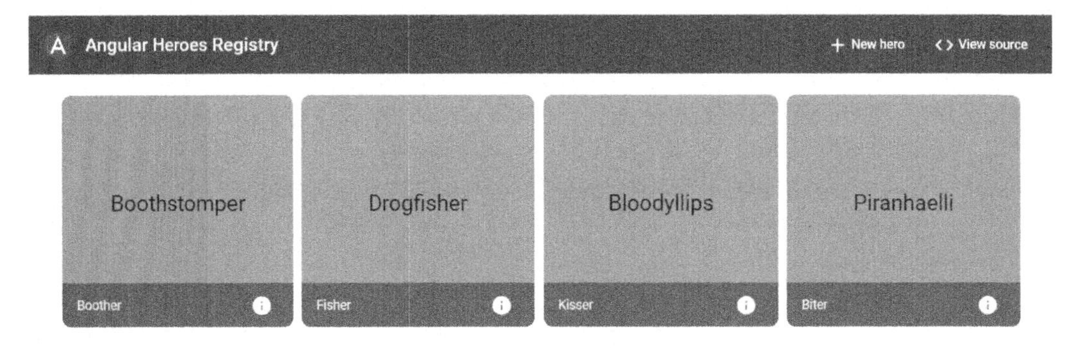

Figure 13.5 – List of heroes

The `heroes` property is set by subscribing to the `getHeroes` method of `HeroService`:

```
ngOnInit() {
  this.getHeroes();
}

private getHeroes() {
  this.heroService.getHeroes().subscribe(heroes => this.
  heroes = heroes);
}
```

Clicking on the selection button of a hero triggers the `selectHero` method of the component, passing the `hero` object as a parameter. The `selectHero` method does two things:

- Sets the `selectedHero` property of the component.
- Opens up the sidebar element. The sidebar is accessed by querying the `mat-drawer` component using the `@ViewChild` decorator. It returns a `MatDrawer` object, which contains an `open` method that we can call to open the sidebar:

```
@ViewChild(MatDrawer) private drawer: MatDrawer;

selectHero(hero: Hero) {
  this.selectedHero = hero;
  this.drawer.open();
}
```

In the following section, we'll learn more about what the `selectedHero` property does.

Taking actions on a specific hero

The `Details` tab of the sidebar contains the `app-hero-detail` component, which displays details about a selected hero:

hero-detail.component.html

```
<mat-card *ngIf="hero">
  <mat-card-header>
    <img mat-card-avatar src="assets/hero.png">
    <mat-card-title>{{hero.name}}</mat-card-title>
    <mat-card-subtitle>{{hero.alias}}</mat-card-subtitle>
  </mat-card-header>
  <mat-card-content>
    <p>{{hero.shortBio}}</p>
  </mat-card-content>
  <mat-card-actions>
    <button mat-button>Assign</button>
```

```
    <button mat-stroked-button color="warn" (click)
    ="deleteHero()">Delete</button>
  </mat-card-actions>
</mat-card>
```

It uses the `mat-card` component of Angular Material to display the hero details in a card style. The title of the card displays the name of the hero, and the subtitle displays the alias. The main content of the card displays the short bio of the hero. Finally, the card contains two action buttons. The `Assign` button assigns a new mission to the hero, which we will see in the following section. The `Delete` button deletes the hero completely. The following is a visual representation of what it looks like when selecting the **Boothstomper** hero from the list:

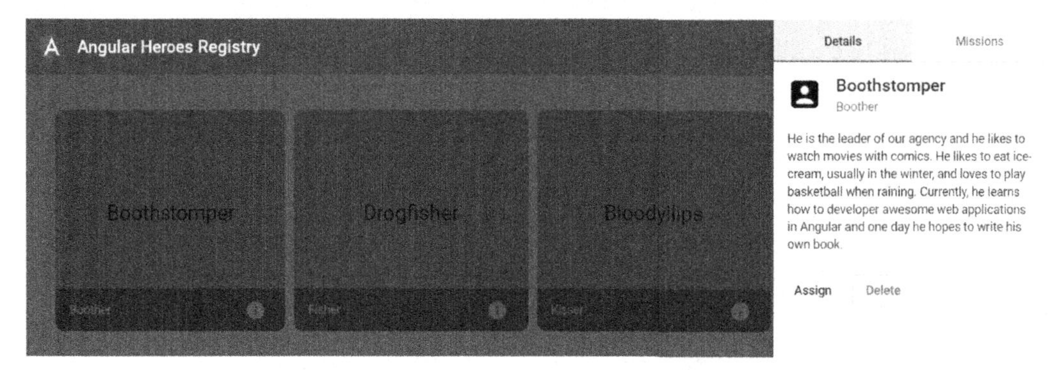

Figure 13.6 – Displaying hero details

The `HeroDetailComponent` contains an `id` input binding that is set from the `selectedHero` property. It subscribes to the `getHero` method of `HeroService` and gets hero details based on that `id`. We make a call to that method inside the `ngOnChanges` lifecycle hook because the value of the `id` changes each time the user selects a different hero from the list:

```
ngOnChanges() {
  this.hero = null;
  this.getHero();
}

private getHero() {
  this.heroService.getHero(this.id).subscribe(hero => this.
  hero = hero);
}
```

The component also contains a `delete` output binding that is triggered when we delete a hero. Upon clicking on the `Delete` button, we subscribe to the `deleteHero` method of `HeroService`. As soon as the hero is deleted, it emits the `delete` event:

```
deleteHero() {
  this.heroService.deleteHero(this.hero.id).subscribe(() =>
  this.delete.emit());
}
```

The `HeroesComponent` listens to the `delete` event and triggers its `onHeroDeleted` method, which fetches a fresh copy of the heroes list and finally closes the sidebar:

```
onHeroDeleted() {
  this.getHeroes();
  this.drawer.close();
}
```

A hero usually needs a mission to accomplish; otherwise, why should we have them? In the following section, we'll learn how to create a feature module that manages missions.

Integrating the missions module

According to the specifications of our application, a user should be able to do the following:

- Assign a new mission to a hero
- Mark a mission in progress as completed

So, we need to create a new feature module that contains functionality about missions. The folder structure of the module should be as follows:

Figure 13.7 – The missions folder structure

It contains the following Angular artifacts:

- `mission`: A component that is used to assign a new mission to a hero.
- `mission-list`: A component that is used to display a list of missions. It also allows us to complete a mission.
- `missions.service.ts`: A service that uses the HTTP client to manipulate the missions of a specific hero.

In the following section, we'll explore the first component, which allows us to assign a new mission.

Assigning a new mission

We can assign a new mission to a hero by clicking on the **Assign** button of the `HeroDetailComponent`. It calls the `assignMission` method, which uses the `MatDialog` service of Angular Material to open `MissionComponent` as a dialog:

```
assignMission() {
  this.dialog.open(MissionComponent, { data: this.hero });
}
```

It also passes the current `hero` object as a parameter to the dialog using the `data` property of the `MatDialogConfig` options.

The application displays the following form for entering the details of a new mission:

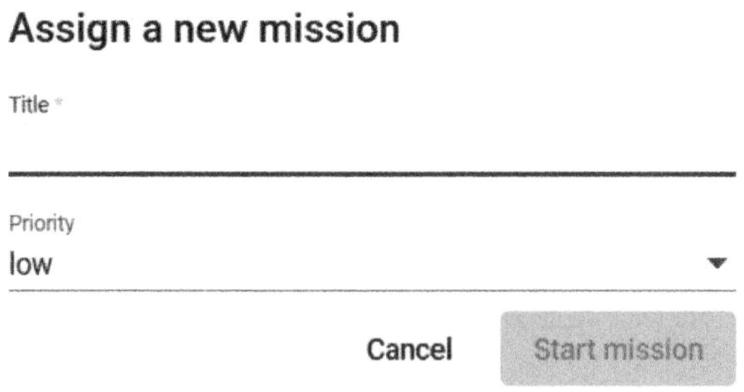

Figure 13.8 – Assign a new mission dialog

The details of a mission are part of the `Mission` model that exists in the `core` folder of the application:

mission.ts

```
export interface Mission {
  title: string;
  priority: 'low' | 'medium' | 'high';
}
```

The **Start mission** button is disabled until we enter a value in the **Title** field. The application sets the value of the **Priority** field to **low** by default, but we can change that according to the needs of the mission. The **Cancel** button closes the dialog without creating the mission, opposite the **Start mission** button.

The template of the `mission` component is shown here:

```
<h2 mat-dialog-title>Assign a new mission</h2>
<mat-dialog-content class="mat-typography">
  <form [formGroup]="missionForm" (ngSubmit)="save()">
    <mat-form-field>
      <mat-label>Title</mat-label>
      <input matInput formControlName="title" required>
    </mat-form-field>
    <mat-form-field>
      <mat-label>Priority</mat-label>
      <mat-select formControlName="priority">
        <mat-option *ngFor="let priority of priorities"
        [value]="priority">{{priority}}</mat-option>
      </mat-select>
    </mat-form-field>
    <mat-dialog-actions align="end">
      <a mat-button mat-dialog-close>Cancel</a>
      <button mat-raised-button color="primary" type="submit"
      [disabled]="missionForm.invalid">Start mission</button>
    </mat-dialog-actions>
  </form>
</mat-dialog-content>
```

We have used several directives of MatDialogModule to style the component as a dialog. At the top of the template, there is a mat-dialog-title directive that indicates the title of the dialog. The mat-dialog-content component indicates the main content of the dialog, and it primarily consists of a form element that is connected to a formGroup in the component class.

The missionForm form group contains an input element for the title and a mat-select component for the priority of the mission. The mat-select component iterates over a list of priorities to display them in the select control. Both form controls are built using the FormBuilder service:

```
ngOnInit() {
  this.missionForm = this.builder.group({
    title: ['', Validators.required],
    priority: ['low']
  });
}
```

The save method of the component, which is bound to the ngSubmit event of the form, subscribes to the assignMission method of MissionService. After the mission is assigned successfully, it uses the MatDialogRef service to close the dialog:

```
save() {
  this.missionService.assignMission(this.missionForm.
  value, this.data).subscribe(() => this.dialogRef.close());
}
```

The assignMission method of MissionService adds a new Mission object in the missions property of the hero and updates the hero using a put method:

```
assignMission(mission: Mission, hero: Hero): Observable<any> {
  if (!hero.missions) {
    hero.missions = [];
  }
  hero.missions.push(mission);

  return this.http.put<Hero>(`${this.missionsUrl}/${hero.id}`,
  hero);
}
```

A mission in progress needs to be completed at some point. In the following section, we'll learn how to accomplish this task using the next component of the `missions` module, the `mission-list` component.

Marking a mission as completed

The `Missions` tab of the `HeroesComponent` displays a list of missions that are assigned to the selected hero, using the `app-mission-list` component. The template of the `MissionListComponent` is as follows:

mission-list.component.html

```
<mat-selection-list (selectionChange)="completeMission($event.
option.value)">
  <mat-list-option *ngFor="let mission of hero.missions"
  [value]="mission">
    <span [style.color]="getPriorityColor(mission)">{{mission.
    title}}</span>
  </mat-list-option>
</mat-selection-list>
```

It uses the `mat-selection-list` component of Angular Material to display a list of missions. It iterates over the `missions` property of the `hero` object and displays a `mat-list-option` component for each hero. Each `mat-list-option` component contains two things:

- A checkbox that, when checked, calls the `completeMission` method of the component passing the `mission` object that corresponds to the checked option as a parameter.
- A `span` element that has an appropriate `color` according to the priority of the mission:

```
getPriorityColor(mission: Mission): string {
  switch(mission.priority) {
    case 'medium':
      return 'yellow';
    case 'high':
      return 'red';
  }
}
```

The `selectedHero` property of `HeroesComponent` sets the `hero` input binding of `MissionListComponent`.

The `completeMission` method subscribes to the `completeMission` method of `MissionService`. After a mission has been completed, we filter the `missions` property of the current `hero`, to exclude the completed mission from the list:

```
completeMission(mission: Mission) {
  this.missionService.completeMission(mission, this.hero).
  subscribe(() => {
    this.hero.missions = this.hero.missions.filter
    (m => m !== mission);
  });
}
```

Marking a mission as completed essentially removes the mission from the hero and updates the hero:

```
completeMission(mission: Mission, hero: Hero):
Observable<any> {
  hero.missions = hero.missions.filter(m => m !== mission);
  return this.http.put<Hero>(`${this.missionsUrl}/${hero.id}`,
  hero);
}
```

As we saw earlier, assigning a new mission to a hero and displaying the list of missions for that hero are handled in different components. If we assign a new mission from the `app-hero-detail` component, how can the `app-mission-list` component know about the new mission? How can we keep both components in sync? Well, we use the `Subject` and `Observable` objects in `MissionService`, maintaining a state management service. Let's look at that in more detail.

We have declared a `Subject` property and its `Observable` counterpart in `MissionService`:

```
private missionAddedSource = new Subject<Mission>();
readonly missionAdded$ = this.missionAddedSource.
asObservable();
```

The `missionAddedSource` `Subject` is used internally from `MissionService`, whereas the `missionAdded$` observable is used from external subscribers to the service. Whenever a new mission is assigned to a hero using the `assignMission` method, we notify any subscribers by emitting the newly assigned mission using the `missionAddedSource` property:

```
assignMission(mission: Mission, hero: Hero): Observable<any> {
  if (!hero.missions) {
    hero.missions = [];
  }
  hero.missions.push(mission);

  return this.http.put<Hero>(`${this.missionsUrl}/${hero.id}`,
  hero).pipe(
    map(() => this.missionAddedSource.next(mission))
  );
}
```

The `MissionListComponent` subscribes to the `missionAdded$` observable inside its `ngOnInit` lifecycle hook:

```
ngOnInit() {
  this.missionService.missionAdded$.subscribe(mission => {
    if (!this.hero.missions) {
      this.hero.missions = [];
    }
    this.hero.missions.push(mission);
  });
}
```

When the `missionAdded$` observable emits a new mission, we add it in the `missions` property of the current `hero`, causing it to appear on the list.

Summary

In this chapter, we used the knowledge that we gained in previous chapters to create a full Angular 10 app from scratch. Throughout building this application, we applied different techniques that we have learned in this book.

We used the Angular Material 10 library to style the application and give it a unique look and feel. We added routing to enhance its navigation experience and used forms to collect user data. We learned how to override the Angular in-memory Web API and implement custom logic for handling HTTP methods. But most importantly, we saw the benefits of using the Angular framework to build a web application.

Unfortunately, our journey with the Angular framework ends here. However, the possibilities of what we can do are endless. The Angular framework is updated with more new features in each release, giving web developers a powerful tool in their toolchain. We were delighted to have you on board, and we hope that this book broadens your imagination about what an excellent framework such as Angular can offer!

Other Books You May Enjoy

If you enjoyed this book, you may be interested in these other books by Packt:

Angular for Enterprise-Ready Web Applications

Doguhan Uluca

ISBN: 978-1-83864-880-0

- Adopt a minimalist, value-first approach to delivering web apps
- Master Angular development fundamentals, RxJS, CLI tools, GitHub, and Docker
- Discover the flux pattern and NgRx
- Implement a RESTful APIs using Node.js, Express.js, and MongoDB
- Create secure and efficient web apps for any cloud provider or your own servers
- Deploy your app on highly available cloud infrastructure using DevOps, CircleCI, and AWS

Angular Projects

Zama Khan Mohammed

ISBN: 978-1-83855-935-9

- Set up Angular applications using Angular CLI and Angular Console
- Understand lazy loading using dynamic imports for routing
- Perform server-side rendering by building an SEO application
- Build a Multi-Language NativeScript Application with Angular
- Explore the components library for frontend web using Angular CDK
- Scale your Angular applications using Nx, NgRx, and Redux

Leave a review - let other readers know what you think

Please share your thoughts on this book with others by leaving a review on the site that you bought it from. If you purchased the book from Amazon, please leave us an honest review on this book's Amazon page. This is vital so that other potential readers can see and use your unbiased opinion to make purchasing decisions, we can understand what our customers think about our products, and our authors can see your feedback on the title that they have worked with Packt to create. It will only take a few minutes of your time, but is valuable to other potential customers, our authors, and Packt. Thank you!

Index

A

B

C

D

E

F

G

H

I

J

K

L

M

N

O

P

Q

R

S

T

U

V

W

X

Z

Made in United States
North Haven, CT
08 September 2022

23809691R00235